GLASTONBURY
and
DISTRICT
MAIL

The POST OFFICES
and
THEIR PEOPLE

Allen Cotton O.B.E.

ISBN 978-1-906069-12-4 Paperback
ISBN 978-1-906069-13-1 Hardback

Published by Allen Cotton
in association with
The Squeeze Press, West Bradley, Glastonbury, BA6 8LT

Printed in Great Britain by
Henry Ling Ltd, The Dorset Press, Dorchester, DT1 1HD

ACKNOWLEDGEMENTS

I would like to show my appreciation to the many people and organisations who have encouraged and helped me in the preparation of this history of the Glastonbury and District Postal service. Without exception, all the people I have met in my studies have been helpful in answering questions, producing documents, even photographs, in support of the project. Many of these are mentioned at the end of the relevant chapters but to those I have missed, my apologies and thanks.

Firstly to my wife, Mary, who has given me tremendous support and encouragement, showing great forbearance during the time spent on research and writing this volume.

To my friend and fellow member of the Wells Philatelic Society, noted Somerset Postal Historian, John Millener who has helped me immensely with help and advice. John has given freely of his time but also allowed me to copy items from his collection providing many of the illustrations used.

To my friend of over 60 years and also my son's father-in-law, Svend Bek Pedersen, from Denmark, who has chivvied and encouraged me to commit to paper the result of over 30 years of research before, as my wife also puts it, it is too late.

To Bede MacGowan, the editor of the local weekly newspaper, the *Central Somerset Gazette*, who has given permission to reproduce material gathered from recent press cuttings but also from the archive held in the office in Wells.

To Adrian Howe of Ashcott, a very keen collector of local history, who did much to help, provide material, and encourage me in this project.

To Nick Bridgwater, another Postal Historian with a deep interest in Somerset, with whom I have co-operated in the study of the Glastonbury Penny Post system. Many thanks for all your help.

To the Somerset Heritage Centre at Taunton which carries a complete set of Parliamentary Electoral rolls for both the Wells and the Bridgwater Constituencies. These contain a lot of valuable information when one is studying the family history of people formerly associated with the local postal service.

Also much used was their micro-film collection of past copies of the *Central Somerset Gazette*, dating back to its original founding in the middle of the 19th century.

Over the years I have paid a number of visits to the British Postal Museum and Archive at Mount Pleasant in London, This archive holds records dating back over the centuries and is a great resource for researchers. Relevant to the archives I must mention, not only the illustrated book of *"Postmarks of Somerset"*, but also the transcribed *"Freeling Reports"* both of which were researched in London by Mike Welch of Bridgwater. These documents were published by The Somerset and Dorset Postal History Group in book form and have been particularly helpful. The S & D group also regularly produce a Journal based on research by its members.

It is courtesy of The British Postal Museum and Archive (© Royal Mail Group 2014) that I reproduce much of the research material, not only from Mike Welch's books but also from the historic documents in their possession.

For the opportunity to search the National Archives census returns, by means of the internet, through membership of Ancestry.co.uk.

To the Somerset County Council who run the local library service. On each of their outlets they have, available for researchers, extracts from the Local Trade Directories dating back to the early 1800s These record in detail local businesses and postal arrangements in the towns and villages in the county. They proved to be a mine of useful information.

With especial thanks to John Martineau, of Wooden Books Ltd., who has offered much helpful advice, as well as practical help, in the preparation of this book.

Allen Cotton

TABLE of CONTENTS

1. Acknowlegements   iii

2. Introduction & Map   1

3. Glastonbury   11

4. Ashcott   69

5. Baltonsborough   85

6. Butleigh   101

7. Meare   117

8. Middle Leigh   129

9. Parbrook   139

10. Shapwick   149

11. Street   165

12. Walton   201

13. West Pennard   217

14. Westhay   233

15. Windmill Hill   245

16. Index   249

Introduction

A Brief History of the Postal Service.

An illustration on early writing paper.

The history of the postal service in Glastonbury, and its surrounding villages, is very much tied in with the development of the service nationwide. Locally for over 300 years it is to Glastonbury that the inhabitants, not only of the town itself but also the surrounding country area, have looked for their letters and, in more recent times, the many other services operated by the Post Office.

Prior to 1600 there was virtually no system of posts in this country excepting that used by the king and the state, hence the name which has passed down through the ages, The Royal Mail. Merchants used their own employees, travellers or carriers to convey their letters. By 1635 King Charles 1st had opened up his mail service to the public in order to raise revenue and under Cromwell the General Post Office was brought into being. A network of posts had become established along the six main Post Roads leading out of London, letters being delivered out to other main Post Towns from various staging posts along the route. A feature of the early posts was the practice of an individual, probably fairly wealthy, making a bid to run the postal service for his own benefit.

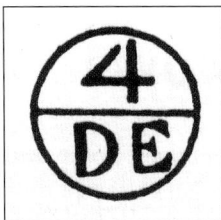

The first reference found to a Postmaster paying for the privilege of running the monopolistic service was when Edmond Prideaux "farmed" the Post for a fee of £5,000 per annum. He was later to build Forde Abbey in south Somerset, so it must have been profitable. In 1653 his successor agreed to pay £10,000 for the privilege and by 1660, the year when the first Post Office Act was passed, one Henry Bishop agreed to "farm" the posts for an annual fee of some £21,500, no mean sum in those days. His name goes down in the history of the postal service as the one who instigated the idea of using a date stamp on all letters received. This enabled a check to be made of the time taken in transit.

From 1668, the system progressed to the extent of contracts being drawn up between the Postmaster General and the postmasters in the major towns; the former holding the monopoly of letter carrying for all letters to outlying towns within 10 miles of the Staging posts. Letters would be delivered and collected for a fee of 2d. from these town post offices. The postmasters could also set up other offices and sub-offices from which letters could be collected or local deliveries be organised. It is important to note that all the six main postal routes were based on London, much as the spokes of a wheel; with no rim and with no means of joining the outer edges. Not only was the cost of sending a letter great but it was also very slow, all letters not on the same Post Road first going up to London and then being sent out again.

In a Post Office pamphlet issued in 1669 of *"Post stages.... and Market Towns served"* Glastonbury's mail connection appears to have been through Wells and Shepton Mallet, thence to Mere in Wiltshire via Wanstrow, connecting with the Western Road at the Shaftesbury stage. The Western Road was one of the principal mail routes which ran from beyond Plymouth to London via Exeter, Honiton, Chard, Crewkerne, Yeovil, Sherborne and then Shaftesbury en route to London.

It was not until the latter half of the 17th century that the cross post system was set up to join the outer spokes of the main post routes. Around 1700, the Postmaster General was seeking a person to farm a new Cross Post which was to run between Exeter and Chester. The Post Office notice said it was to begin from Michaelmas 1700 and to continue twice weekly through Tiverton, Wellington,

Taunton, Bridgwater, Wells, Bristol, Wootton under Edge, Gloucester, etc. to Chester. Letters sent from Exeter would be in Chester on Sunday mornings and answers returned to Exeter on Wednesday mornings.

The P.O. account books of 1707 show that a Joseph Quash farmed the cross post on an annual rental of £600 but it obviously did not prove to be the gold mine one might imagine. It is recorded that Joseph was adjudicated bankrupt in 1713, after which time the service reverted to being run by the General Post Office. There can be little doubt that in getting from Bridgwater to Wells, the mail would have passed through Glastonbury and thus be available to the local residents.

A well known name, Ralph Allen of Bath, reputedly a distant relative of the author (whose mother's maiden name was Allen) was granted the "Farm" of all the cross posts in 1720 . He seems to have fared rather better than Mr Quash as he was able to build the large mansion of Prior Park in Bath, no doubt aided by his profits from the service.

Around this time great strides were made in the speeding up of the mail, improvement in the roads going hand in hand with an improvement in the means of transport. John Palmer was instrumental in introducing the first Mail Coaches on the Bath Road in 1784 and it was not long before these became the normal means of transport on all the main post routes.

Glastonbury 134
handstamp with
5d. postage to be collected.

Below is an example of the
Glastonbury 135
handstamp

As the use of mail for business and industry was greatly increasing, many places could see the benefit to their locality and petitions were raised for improvements to the service. In answer to this need an act of Parliament had been introduced in 1765 allowing the Postmasters, mainly based on existing businesses in the Post Towns, to establish what came to be called "*Penny Posts*". This enabled them to run a local system for the delivery, and collection, of letters to the outlying villages for a charge of 1d. over and above the postage rate, if it was considered to be economic to do so. These did not really take off until the early 1800s.

As postal charges were still based on mileage travelled and they were mostly collected from the recipient, new handstamps for postmarking the letters were issued to "*Letter Receiving Houses*". These all showed the distance the office was from London. When it arrived at its destination the clerk could check that the charge was correct by adding the mileage on the letter to the known distance of his own office from London. There must have been a lot of dissension about the measurements as the issue of these mileage stamps was soon suspended. Only after a John Cary was commissioned to measure every post road in the country, around 1801, was the issue of mileage stamps was resumed. Even this was not the end of the story as the Glastonbury mark, the earliest of which known is dated 21.6.1811, has 134 as the distance from London, only to be amended to 135 in late 1822.

One has to appreciate that postal rates around this time were very expensive indeed. In 1812 the lowest cost for sending a 'single sheet' letter, if the distance involved was not more than 15 miles, was 4d. If it was between 300 and 400 miles it would have cost Is/Id. with an addition of Id. for each additional 100 miles. The reference to a 'Single Sheet' was that, because of the system then in use, the charge was per sheet, regardless of weight, even the use of an envelope would have doubled the rate.

The mail service, although it had made great strides, was still not much used by the public as the cost was high in relation to the general level of wages. In 1839, following Rowland Hill's suggested reforms of the Postal system, a uniform 4d post, for letters up to 1 oz, was introduced to cover the whole of Britain on the 5th December of that year, very quickly to be followed by a Uniform 1d rate on 10th January 1840. On the 6th of May of that year, with the introduction of the 1d. Black stamp whereby the postage was now prepaid, sending a letter became very much simpler.

The treasury were very much opposed to Rowland Hill's suggested reform as the system that existed before 1840 had shown a very good profit for the state.

Indeed Francis Freeling, who virtually ran the service and whose meticulous records are now in the National Postal Archives, felt that it was his duty to raise the maximum amount of revenue possible whilst still running an efficient service. Up to a point the opponents of change were vindicated as, indeed, the revenue to the treasury did drop dramatically; it was not until nearly 30 years had passed before the service was again in profit but the advantages to business as well as the public were immeasurable.

The use of horse-drawn mail coaches continued throughout the 19th century although, increasingly, the development of the railway network and the postal system followed a parallel course being, very much, inter-dependent.

After the commercial development of the electric telegraph one of the worries to the postal authorities was the growing use of telegrams to send messages. The telegraph system in Britain had been quickly built up by a series of local operators based on towns and cities on a piecemeal basis. Whether it was to rationalise the service or to cut out competition, the decision was made to nationalise almost all the companies concerned in 1872. These were then brought under the auspices of the G.P.O., the foundation of the "Post Office Telephones" service although it was not until 1912 that a national service was complete.

An early telegram from a company founded in Exeter in 1844

In former days all the telephone exchanges were manually operated, being based on Post Office premises. In the villages many being operated by a family member of the postmaster or postmistress. The service was to remain a subsidiary of the Post Office until 1981 when BRITISH TELECOM was formed after the decision to privatise the service. Its original purpose, the sending and receiving of telegrams, had finally ceased being available in 1977.

As will be seen, the Post Office was the main vehicle through which many of the government services were operated. Licences for carriages, dogs, guns, etc., the sale of government annuities and insurance, money orders and, later, postal orders and even business for the Post Office's own Savings Bank being but a few.

A Parcel Post Label issued to Glastonbury under Bridgwater.

The initials "GAZ" were the Glastonbury telegraphic address.

PARCEL POST.
Glastonbury (GAZ)
(under Bridgwater)

FOR POSTAGE STAMPS.

Initially the Post Office only carried letters, for which they held the monopoly, and it was not until 1883 that they began a parcel service. Originally local carriers had operated throughout the country and it was to them that one turned for the delivery of larger items before the coming of the railways. These same railway companies were very opposed to the idea of the Post Office operating a parcel service but an act of Parliament was passed in 1882 which laid down the foundations for its formation and implementation on 1st August 1883. Up until that time all deliveries had been carried out by "Letter Carriers" but from then on the employees who did this work became known as "Postmen". Starting a parcel delivery service entailed big changes in the organisation: from the small matter of providing all Post Offices with large scales to the introduction of high value stamps, let alone having to provide postmen with the means of carrying a far greater load than previously. As much of the wrapping paper used was of a coarse nature the Post Office produced special labels for each office which could be stuck on securely and have the correct postage stamps applied.

After much lobbying, following their introduction on the continent, Britain got its first Postal Cards in October 1870 carrying a halfpenny pre-printed stamp. These were only sold by the Post Office and their use was restricted to so that only the address could be written on one side whilst the message had to written on the reverse. According to a letter published in the *Central Somerset Gazette* in 1880, following the suggestion that the cards should be sold at the cost of the postage alone, the reply from a Mr Hardy from the General Post Office said that initially this was the case but after complaints from the "*Committee of Wholesale and Retail*

Stationers of the United Kingdom" the Treasury decided that *"as a matter of justice and policy a small charge must for the future be made for the card itself"*

With the number of mail deliveries a day increasing all the time these cards proved very popular for sending short messages locally as well as being used for advertising and circulating dates of meetings and the like.

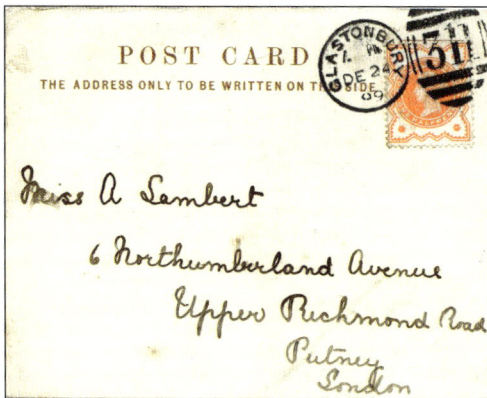

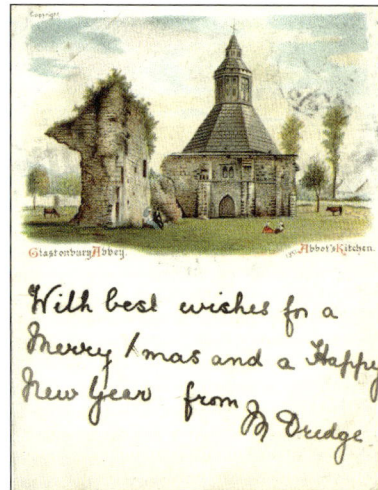

It was not until 1894 that manufacturers were allowed to produce the first picture cards on to which postage stamps could be affixed. This was the beginning of the picture post card era although the rule of only the address on the front was still strictly enforced. It was not until 1902, when what is now known as the "divided back" card was first allowed, that the post card collecting craze started, reaching a peak before the outbreak of the first world war.

The introduction of decimal coinage in the United Kingdom in February 1971 coincided with the first national postal strike. Following a decade of worsening industrial relations and increasing inflation, the union's demand for a 15% wage increase was rejected which resulted in a strike which lasted for seven weeks. This was the only time since 1840 that the Post Office monopoly on the carriage of letters had been suspended. Many small enterprises took advantage of this - some more efficiently than others.

Having built up a massive nationwide service, indeed world-wide one, the pattern was to remain throughout most of the 20th century. It was in 1986 that it was decided to break the postal service down into three distinct parts; The G. P. O. (General Post Office) for the postal service and running the M.L.O.s (Mechanised Letter Offices), and two limited liability companies, Parcelforce Ltd. and Post Office Counters Ltd.

Various experiments were made over the years to help with the very labour intensive task of mail sorting. The introduction of stamps incorporating phosphor bands, in 1959, replaced the short-lived experiment of applying graphite lines to the back of stamps in 1957. Both of these systems enabled letters to be mechanically "faced" so that the address appeared at the front with the stamp in the top right corner ready for machine cancellation.

The next big move to aid delivery was the introduction of "Post Codes" in 1974. The whole country was attributed with a 6 or 7 figure code, each based on a major post town. Glastonbury was designated BA6, i.e. number 6 under the Bath postal area. The second three or four digits then broke this down in to very specific areas. e.g. West Bradley BA6 8LT.

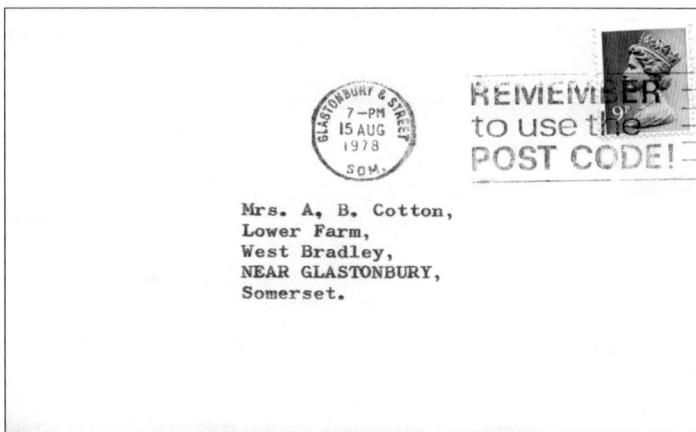

An envelope with the slogan cancellation
'REMEMBER TO USE THE POST CODE"
but without it in the address!

After centuries of holding the closely guarded monopoly on postal deliveries the service was opened up to competition in 2006 although the G.P.O. was still obliged to maintain the national six day delivery service.

The next major change came about when a new company, Royal Mail Ltd., was launched on the stock exchange in 2013. The increasing use of electronic means of communication such as "Email" has also put the service under increasing financial pressure. So much so that in 2014 the cost of sending a letter, for next day delivery, had risen to 63 pence, the equivalent of over 12 shillings in the currency of 1840. What would be Rowland Hill's thoughts be on that fact one wonders?

The successor to the postage stamp. The counter-printed "Postage Paid" label.

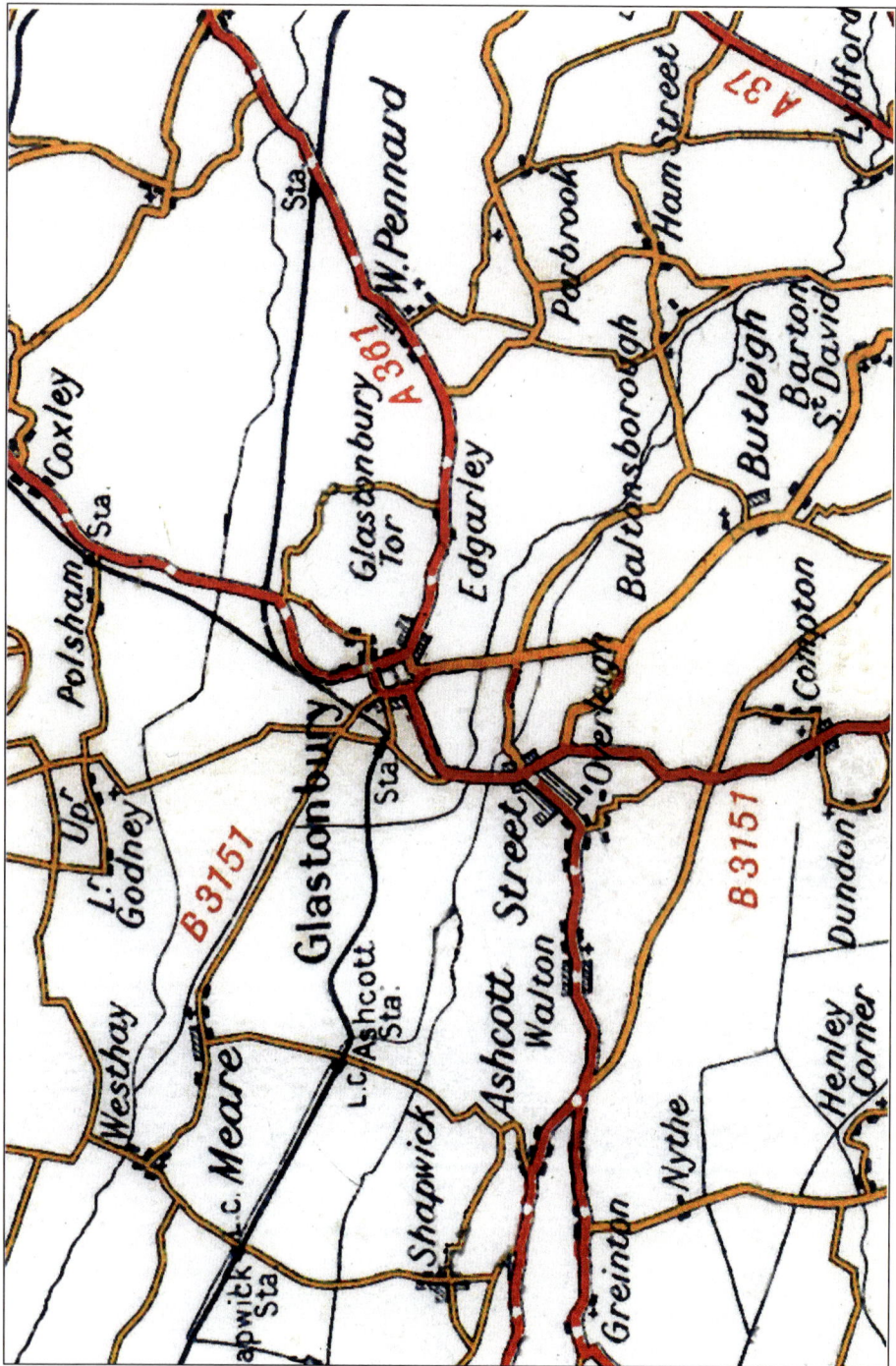

A Map of the Glastonbury District of Somerset. circa. 1938

Glastonbury

GLASTONBURY, a town, a parish, and a sub-district, in Wells district, Somerset. The town stands on a peninsular tract, engirt by the river Brue, and on the Somerset and Dorset Railway, at the junction of the branch to Wells, 5½ miles SSW of Wells, and 25 SW of Bath. It occupies eminences, connected with the inferior oolite of the county; but is largely environed by marshes, and is flanked on one side by Weary-all-Hill, on another by Glastonbury Tor.

From:- *"The Imperial Gazetteer of England & Wales"* by John Marius Wilson.
Pub. A. Fullarton & Co. 1872)

THE FIRST REFERENCE to Glastonbury's postal arrangements is found in a Post Office pamphlet issued in 1669. It stated that letters from London on their way to Plymouth and beyond came along the Western Road through Hartford and Salisbury to the Bye Post town of Shaftesbury. Included in this same pamphlet is the following reference: *"Post stages.... and Market Towns served.... Glastonbury"* The mail connection appears to have been through Wells and Shepton Mallet, thence to Mere in Wiltshire via Wanstrow, connecting with the Western Road at the Shaftesbury stage. The Western Road was one of the principal mail routes which ran from beyond Plymouth to London via Exeter, Honiton, Chard, Crewkerne, Yeovil, Sherborne and then Shaftesbury en route to London.

This was a time when, following the Post Office act of 1660, great strides were made in the improvement of the postal service throughout the country. By 1784 the *Universal Directory* has an entry which reads: *"The mail coach comes through Glastonbury from London every day".* This is very much supported by the 1787 edition of *Cary's English Atlas* where, under the heading of Glastonbury Sub Office - Posts from London next day - Arrives 1.0pm. Departs 1.0pm.

At this time Glastonbury was still a sub-office under Wells. In the 1791 "Survey of riding work" there is an entry entitled *"Salaries paid for jobs "* and under the heading of "WELLS"

A letter dated 1st April 1785 posted from Glastonbury to Kent with the
GLASTON
BURY
double lined postmark measuring 50 x 18 mm. Also a "Bishop Mark" dated the 4th April as well as a London time mark. The charge of 5d. to be collected from the recipient.

Mails to and from Bristol. 7 days, 21 miles	£98
Office	£24
Sub-Office Glastonbury	£4

Extracts from the old business directories have been produced by the Somerset Library Service and they are a mine of information. In the copy of *The British Directory* c.1793 it says that Ann Shave ran The George (White Lion) and a year later, in the *Universal British Directory* Mrs Elizabeth Bridgeman's occupation was that of Victualler at the George Inn and Thomas Bridgeman was a Postmaster & Maltster. This same entry also supports the *"Survey of riding work"* above that the Glastonbury facility was a sub-office of Wells.

It is possible that The George Inn continued to be the Glastonbury Receiving House although it is believed that at one time the White Hart inn, on the other side of the High Street, held this position. There is an entry in the minute book of the Post Office, held in the Archives, dated 30th December 1820 which states that Glastonbury was to continue as a Sub-Office of Wells until 20th February 1821 when, because of the "Acceleration of the Mails" to Exeter and Falmouth via Bath, Glastonbury should be raised to the status of a Head Office. It seems that, due to pressure of work, time needed to be saved at Wells.

A Bill head from the George Hotel in 1880.

The London bag to Minehead was to be taken away and a bag for Glastonbury substituted. It was also necessary, at the same time, to extend the Somerton and Street Ride to Glastonbury.

In this report it was also recommended that, as he had *"conducted the Sub-office for several years to the satisfaction of the town and neighbourhood, that James Rood, the Sub-deputy be appointed the Postmaster"*.

Confirmation of this is found in the list of Post Office appointments held in the National Postal Archives when James Rood, whose occupation is put as Shop keeper, is recorded as the "Deputy" i.e. Receiver, on the establishment of the office. This was probably the establishment of the *"Penny Post"* system and his bond stood at £400.00.

The Penny Post system was introduced by an act of Parliament in 1765, Post Towns were enabled to establish what came to be called Penny Posts which allowed them to run a local system for the delivery, and collection, of letters to the outlying villages at an additional cost of 1d. if it was considered to be economic to do so.

Town	Deputy	Nominated	Occupation	Late Deputy	Cause	Date	Bond
Glastonbury	James Rood	28 Feby 1821	Shopkeeper	On the Establishment of the Office			400

The Glastonbury Penny Post was established in 1826 serving Ashcott and Street as receiving houses Nos. 1 & 2. In 1832 Shapwick (No.3) was added, and Walton (No.4) in 1835. In 1836 Butleigh and Baltonsborough were added with the No.5. The postal historian Geoff Oxley, in his book, also identifies Street as being in the Somerton Penny Post from 1821.

In June 1821 there was a further note to the effect that as the Sub-office salary was £20 annually this should now be increased by £15, "*to commence from February last*" This is supported by the entry in the 1830 edition of *Pigot's Directory*:-

> *Post Office High Street. James Rood, Postmaster (in a later directory he is listed under the heading of Chemists and Druggists). Letters from London & Co arrive every morning at half past eleven and are despatched every afternoon at a quarter past two. Letters from Exeter arrive every afternoon at half past two and despatched every forenoon at half past eleven.*
> *Letters from Ashcott & Shapwick arrive every morning at eleven, and are despatched every day at twelve.-Letters from Somerton and Langport arrive every morning at eleven, and are despatched every afternoon at twenty minutes to three*

It seems that all did not go well as planned as on 5th February 1829. Freeling wrote that the matter of the Glastonbury Postmasters salary following the up-rating to a main office in 1821, the recipient had still not received any extra money due. This was non-approval by their Lordships and suggested that the incumbent should retain £50 from his next remittance and also retain at the rate of £15 a year quarterly until the treasury confirm the augmentation recommended. Obviously nothing, other than the above, happened because we find a note, dated 20 May 1833, in the Index referring to the fact that the Postmaster was still awaiting back pay of £67-14-2. The Auditor General had checked the figures and the recommendation was that he should receive £54.16.9d. - a not inconsiderable sum at that time.

Things had been sorted out by 1834 as it was acknowledged that the Postmaster's salary was £35 per annum. At that time Glastonbury still had a Town Delivery Charge of ½d on letters but it was proposed in April of that year that he should receive an extra £9 and this should allow for free delivery in the town.

On the 22nd January 1836 Ellen Ball, described as a "Bookseller" on her appointment, replaced James Rood in running the Post Office in Glastonbury. According to the local directory she was a Commercial and General Newsagent, listed in the 1840 *Somerset Gazette* under "Booksellers and Stationers" as "*Ellen*

Ball, High Street. Agent for Standard of England Life Assurance." Also in Bragg's Directory of the same year:

> Ellen Ball. High Street; Hours of post: The box for the Western letters closes at 10. Post departs at half past 10. The London box closes at half past 3 and the post departs at 4.

An interesting note from Ellen Ball, sent to Mr Whitehead, the cheese factor (merchant) concerning his "Private Bag" which was collected from Glastonbury, the contents of which are included in the chapter on Baltonsborough.

A small insight into the running of a local Post Office can be gleaned from an entry in the Postmaster General's minute book for 7th May 1840 concerning "Mr J. Reeves application to Mr Gordon, of the Treasury, that the Bond which he had entered into for the Postmaster of Glastonbury may be given up to him". In the event his request was turned down; "It had been the practice for many years .... to refuse giving up any bond while the officer remains in the service". Rather surprisingly, "explain also the circumstances of Mr Reeves having been an applicant for the postmaster of

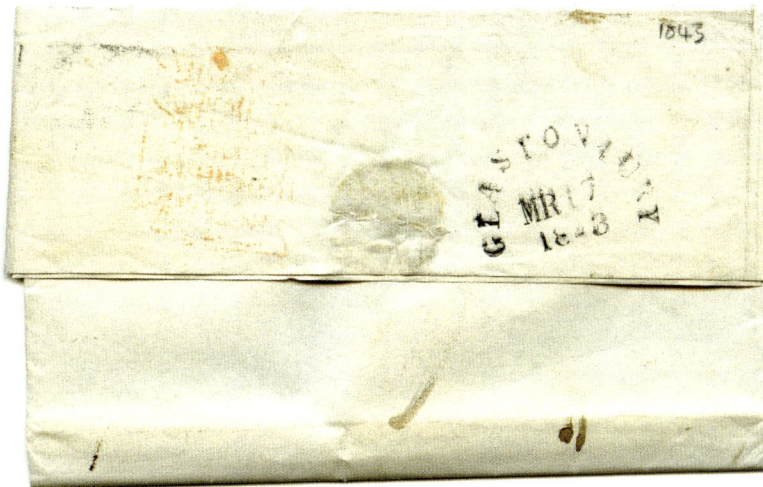

A letter from the "Whitehead" correspondence with a "Skeleton" postmark of Glastonbury. Skeleton marks were of a temporary nature in use for only a limited period, usually when the regular handstamp was not available.
Seen dated March 14th - 17th 1843

THE POSTAL REFORM ACT OF 1840 INTRODUCED THE UNIFORM PENNY POSTAGE RATE

*The Twopenny Blue
for use on letters up to
1 oz. in weight*

*A letter from the "Whitehead" correspondence, posted at Baltonsborough in October 1840 with
the Maltese cross cancellation in red on the 1d. Black.*

*An example of the "Mulready" Letter Sheet, issued in May 1840, sent from
Glastonbury to Street.*

Glastonbury's situation." The Mr Reeves referred to was probably John Fry Reeves, a member of the comparatively wealthy family who lived at Edgarley Hall, the property they had built around 1820.

After the major reform of the postal service in 1840 and the introduction of the Penny Black and Twopenny Blue stamps the increase in business was quite dramatic. By 1842 the *Pigot & Co's Directory* lists Ellen Ball as now in Magdalene Street, and the post was getting organised as it states that: *Letters are delivered to all parts every morning at half past seven and despatched every evening at half past seven.*

Another entry in the Postmaster General's minute book dated 6th June 1842 - "*Glastonbury Deputy remonstrance against suspicions entertained against her office*" followed by the reply "*I have again attentively considered this case; the suspicions against the Postmistress of Glastonbury appear to me to be well founded & if you approve I submit she may be informed that your Lordship sees no reason to change your former opinion*"

Another intriguing reference in the archives headed "*Glastonbury and Somerton Mail Cart driver reprimanded for carrying the bags to Somerton*". Signed: W. Cresswell 30th November 1841 and the letter sent subsequently to the Postmaster General: "*I presume your Lordships will approve the course taken by the surveyor to this case & consider the severe reprimand & caution given to the driver of the Mail cart sufficient to ensure his proper attention to the duties of his situation in future*". One does wonder as to the nature of his sin; had he forgotten to drop the bags off at Street on the way, perhaps?

One of the major worries of the authorities was that people would clean cancelled stamps and re-use them. The use of control letters in two corners of the design, later in all four, was also to prevent forgery or even the joining together of two clean halves of used stamps. Within a year of being first issued, the colour of the 1d. stamp was changed to what is referred to in philatelic circles as "Red" although in reality is closer to brown. Being a breeder of cattle all my life I fully understand the terminology: all cows of a similar hue are referred to as red. We do not have brown cows in Britain!

After the change of colour, initially, the Post Office continued with the "Maltese Cross" cancellation on stamps but used solid black to replace the red ink. The Glastonbury Maltese Cross handstamp always seems to appear as a solid blob of ink whereas in some towns the pattern is very clear. Perhaps they just failed to clean it

*A letter posted in **Street** (No.2 still being used) on 31st May 1843 with the **Somerton** rather than the Glastonbury date stamp applied. Note also the neat Maltese Cross cancellation applied at Somerton Post Office*

but it certainly achieved the objective; it most certainly prevented anyone cleaning the stamp and re-using it. Each Post Office was obliged to make its own ink as the following instructions show although this was for the black ink that followed the use of the original red. Possibly the staff at Glastonbury failed to get the recipe right.

The local G.P.O. surveyor, George Louis, issued a list of general instructions, printed in Yeovil, to *"Penny-Post and Other Receivers"* including the following:

MIXTURE TO BE USED FOR STAMPING.
Lamp Black and Olive or Sweet Oil, in proportions of ¼ of an ounce of the former, to half a pint of the latter; a little common ink would improve the mixture.- The ingredients should be incorporated over a slow fire, stirring them well during their time; the liquid will in consequence become dry quicker, and the impression less likely to smear He went on to suggest: *MATERIALS TO CONTAIN THE MIXTURE""* that *"Three, four or more pieces of Hat or Cloth put in a tin or other dish, with a cover to prevent the dust collecting when not in use; the mixture should be well stirred, and applied to the under pieces - it will by pressure rise to the top; this should be done invariably many hours before the stamping commences"*

In 1844 all "Post Towns" in the country were allocated a number. These were firstly given out in alphabetical order, Glastonbury's being **311**. After its introduction this number was used throughout the Victorian era to cancel postage stamps although the design was to change throughout the period.

It appears that Ellen Ball resigned her position on the 8th September 1843 as again recorded in the list of appointments in the Post Office archives, we find that William Cruse, described as *"Man Milliner and Woollen Draper"* taking over the office on 10th October 1843 with a surety bond of £300.00. It seems that the position was not without its troubles as in the archives in London is a book entitled *"Deputy Order Book"* quoted in the journal of the Somerset and Dorset Postal History group, with the entry:-

15.1.1848. Page 5. Suspension of deputy
William Cruse . Deputy suspended

5.5.1848. Page 9. William Cruse, Deputy restored.
Date of commencement 6.5.1848.

8.5.1848 Page 9. De Lisle Bermore. Officer in Charge.
Date of commencement 16.5.1848.

William features again in the archives, this time dated June 7th 1849, *"for the account of one, William Cruse, to cease"* followed by *"Resignation of Deputy"* After his resignation William, who was born in Horningsham in Wiltshire, continued to live in Glastonbury where his business was that of Estate Agent and Auctioneer and, at one time, held the position of Deputy Registrar. His wife, Sophia, came from Babcary, near Somerton. In the 1881 census they are recorded as living in Glastonbury and having 6 daughters and one son. The eldest daughter, the wife of a colliery manager from Glamorgan, was visiting her parents on the day the census was taken.

The following entry appears in the archives dated June 2nd. 1849 *"Accounts to commence: William Carroll. Officer in Charge".* The local directory entry of the time states that *"letters are delivered at 7.0am in summer & 7.30am in winter".* It seems that William Carroll was only a temporary appointment as on 10th June 1850 William Vernon, a grocer and draper, was appointed to the position. This is verified by the entry in the census of 1851 where William Vernon is credited with running the Post Office and a grocer's shop in the High Street.

William was an interesting character. He born in Scotland and his wife, Mary Ann, in Madiera and, it seems, they did not stay long in the town as by 1861 they were living in Fordington Green in Dorset and had set themselves up as tea dealers as well as drapers by then employing 3 men.

We next find, in the archive minute book dated 10th May 1853 under Glastonbury, *"The vacancy reported to the Treasury."* and obviously someone else had taken over

1863. Wm. CRUSE,
Estate, House, Emigra-
tion & General Agent
Accountant & Auction-
eer
GLASTONBURY

the role as Postmaster because the following entry in the Minute Book dated 15th August 1853 states -

> "Under the report of Mr Cresswell, (the P. O. Surveyor) I submit that the office at Glastonbury may be reduced to the condition of a Sub Office under Bath and the future salary fixed at £27 a year. It is to be regretted that Mr Cresswell had not suggested the reduction of the office and consequent adjustment of the salary before the new appointment was made.
>
> I submit that the memorialists be informed that the intended reduction of the Post Office at Glastonbury to the condition of a Sub Office will not in any way diminish their accommodation being a measure exclusively affecting the interior arrangements and that there appears to be not sufficient reason for not carrying it into effect."

How many times have we heard similar words being used when major changes are contemplated? A year later, in 1854, Glastonbury was again mentioned :-

> "Under the circumstances of the case I think it will be the best plan to separate the situation of the Sub Postmaster and Letter Carrier at Glastonbury (which under a recent arrangement has been combined) and to fix the salary of the former at £20 and the wages of the latter at £10 agreed as Mr Cresswell proposed."

Presumably, up until then, the letter carrier had been paid out of the basic salary of the Sub-Postmaster.

Referring back to Mr Reeves' application for a return of his bond in 1840 the following entry is very relevant and shows the amount committed-

> "It appears from the enclosed return that a less (security?) than the present amount of £300 will not be sufficient to cover the liabilities of the Glastonbury Office upon

it becoming a Sub Office. I intend therefore that the penalty for their bond may remain as at present."

As mentioned earlier, Post Office business was increasing all the time and the next major step to assist the use of the postal service was the introduction of Post Boxes. Initially proposed by Anthony Trollope, a clerk to the Post Office who later become a well known novelist, was the first to suggest introducing these collection boxes in this country. Apparently he had travelled extensively across Europe where he first saw their use. Introduced initially in the Channel Isles in 1853, they proved so popular that it was not long before they came into general use in mainland Britain. Although they were brought in gradually in Glastonbury, as we shall see later, there were at least 21 in use in the town at the end of the 20th century. The aim, in urban areas in recent times, has been that

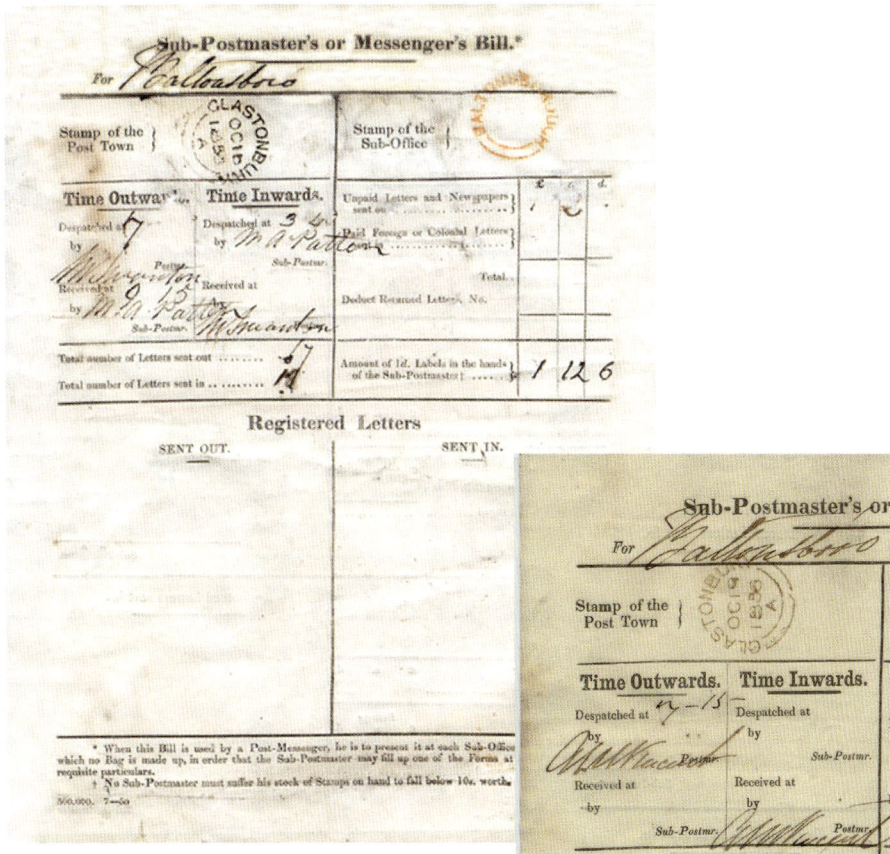

Sub-Postmaster's or Messenger's Bills.
Items carried by the Butleigh - Baltonsborough letter carrier. The first signed by Thomas Swanton and the second one by Anna Maria Vincent

no-one would need to walk more than a quarter of a mile to post a letter. *(see Appendix ii re; Glastonbury Post Boxes.)*

Previously almost exclusively dependant on horse drawn transport, another major advance for Glastonbury was when, in 1854, the Somerset Central Railway was opened. A broad gauge line from Highbridge - where it connected with the Bristol & Exeter line built in 1841 to Glastonbury, along the line of the Glastonbury canal was opened in 1854. Extended in 1858 to Burnham on Sea to connect with steamers from S. Wales. The line was, later, connected to the Dorset Central at Cole, near Bruton, in 1862 and amalgamated as the Somerset & Dorset Joint Railway. Although the coming of the railway to Glastonbury did not have an immediate impact on the postal service it certainly did so in the long term.

An early design of Letter Box still in use in Bath, Somerset, in 2012

The mention of the Glastonbury Canal, first opened in 1833, was interesting. It had a lot of problems during its construction across the peatlands and was never a financial success. Eventually it was bought by the new company, who used it in the construction of their railway line, before its final closure in 1854.

Referring again to the local directories, in 1859 *Messrs Harrison-Harrad & Co* named Thomas Swinton as running a Grocers and Confectioners shop together with the Post Office in the High Street. Sometimes the facts in the directories are of doubtful value as the 1861 census definitely gives us the name of Stephen Swanton in the Post Office living with his wife, Maria, and "daughter-in-law" Anna Maria Vincent as the Postmistress. In the 1851 census return Anna Maria had been described his "sister-in-law". One suspects that she was actually Maria's daughter from before her marriage. By the time of the 1871 census Anna Maria Vincent had married John Baily and twenty years later, in 1891, Maria, now widowed, was living with John & Anna and was referred to as John's mother-in-law.

The 1861 Census return for Glastonbury High Street

Certainly Maria Swanton, although not named as Postmistress, was thought to be in charge as a report in the *Central Somerset Gazette*, the local Glastonbury newspaper, dated 8th December 1866 has this entry:

POLICE REPORT.

Emily Bailey, a young girl, was summoned by Mrs Swanton, of the Post Office, High Street, for breaking a pane of glass in her shop window, valued at 6s.

The defendant acknowledged breaking the glass but said it was an accident.

John Baily, who was born in Wells, Somerset around 1838, was a man of many talents. The son of Alexander Baily who kept the George & Pilgrims Hotel in the town and who, in 1861, was also farming 60 acres of land with two labourers. John himself, as we see above, had married the daughter of Mrs Swanton some time before 1871 and he and Anna Maria, nee Vincent, were now respectively named as Postmaster and Postmistress of the Post Office in the High Street in the directories of the time.

In 1872, after 19 years as a sub-office under Bath, the Glastonbury Post Office was deemed to be important enough to be raised, once again, to the status of a Head Office. Certainly the workload of anyone running a town Post Office was far greater than it had been 20 years before.

The directory produced by *Morris and Co.* lists many of the tasks carried out by the office at this time over and above the normal weekday deliveries there was also:-

On Sundays. One delivery only, at 7.0am and one dispatch at 6.15pm

Money orders granted and paid, and savings bank and annuity business transacted from 9.0am to 6.0pm, and on Saturdays until 8.0pm

Postal Telegraph office open from 8.0am to 8.0pm, on Sundays from 8.0am to 10.0am

By 1881, when John Baily was 43 and his wife 46, John was not only listed as the Postmaster but also as: *"Corn Merchant, Farmer of 85 acres employing 5 men and a boy"* as well as being a town councillor! By this time they had three children, Agnes aged eight, John seven and Mary, three. To help run the household Maria had an 18 year old nursemaid, Ellen Billings as well as a general servant, Susan Golledge, who came from West Bradley. Also boarding was Clara Eyers, listed as a Post Office clerk, who came from Westbury in Wiltshire. With John's many occupations it is fairly clear that Anna Maria was running the Post Office, something she was well qualified to do with her long experience of carrying out the work.

Meanwhile the telegraph system had been expanding at a great rate and, because of this greater use, the Post Office was able to halve the price of sending a telegram. On 19th September 1885 the *Central Somerset Gazette* carried this short article:

SIXPENNY TELEGRAMS
On the 1st of October next the new rate for inland telegrams will come into force, and the charge will be 6d. for 12 words or less and ½d per word afterwards.

At that time the basic salary for a postmaster was somewhat higher than that of a postmistress, no doubt the reason for John to remain as the nominated holder of the office. Around this time the population of the borough and parish was 3828, a figure that had increased dramatically over the previous 50 years.

In spite of severe opposition from both the general carriers still operating in the district and the railway companies, the Post Office introduced a Parcel Post into the system on 1st August 1883. This meant that a far greater volume of mail passing through their many offices.. The railways did manage to negotiate a deal whereby they received some 55% of the revenue if any parcels were carried by them which, increasingly, many did. The main carrier still operating in 1906 was listed as:-

Royal Mail Omnibus: Thomas Cridland, Proprietor, from Magdalene Street daily 8.30am to Bridgwater via Street, Walton, Ashcott, Shapwick, Catcott, Edington, Chilton Polden, Cossington & Knowle returning the same day

The business of the Glastonbury Post Office continued to increase and the decision was made to have a new purpose-built Post Office. This was built in the High Street just below St. John's Church and completed in the year of Queen Victoria's Golden Jubilee, hence the plaque at the top of the facade. Although the lower storey was exclusively used by the Post Office, the upper rooms were let out as office accommodation. In the back premises of this new building was to be found the mail sorting room and the manually operated telephone exchange.

Over the main entrance door was a sign "POST OFFICE" as illustrated on the next page. This sign has an interesting later history.

It was found, many years after the construction of the replacement building in the High Street, in an outbuilding of the house that had formerly been the Post Office in the village of Butleigh. The local sub-postmaster most probably rescued it with a view to erecting outside his Post Office but never got around to doing so.

A letter in the *Central Somerset Gazette* in April 1897 *"With the temporary Post Office situated nearly at the top of the High Street...."* and asks if the authorities could place a Pillar-box in the Market Place for the convenience of the public in the lower part of town. This temporary office was probably only open whilst the new premises were being built.

The Post Office opened in the High Street in 1897, the year of Queen Victoria's Diamond Jubilee.

Kelly's Directory of 1906 lists the duties and services offered and the hours the office was open which were very extensive:

> *Post, Money Order & Telegraph Office, Telegraphic Money Order, Savings Bank and Insurance and Annuity Office.*
>
> *Letters delivered at 7, 8.45 & 9a.m. (parcels) & 4.30 and 7.25 p.m.*
>
> *Dispatched 7.15 & 10.15 a.m. and 12.30, 3.25, 4.55, 5.15 and 7.0, and 7.30 p.m.(with extra stamp)*
>
> *Money orders are issued and paid from 7.0 a.m. to 8.0p.m.,*
>
> *Telegraph from 8.0 a.m. to 8.0 p.m.*
>
> *Sundays, dispatched 7.0 and 7.30 p.m. (with extra stamp)*
> *Delivered 7.0 a.m.*

The term "with extra stamp" refers to the fact that if one paid an added sum, a "late fee", you were able to get catch the post up to half an hour after the official closing time.

The mention of 4 letter deliveries, plus a separate parcel delivery, every weekday tallies with what was written in the sale catalogue when the Abbey House and Abbey Ruins were sold in 1907.

Postal Arrangements and Railway Accommodation. There are four deliveries a day. The Post Office is near, and a Post Office Telephone installation is laid on to the Mansion.

There had been a complaint raised around 1900 that John Baily was not devoting much time to the affairs of the Post Office, which was probably correct as he, by this time, was also actively involved with his late father's hotel in the town. With his other interests as well, the Post Office surveyor surmised that he was neglecting his duties and suggested that the position should only receive the pay of a postmistress rather than that of postmaster. Somehow he seems to have survived this as he continued to be the named holder of the position until around 1906 when a vacancy was declared.

The entry in the Postmaster General's Minute Book, No. 26829, was quite telling:

> I submit for your approval a proposal to reduce Glastonbury to the rank of a salaried Sub Office. The office is now vacant owing to the retirement of the Postmaster and the present occasion is opportune for affecting the change.
>
> Glastonbury is a small town, with no special industry. Its subordinate area is small and unimportant, containing only 5 Sub Offices, the control of which has for some time past devolved temporarily on the Postmaster of Bridgwater on account of the inability of the late Postmaster of Glastonbury to undertake the necessary surveys. It is proposed to make this arrangement a permanent one; the whole area is easily accessible by rail from Bridgwater and its administration will present no difficulty.

A comment written at the side of this entry reads:

> "Geographically Wells would be the proper Head Office but the present Postmaster of Wells is not equal to the control of a larger office"
>
> The change involves no alteration of vouching or curtailment of postal facilities, nor does it in any way effect the outdoor staff.
>
> It will be possible to reduce the attendances of the indoor staff, consisting of 1 male and 2 female Sorting Clerks and Telegraphists, by two hours a day, and to employ an Assistant working 6 hours in place of a Female Sorting Clerk and Telegraphist.
>
> The salary warranted for a Postmaster is now £150, while if the reduction were carried out the salary would be £130; so the reduction would result in a saving of £20 on the salary alone, irrespective of that consequent on the substitution of a part time Assistant for a Female Sorting Clerk and Telegraphist
>
> *November 1906.*

The part in the middle *"on account of the inability of the late Postmaster of Glastonbury to undertake the necessary surveys."* does perhaps reflect a certain dereliction of duty by the late postmaster!

So after 34 years as a Head Office, Glastonbury was, once again, reduced to the status of a sub-office

In the picture of the Post Office staff, probably taken around 1907, the gentleman sitting in the front row is reputedly Harold Baker. The picture was found by Ken

& Joan Baker of Westhay in an old frame with another picture in front of it, Harold being one of Mr Baker's relations. There appears to be eight or 9ninepostmen in their smart uniforms and two or three telegraph boys. The ladies sitting at the front were either telegraphists or counter staff. This does not quite tally with the staff numbers quoted by the surveyor in 1906! As to whether Harold Baker was then Acting Postmaster rather than in a permanent position is open to question. Harold Luke Baker was a local lad from Meare who was employed by the Post Office in Glastonbury and referred to as a "Learner" in 1901 and he is recorded as moving to Glastonbury, under Bridgwater, as a qualified Post & Telegraph Officer in 1907 later moving to Weston-s-Mare in 1914. Eventually he returned to his home village and ran the Post Office and a confectioners shop.

The Post Office guide of the time, issued annually, contained a wealth of information; it names Miss E. Griffin as being appointed to the position of sub-postmistress for Glastonbury on 20th January 1907. Usefully the same guide also gives the date of birth of these appointments - Emily Griffin was born on the 28th July 1871 so was aged 35 on the date of her taking on the role. Carrying out research on the internet reveals that her parents were Edward and Emma Griffin, father being a solicitor's clerk. One of two children born in Glastonbury, Emily, then aged 19, had left home and was working as a Post Office clerk in Street by 1890. She was one of two clerks and a telegraph boy boarding with Mrs Caroline Boyce, the Postmistress. By the time of the 1901 census Emily, still described as a Post Office clerk, had returned to live with her now retired parents at No. 70 High Street, Glastonbury. She was most probably now working in Glastonbury and when the vacancy occurred Emily, with her many years of Post Office experience, would have been an obvious choice to become the new Postmistress. Emily was to continue in this role until she retired in 1926 after 19 years in post, her salary for her final year being £177.00. During her tenure she had seen a number of changes due to the upset caused by the Great War, especially the greater role played by women in the workforce and also the cost of postage. Since its first introduction in 1840 the basic rate for a letter had remained at 1d. but, due to the demands from the treasury, the Post Office was obliged to increase this to 1½d. in 1918; only for it to increase further to 2d. in 1920. This latter increase was short-lived as by 1922 the rate had again reverted to 1½d.

Picture believed to be of Emily Griffin whilst she working at Street Post Office in 1895

Nationally, in 1880, the Post Office first used the bicycle for postal deliveries but their introduction in Glastonbury did not take place until 1900. As with so many things to do with the running of the postal service, there is a manual with very specific instructions even for the maintenance of the humble bicycle.

In the P.M.G.s minute book for 1923 there is a reference to obtaining, in Magdalene Strret, a garage for a "Motor Cycle combination"; this would have been a motor cycle and side-car and one wonders as to which part of the service would use it?

In August 1926, following Emily Griffin's retirement, the Post Office appointed Ernest A. Boon, born in 1871, as the new Postmaster. Ernest, originally came from Modbury in South Devon and had started his Post Office career in Bideford in 1893. By the time the 1901 census was taken he had progressed to being a sorting clerk and telegraphist, now living with his wife, Clara, and their seven month old son. ten years later, with 3 children, all at school, Clara was also working at the Post Office as a sorting clerk and telegraphist. By the time of his appointment to Glastonbury, aged 55, Ernest had risen to become manager in charge of the postmen whilst still in Bideford.

In the year when Ernest Boon retired, 1931, his salary was stated to be £202.00 a year. He was replaced in March that year by Henry Passmore who had first

1.—Handlegrip.	15.—Front rim.	28.—Right pedal.
2.—Handlebar.	16.—Tyre cover.	29.—Left crank.
3.—Handlebar stem.	17.—Front mudguard.	30.—Left pedal.
4.—Head lock nut.	18.—Mudguard stays.	31.—Seat stay—left.
5.—Head washer.	19.—Splashguard.	32.—Chain.
6.—Head adjusting race.	20.—Top tube.	33.—Chain stay—left.
7.—Top head lug.	21.—Saddle pillar.	34.—Back rim.
8.—Head tube.	22.—Seat lug.	35.—Back mudguard.
9.—Bottom head lug.	23.—Seat lug bolt and nut.	37.—Reflector.
10.—Fork crown.	24.—Seat tube.	38.—Saddle clip.
11.—Fork blade left.	25.—Bottom tube.	39.—Free wheel.
12.—Spokes.	26.—Bottom bracket axle.	128.—Lamp bracket
13.—Spoke nipples.	27.—Right crank and ft.	(front).
14.—Valves.	chain wheel.	

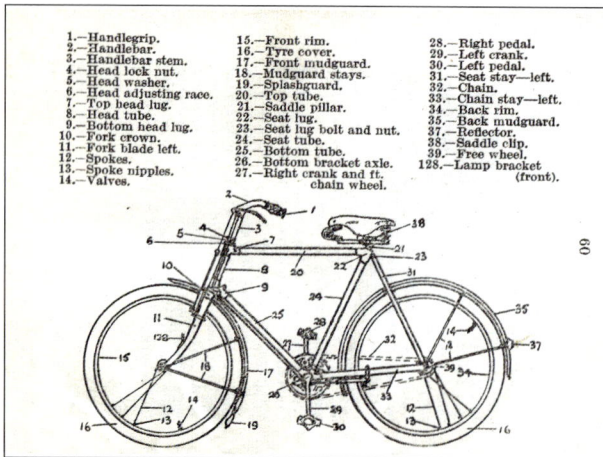

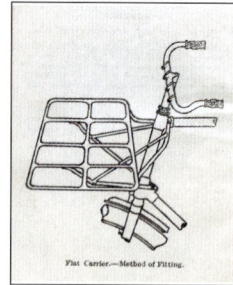

Illustrations from the bicycle maintenance manual.
Courtesy of Ron Talbot of Street. 2014

started working for the Post Office in Taunton in 1905, aged 16, classed as a "Learner". His father, originally from Marazion in Cornwall, had married a girl from Taunton who also worked for the Post Office. Henry progressed to Wellington, being first posted there in July 1908, and he was one of two boarders in lodgings in the town in 1911, both of whom worked in the Post Office. Unfortunately it seems that Mr Passmore did not perform to the standard required by the service as in 1934 we find the entry: *P.M.G. Minute Book E16307/08: "Glastonbury. Passmore H T, Sub Pm. Irregularities in A/cs and improper conduct to female staff. Reduced to rank of S.C.T.(P) and compulsorily transferred to Plymouth"* and no more was heard of him in Glastonbury.

And so it was that on 18th April 1934 Stuart Barringer was appointed postmaster at Glastonbury. Stuart was originally from the London area where both his father and his sister worked for the G.P.O. His father was a telegraphist and his sister, Gladys, was a clerk with the P.O. Savings Bank. Whilst living in Hornsey in 1900, at the age of 16, Stuart was taken on by the G.P.O. as a learner, according

A picture from the Internet of a Postman outside the Post Office. Circa 1932.

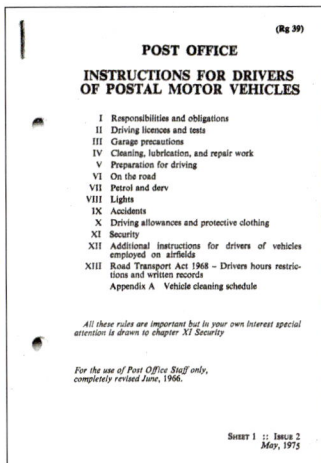

As with bicycles, so it was with motor transport; a seriously comprehensive guide to the use of Post Office vans, their loading and use.

to the P. O. records. In the census of 1901 he is described as a telegraphist like his father. In 1911 he had become a counter clerk, still in the London District. Between that time and his move to Glastonbury no records could be found but in the P.M.G. minute book (3603) for 1934 is this bare statement:- *Glastonbury. Barringer. S. Postmaster Torrington appointed Postmaster* - and his salary for 1935 was £274.6.0.

The major postal event during the time that Stuart was Postmaster was the opening of the new Post Office in 1938. The site for the new office in the High Street had been bought earlier and was, at that time occupied by the three storey shop known as London House. Here Messrs Brooks and Sons ran a drapery business. It is reputed that the original John Lewis, the father of John Spedan Lewis who founded the John Lewis Partnership chain of shops, as a young man, learnt his trade here. As he was born in Shepton Mallet, only a few miles away, this is entirely feasible.

The new Post Office, built by local builders, Messrs D. R. Dunthorn, was opened on 17th August 1938 amongst great pomp by the Mayor of Glastonbury, the occasion chaired by Lt.-Col. W. R. Roberts, the Post Office Surveyor for the Western District.

The Official Opening was carried out by the Mayor of Glastonbury, Wm. A. L. Hucker, Esq, J.P. whose address included reference to the increased business carried out in the Glastonbury Post Office in recent times: In 1937 they had 44,000 letters and 1,800 parcels delivered a week as compared with 33,000 letters and 1,400 parcels a week in 1936.

A Postcard of the High Street, c. 1910,
showing Brooks & Sons shop, London House, on the left hand side

Mr. H. E. Seccombe, architect to H.M. Office of Works, spoke about the building and described his first visit to Glastonbury. He said he was disappointed on seeing so many petrol pumps in the High Street which gave visitors a wrong impression, and he also felt that the existing "London House' spoiled the line of the other building around. In pulling it down and erecting the present building he thought he had done the town a service.

Mr. Turnbull, the Postmaster of Bridgwater proposed a vote of thanks and this was seconded by Dr. Eglington, the Medical Officer to the Street Post Office. The Mayor was then presented with a silver-gilt key by Mr. Seccombe.

Stuart Barringer, the Postmaster of Glastonbury, did have the opportunity to speak when he seconded the vote of thanks to the Chairman.

After the formal opening of the main door from the street, the first sale over the counter was made by the Deputy Mayoress (Mrs. J. Alexander) to the Mayoress (Mrs. W.A.L. Hucker) and then Miss Rocke, Lady of the Manor of Glastonbury, handed in the first telegram, which was addressed to the Postmaster General. After the party had made an inspection of the building and partaken of tea a reply had been received and this was read out to those attending.

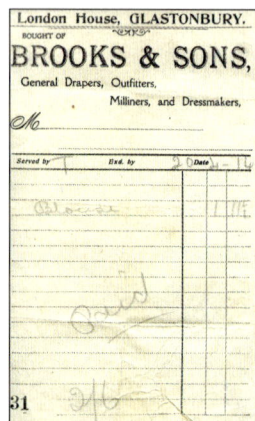

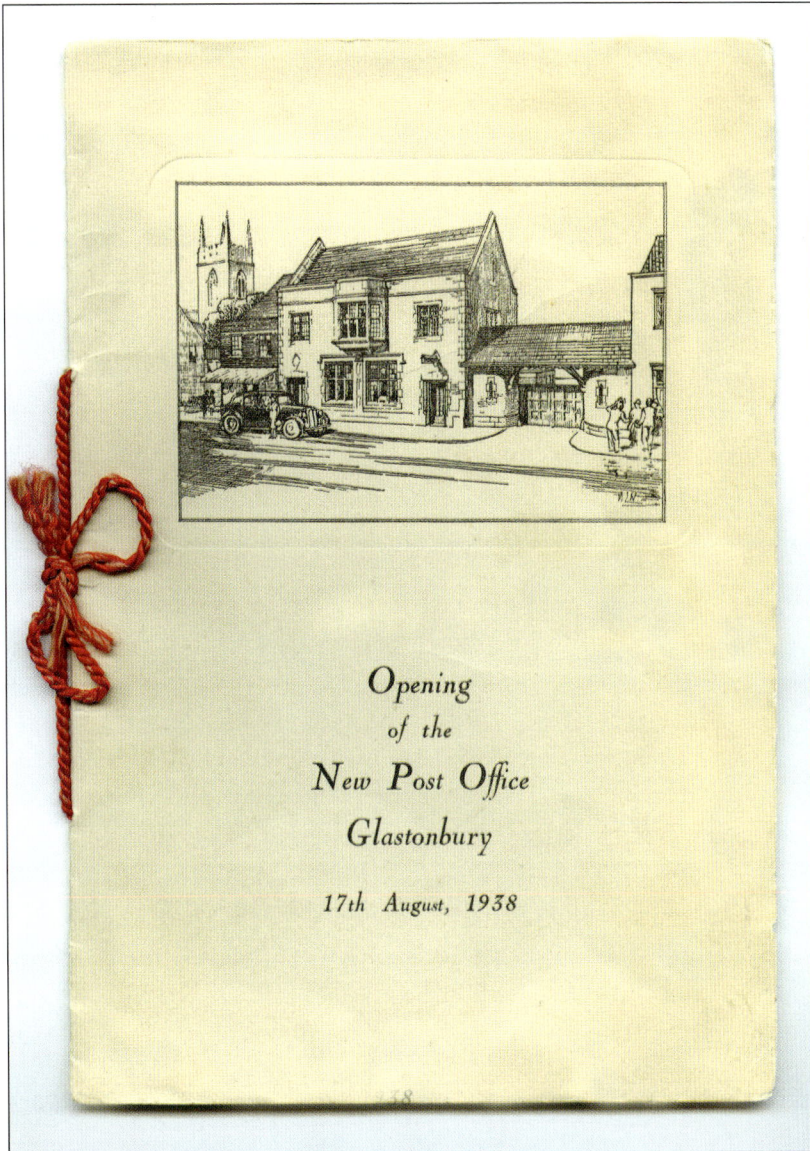

Opening
of the
New Post Office
Glastonbury

17th August, 1938

Graham Carroll

*A copy of the Programme issued to the staff and the
townspeople taking part.
This copy belongs to Graham Carroll, himself a former
Glastonbury Postman, whose wife's late uncle was on the staff
at the Post Office in 1938. There is another copy to be found
in the "Glastonbury" folder in the Post Office Archives.*

In the original printed programme the Rev. Lional S. Lewis, the vicar of St John's church, was expected to give a vote of thanks to the mayor. As to why he was not present no reason was given. He had previously had an input into the design of the new building. It is believed that, when the plans were first published, the frontage was going to be of brick. This the Rev. Lewis objected to strongly and, having a direct connection to the Postmaster General in London, he was able to have major amendments made. To have a building more suited to the historic town was said to be his opinion.

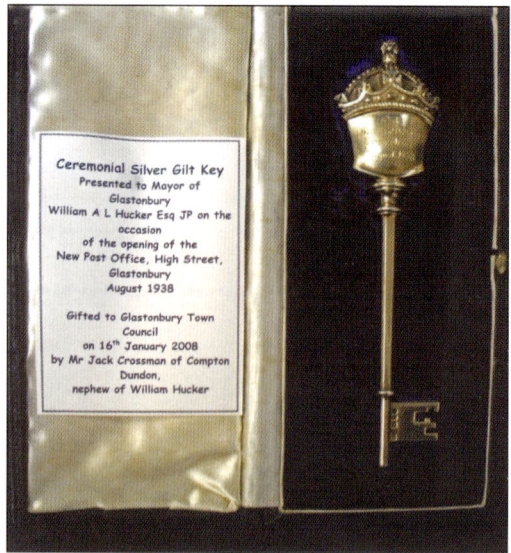

Ceremonial Silver Gilt Key
Presented to Mayor of
Glastonbury
William A L Hucker Esq JP on the
occasion
of the opening of the
New Post Office, High Street,
Glastonbury
August 1938

Gifted to Glastonbury Town
Council
on 16th January 2008
by Mr Jack Crossman of Compton
Dundon,
nephew of William Hucker

The Silver Gilt Key presented to the Mayor at the opening ceremony. Presented to the town by his nephew, Jack Crossman, in January 2008, and now kept in the Town Hall

During the ceremony reference had been made to the new building at the back of the yard where the replacement of the manual telephone exchange by an automatic one was to be housed. Due to the outbreak of war in 1939 this was very much delayed and the existing exchange continued in use at the rear of the old Post Office below St John's Church. When Glastonbury did get its new S.T.D. (Subscriber Trunk Dialling) Exchange, which was not until the late 1960s, it was built on an entirely different site in the town.

After 45 years of service to the G.P.O., Stuart Barringer's salary, in his final year before retiring at the age of 61 in 1945, had risen to £327.8.0 per annum. On the 26th June 1945 Walter C. G. Simons, aged 47, was appointed as the new postmaster with his salary slightly less than that of his predecessor at £325.0.0 but

Two of the many design features set in the mosaic floor.

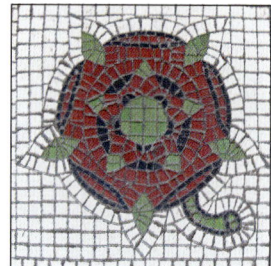

The scene outside the new Post Office on the afternoon of the opening

this was to rise quite quickly as by 1948 it was £510.0.0 p.a. This information was all published in the Post Office guides of the time.

Walter Simons originally came from Weston-s-Mare, born in the town in 1898. He started employment for the G.P.O. as a postman there in 1914. It was unusual to be placed in this position quite so young but, probably due to the outbreak of the war, there was a severe shortage of staff in many industries, including the Post Office. We find that he was to remain at Weston until 1927 when the records show him being appointed to a position in Newton Abbot in Devon. Very probably he had been to Letchworth in Hertfordshire before that. The distinctive initials of his name are clear so the W.E.G. Simons, who was Postman Manager in Southampton in 1929, could well have been the Walter Simons who was later to come to Glastonbury.

Following Walter Simons we find Charles Gooch being appointed to the position of Postmaster at Glastonbury on the 28th June 1948 just before his 50th birthday. He started his Post Office career in Malvern in 1917 as a "Leaner"and then qualified as a Sorting Clerk and Telegraphist at Tewkesbury, Gloucestershire, in April 1919.

After eight years the position at Glastonbury was again declared vacant and was taken up by Basil Southgate whose appointment commenced on 10th July 1956. It is believed that Basil, who was born in February 1910, came from the East of England and that he qualified as a Sorting Clerk and Telegraphist in

The Post Office as seen in March 2003.

Norwich in 1929. Little is known as to where he went after leaving Glastonbury but he is recorded as dying in the town in which he first qualified, Norwich, in 2005.

At some time between Basil Southgate leaving and Les Garrett taking over in 1973 a Mr Cunningham was the Postmaster. I was able to visit Les in June 2014, then living in retirement in Paulton, near Radstock. Tracing his life history certainly gives a very good insight into the Postal system and the career path that many of its employees followed.

Les started work in the Post Office in Frome at the age of 14 in 1942 as a temporary Boy Messenger and rose to be Postmaster at Glastonbury. A boy Messenger could only hold this position, which entailed delivering telegrams around the district as well as other duties, until the age of 16, after which they were expected to join the regular staff. In order to progress to the position of Postal Sorting Clerk and Telegraphist Les had to first pass a Civil Service Commission examination which covered not only his writing ability but also the skill needed to précis a short story. It also tested his ability with figures, having to add up 3 separate columns of figures in pounds, shillings and pence, answer questions about surface area from an example given concerning kites and lastly, his knowledge of geography with such questions as: *On the accompanying map of the British Isles (a.) Mark clearly and name Barrow, Bristol, Larne, Oldham, Southend and Sunderland.* Also, for instance, *(e.) Show by a dotted line a railway route from London to Penzance through Swindon, Bristol and Plymouth and mark and name these 5 towns.* There were also questions on world geography; I liked the one where he had to clearly mark and name on the world map provided the following: *Algiers, Brisbane, Calcutta, Istanbul (Constantinople), Montevideo, Nanking and Rangoon!*

After taking the exam he received a letter from the Civil Service Commission informing him that he now held *"A Certificate of Qualification for employment in the situation of Temporary Postman Messenger".*

Sir,
Madam,
        I have to inform you that your son *Leslie R G Garrett* has been
appointed to the regular Messenger Staff at the *Frome Same.* Post
Office with effect from *14 February* 1942.

I am, Sir,
~~Madam~~,
Your obedient Servant,

C.H. Annington
Head Postmaster.

*[4007] 19096/P3902 3000 9/36 1195 G & S 625

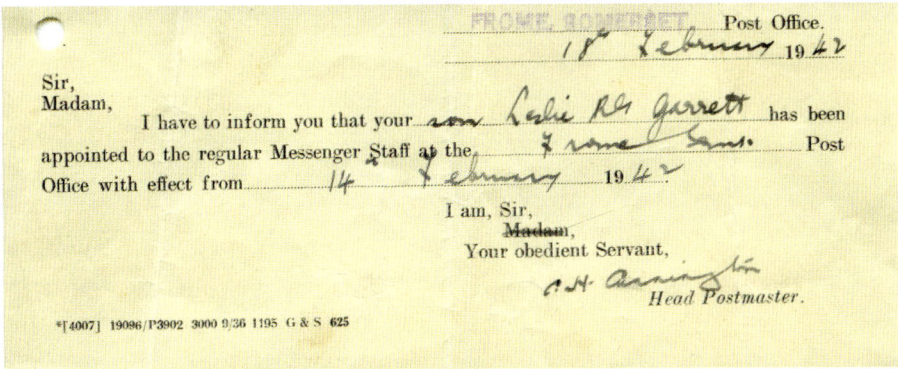

Anyhow, following the exam, Les was pleased to receive the letter and this
was followed up by a further letter, dated 3rd November 1944, from the Civil
Service Commission to the effect that he was now qualified as a *"Sorting Clerk &
Telegraphist"* and was taken on for a six month probation period at 25/- a week
from 28th January 1945. *"Your next increment will be due when you have qualified,
provided that a fully effective duty is performed or you have given 6 months' service,
your normal date of increment will be 13th July."*

In 1946, like most of the youth of his era, he was called up for National Service,
spending two years in one of the armed services. Les opted for the Royal Air
Force and, after serving his time, returned to his job in Frome Post Office where
he soon qualified as a Post & Telegraph Officer, receiving confirmation of this in
May 1949 and, over time, was promoted to the position of overseer.

BOY MESSENGERS' GENERAL EXAMINATION
Office. FROME   Messenger L. R. G. Garrett

        In the General Examination held on the 6 June 1944 you
obtained 258 marks including 37 marks for Handwriting.
        The minimum number of marks qualifying for appointment as
Sorting Clerk and Telegraphist is 220 with not less than 25 marks for
Handwriting.
        You have therefore qualified in the Sorting Clerk and Telegraphist
group of the Examination.
        It should be clearly understood that no promise of appointment as
Sorting Clerk and Telegraphist is made, but you will be considered in
turn with other candidates should vacancies occur.

Signed C .H. Trowbridge
Head Postmaster

Les was later to be seconded to the Head Post Office in Bristol and in 1973 he applied for and was appointed to the position of Head Postmaster at Glastonbury, a position he held until his retirement on his 60th birthday, the 13th July 1987.

As Postmaster he was responsible for all aspects of the office which included not only the counter services but also the urban and rural deliveries with a total staff of about 40 people. They also had a large Parcel Post workload as Clarks Shoes of Street sent all their work through the Glastonbury office and, after the closing of Glastonbury Railway station, two large vans were permanently employed on this work. This office also covered the management of Street Post Office, the latter having just a senior clerk in charge of counter services. When the first post of the day arrived from Bristol at 4.30am. there was an assistant inspector, who held the keys to the premises, on duty to let the Postmen begin their work. Les was usually in his office, adjoining the counter services in Glastonbury Post Office, by 8.30am although, technically he was always on duty, 24 hours a day.

The recruitment of staff fell to the Head Post Office in Bath to carry out the advertising of the vacancy and the gathering of references but the final say rested with the postmaster, and an Assistant Inspector when, subject to the passing of an simple test hardly stiff enough to call an examination, the subject was taken on to the pay-roll.

Glastonbury
Somerset.

Post Office		Post Office

Postmaster - L.R.Garrett.

LATEST POSTING TIMES (First Class Letters) normally securing first delivery at:

	Mon-Fri	Sat
LONDON	1830	
Bath	1830	
Birmingham	1830	
Bridgwater	1830	
Bristol	1830	
Cardiff	1830	
Exeter	1830	
Leeds	1600	1245
Liverpool	1830	
Manchester	1830	
Street (Som)	0600	
Taunton	1830	
Wells	1830	
Weston-S-Mare	1830	
York	1830	

RURAL All places in rural area incl.
Baltonsborough
Butleigh
Meare   0600
Walton
West Pennard

HOURS OF BUSINESS
Mon-Fri   0900 - 1730
Saturday   0900 - 1300

Sunday. Christmas Day. Boxing Day.
Good Friday and Bank Holidays
CLOSED

TOWN DELIVERIES (Ex Sunday. Christmas Day. Boxing Day and Bank Holidays)

	Start of Delivery	Latest posting time normally at this office to Connect (First Class Letters)
Letters	0700 1100 Not Sat	0600 1030 Not Sat
Parcels	One Daily	

SECOND CLASS LETTERS Will generally be delivered up to two days later than First Class Letters.

PRINCIPAL COLLECTIONS From the posting box at this office are made at:

Weekdays	Good Friday
0600	1245
1030 Not Sat	
1245	
1600 Not Sat	
1830 Not Sat	

Sunday.
Christmas Day. Boxing Day
and Bank Holidays
NO COLLECTION

TELEGRAMS May be dictated from kiosk at any time.

PUBLIC TELEPHONES The nearest kiosk is in High Street.

Notice outside the Post Office in March 1982
Note: Postmaster L. R. Garrett

Les Garrett in June 2014 living in Paulton, Near Radstock.

The delivery Postmen worked in groups and rotated their rounds between Town and Rural delivery or Indoor duties. Having sorted the mail for their respective round, the aim was to be out on the road by 6.00am and to complete the round by 9.30am. Then came the task of sorting the mail which had been collected from the various letter boxes, particularly finding the letters for local delivery, enabling them be sent out on the second delivery in the afternoon. At that time all the mail collected locally was postmarked with its office of origin before being forwarded on to Bristol.

Before Les retired, in 1986 the Post Office was subject to a major overhaul and the service was broken down into three distinct sections, Post Office Counters Ltd, Parcelforce and M.L.O.s (Mechanised Letter Offices). The latter were where all the mail was dealt with on a regional basis and only the local sorting took place in Glastonbury.

Even Glastonbury Post Office was not immune to the spate of break-ins that occurred around that time. In October 1988 there was a robbery in the High Street Office when a quantity of Visitor Passports and a validation stamp, together with items from postal packets, were stolen.

An insight into the life of a local postman is also illustrated by the visit I paid to Ron Talbot, living in retirement in Street, in March 2013. Ron started as a postman in Glastonbury in 1974 and completed 28 years of service before retiring.

When he first started the staff came on duty at 4.00am. when on the early shift and, after sorting the mail, they completed their rounds and finished at 12.00 midday. They worked a shift pattern of two weeks on the early shift and one week on the late one which ran from 12.00 midday until 8.00pm. and there were two deliveries a day throughout the whole of the Glastonbury area. This applied to the surrounding villages as well. Later on, the start was put back to 4.30am. but an 8 hour shift was still worked. Saturday morning was considered to part of the ordinary working week and, even when taking a week's holiday, one was expected to complete the round before your break started.

Ron Talbot in his Postman's Uniform and his cap and ID badges.

The change from town deliveries to the country areas usually took place about every two to three years and one was expected to know the whole area, especially the whereabouts of the various house letter boxes, let alone the post boxes spread throughout the region.

When Ron was there the Postmaster was Les Garrett as the main office was still designated a "Crown Office" and the sorting office and Post Office were under one management. In later years managers were appointed with out the title of Postmaster.

With the Christmas issue of stamps in November 1986 a stylised depiction of the Glastonbury Thorn appeared on the 13 pence value, the second class rate at the time; millions of copies of these were used that year on Christmas cards giving Glastonbury tremendous publicity.

In 1988 Post Office Counters Ltd put out a consultation document suggesting that Glastonbury Post Office should lose its Crown Office status and become an agency sub-office; much as the village equivalents. A long fought battle under the heading of *"Save Glastonbury Post Office Campaign"* was led by Mr Clive Browning for the town to keep its Head Office. This even entailed a visit to London to meet Sir Bryan Nicholson, the Chairman and Chief Executive of the Post Office, to present a 4000 name petition as well as the deputation going to No. 10 Downing Street. Many stories circulated concerning the siting of a re-graded Post Office; Was it going to be in the in the local supermarket, Safeways, or some other shop in the town? Mr Brian Strange, the district manager of Post Office Counters Ltd dismissed these rumours and described the Glastonbury Campaigners as *"People who probably don't understand the issues"*. He went on to say that the proposed move was a *"re-grading"*, not a *"down-grading"*. He even suggested that the rumoured sub-office in Safeways would have been a supplement to the High Street, not an alternative.

The Christmas stamp of 1986

On what the campaigners referred to as "Black Friday" on Friday, 13th January 1989 Post Office Counters announced that they had finished their consultations and did not feel that any new points had emerged to make them change their minds. Royal Mail, who owned the premises, was allowing Post Office Counters Ltd to take over the shop at the front of the building and therefore the Post Office building in the High Street was still able to operate as normal as far as the customers were concerned.

As reported in the *Central Somerset Gazette* on 22nd. March 1990:

The newly franchised Glastonbury Post Office will be open on April 23rd, with Ken Watkins, aged 51, an office manager at the Wells Post Office, in charge. Ken, who lives in East Horrington, will be taking over the front ground floor area of the building.

Said Ken: "My wife, Margaret, will be working part-time with me and I will be taking on one other part-timer. It will not be possible to take on all the staff that work there at the moment as they have retained their jobs with Post Office Counters at another office. He added: "I am very excited about it. It is a privilege to be able to serve the people of Glastonbury and to be able to

CENTRAL SOMERSET Gazette

THURSDAY DECEMBER 8 1988 PRICE 22p

Thousands rally to protest

Status quo plea in bid to save PO

Story by Tessa Finch

The Central Somerset Gazette of December 8th 1988

work in such a wonderful historic town. I really mean that, I love the West Country, which is why I moved here originally from Brighton".

Ken Watkins had not been, unlike many others, a lifetime Post Office employee. After a career in the Royal Air Force, from which he was invalided out due to injury, he joined an engineering company which manufactured buses. Still suffering from his health he made the decision to seek lighter work. Initially joining the wine trade before taking, with his wife Margaret, a newsagents shop in the New Forest. Seeing an opportunity of working for the G.P.O. Ken took an internal examination and soon rose to the position of office manager in the Post Office in Wells.

Whilst at Wells, Ken was very much involved with Post Office Union affairs, becoming treasurer of the branch at one time. He recalls attending a National Union conference where, because of his background, he found himself much distrusted and suspected of being sent there as a management spy!

With the amendment to the status of the Glastonbury Post Office Ken and Margaret seized the opportunity to take over the business and also to work together. They did find the bureaucratic nature of the management of Post Office Counters difficult to handle. But by having one of the first computers, an Amstrad, he found that did simplify the return of the many forms required.

Whilst at Glastonbury, one of the first moves they made was to incorporate the managers office into retail selling space for cards and related stationery. At that time it could only be accessed through the main door. Ken and Margaret remained at Glastonbury for three years, before moving to Street, and eventually retiring to Wales.

Following Ken at the Post Office we find Jon Oberholzer and his wife, Sue, managing the business whilst Jon's father-in-law, Alan Clark, was the nominated Sub-Postmaster. Jon was born in Rhodesia and had been in the Rhodesian Air Force from the time he left school. It was out there that he met Sue, Welsh by birth, and that is where they got married. With the outbreak of racial tension in the country they were obliged to leave and that is how they came to be in Britain.

Jon found work in the Post Office at Glastonbury and with Ken and Margaret's wish to move, in June 1993, Jon and his family decided to take over the running of the High Street business. During their time there they expanded the trade, even opening the second doorway into the card shop. They continued to run it for the following eight years until eventually selling out to Gerald Cross in May 2001.

Gerald had originally had a career in banking, ending up as Rural Lending Manager at a bank in Shepton Mallet. That job became increasingly frustrating and, following a short time working in Bristol, he decided on a change of career. That was when he became the manager, in 1997, of the village Post Office at Evercreech, near Shepton Mallet. When the opportunity of taking over the Glastonbury Office arose he was only too pleased to take it. In 2015 he employs seven people of which two are full time, the others come in on a part-time basis.

Glastonbury Post Office Counter before re-organisation
in March 2014

One of these full time workers is Jon Oberholzer, the previous manager who, after a short break working in the Wells Post Office, came back to Glastonbury and now has now given over twenty years service to the people of the town

The Glastonbury Post Office staff in August 2004.
From left to right: Pat Manning, Tracey Lambert, Gerald Cross,
Sharon Gainey, Jon Oberholzer.
Photo by Tony Bolton in the Central Somerset Gazette

Things evolve and fashions change. In March 2014 the Post Office was shut for two weeks whilst a complete refurbishment took place. Part way through the re-development a gentleman from English Heritage arrived to question as to what was happening but he was too late to preserve things as they were! Out had gone the glass-fronted counter, to be replaced by a more open plan lay-out. The only exception to this was the section where foreign money transactions take place. The card shop next to the main office now had a counter in the corner where almost all Post Office business could be transacted, again with very little security. This gives four serving positions in all and the hours of business were extended so that, after refurbishment, the office was open from 9.00am. until 5.30pm. including Saturdays. The mosaic floor, of which much was made at the original opening in 1938, was covered except for a small patch just inside the main entrance which can still be seen.

Glastonbury Post Office Counter after re-fitting. Photo July 2014

Royal Mail's sorting and delivery office continues in the premises behind the Post Office in the High Street with the entrance in Archers Way. This is run, in 2015, completely separated from the front office, indeed the door between the two parts is kept locked. The position of what was traditionally called Postmaster, in 2015, is Matt Alford under the title of Delivery/Office Manager. He reports, as was the case in 1853, to the Bath Head Post Office.

Matt started out as a postman in Yeovil in 1995, rising to be assistant manager in that office, a position he held for four years. He then transferred to Taunton, staying for a further two years before moving to Wincanton. He first took up the position of manager in Glastonbury in January 2009.

Ina McLaughlin stood beside the new counter in the former Manager's office where most Post Office transactions can be carried out. Photo taken: July 2014

The Glastonbury delivery and collection office employs 43 full and part-time people and of these 40 carry out regular post deliveries around Glastonbury, Street and the surrounding villages. Normally there are 16 delivery vans based at the depot handling some 130,000 letter and 10,000 parcels a week. This rises to nearly a million items in December, prior to Christmas, when two extra vans and more staff are employed. The use of bicycles on delivery rounds was discontinued in 2008, the form in 2015 being that delivery trolleys are used around towns and all rural deliveries are made by Post van. The Glastonbury office continues, in 2015, to handle a large number of parcels for Messrs Clarks Shoes of Street, particularly the returned items.

Matt Alford in his office

All mail in 2015 is primarily sorted at the Mechanised Letter Office based at Filton in Bristol from where 3 x 7.5 tonne Royal Mail trucks, together with one transit van, arrive at Glastonbury every morning. The Postal delivery staff arrive at 6.00am. carry out their final sort and aim to be on their rounds by 9.00am. Rather more sociable hours than in former days.

The Staff of Glastonbury Delivery Office on the occasion of a visit by Tessa Munt, the Member of Parliament, to open the new Enquiry Office
3rd June 2013.

ACKNOWLEDGEMENTS

With grateful acknowledgements to the many people of Glastonbury who have helped me fill in the details of the history of the Post Office including: Matt Alford, Neil Bonham, Gerald Cross, Ken Gane, Les Garrett, Jon Oberholzer, David Orchard, Ron Talbot and Ken Watkins.

GLASTONBURY POST BOXES

Reference in *Kelly's Directory* of 1906 lists the following:

<u>Wall letter boxes.</u>

Lambrook Street cleared at 6 & 8 a.m. 12 Noon, & 3.35 & 6.50 p.m.
Railway Station at 7.40 & 10.35 a.m. and 1 & 6.30 p.m.
Northover at 11.25 a.m. & 2.55 & 7.0 p.m.
Chilkwell Street at 6.0 & 8.0 a.m., 12 Noon & 3.25 & 6.45 p.m.
Northload Street 11.45 a.m. & 2.45 & 6.40 p.m.
Park Terrace, 5.50 & 11.45 a.m. and 3.15 & 6.50 p.m.
Havyatt, 9.0 a.m. and 12.40 & 6.5 p.m.
Edgarley at 9.30 a.m. and 1.5 and 6.35 p.m.
The Poplars wall box 7.50 & 10.0 a.m. and 3.15 & 6.35 p.m.

In the 1949 paperwork concerning the proposal to close the Street mail sorting office and transfer all work to Glastonbury there is a list of letter boxes in the town: the number in brackets are the Post Office reference numbers.

Street Road (116)	Roman Way (215)
Northover (126)	Station (117)
Benedict Street (111)	Magdalene St. (242)
Northload St. (115)	Wells Road (118)
Brickyard (235)	Bove Town (110)
Lambrook Street (114)	Bere Lane (112)

Glastonbury Post Office
High Street
BA6 1.
March 2014

Tor View Avenue
BA6 292
July 2014

This design is known as a "Lamp Box" is usually attached to a telephone or electricity pole.

Victorian Wall Letter Box
Edgarley, Millfield Junior School entrance. BA6 121. July 2014

Morrison's Supermarket.
BA6 23
July 2014

This design was introduced c. 1979

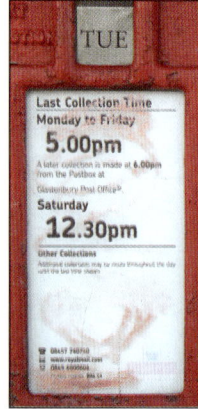

Mornington Road.   BA6 53   July 2014

Bove Town. Glastonbury.   BA6 110   July 2014

Benedict Street
BA6 111
July 2014

Chilkwell Street.
The Victorian Box
BA6 112

March 1982
&
August 1987

Chilkwell Street
The replacement letter box installed in August 1987.
BA6 112
Photo: July 2014

Northload Street
BA6 115
January 2009

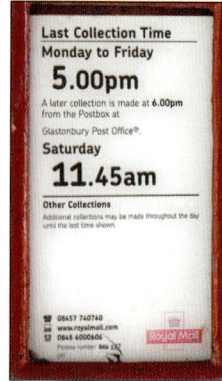

Actis Road BA6 117   July 2014

Wells Road, Glastonbury
BA6 118. January 2009

Ranger Road,
Glastonbury.
BA6 22
January 2009

The Roman Way
BA6 215
January 2009

Brickyard, Wells Road, BA6 235. January 2009

Pillar Box Panel
July 2014

Magdalene Street. BA6 242. March 1982.

Pillar Box. Windmill Hill
Glastonbury
BA6 269
January 2009

Coursing Batch
BA6 113
August 2004

Lambrook Street. BA6 114. January 2009

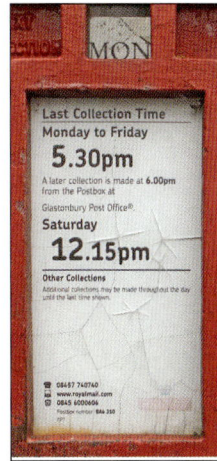

Underwood Road BA6 310 July 2014

Chalice Way,
Actis Estate
BA6 311
January 2009

Some of the
POSTMARKS of GLASTONBURY

GLASTON BURY

The two line
GLASTON
BURY
in use in 1773

The two line
GLASTON
BURY
in use in 1785

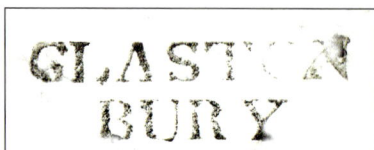

GLASTON BURY

GLASTON BURY

The smaller two line
GLASTON
BURY
in use in 1798

Mileage Mark.
Denoting the distance
from LONDON, the
basis of charging postage
in 1811

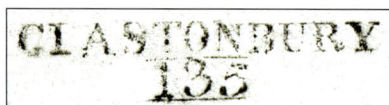

**GLASTONBURY
134**

**GLASTONBURY
135**

Following amendment to the
routes, new Mileage Marks
were issued to Post Towns in
1822

In use after the introduction of the
GLASTONBURY PENNY POST
system in 1832

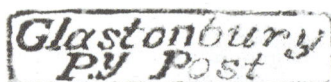

**Glastonbury
P.y Post**

The following two and a half pages are mostly taken from the *Proof Book Impressions* in the Postal Archives as recorded by Mike Walch in *The Somerset and Dorset Postal History Group* publication, 1995.

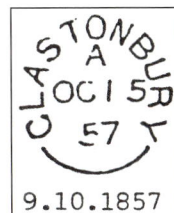

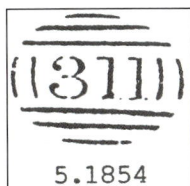

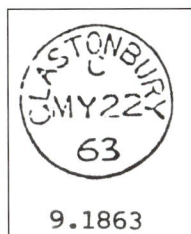

GLASTONBURY
JY 25
1837

27.7.1837

GLASTONBURY
MA 16
1843

16.3.1843
"recut"

GLASTONBURY
MY 8
1849

28.5.1849
"new"

GLASTONBURY
JY 8
1849

GLASTONBURY
SP 5
1853
A

5.9.1853

GLASTONBURY
SP 27
1853
A

GLASTONBURY
AU 2
1854
A

8.1854

GLASTONBURY
A
JA 20
58

GLASTONBURY
A
OC 15
57

9.10.1857

((311))

5.1854

(311)

((311))

23.6.1857

GLASTONBURY
D
AP 25
62

25.4.1862

GLASTONBURY
C
MY 22
63

9.1863

GLASTONBURY POSTMARKS (Cont.)

26.8.1867

30.11.1865

15.5.1872

25.2.1873

13.10.1874

7.4.1876

7.11.1877

10.12.1878

5.6.1880

27.5.1882

GLASTONBURY POSTMARKS (Cont.)

20. 11. 1882

25.2.1887

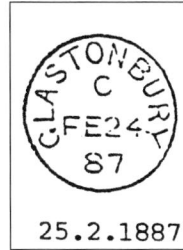

25.2.1887

24.7.1911

SKELETON OR TRAVELLING POSTMARKS
These handstamps were used when an extra one was required due to extra demand or if the regular one was missing

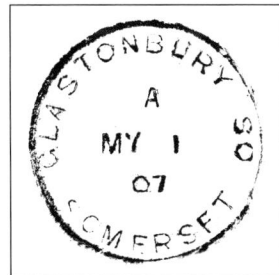

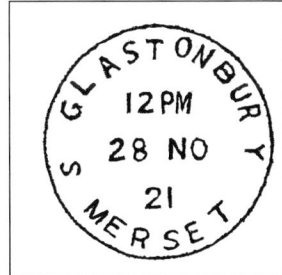

Handstamps used at the counter or in the Sorting Office

GLASTONBURY POSTMARKS (Cont.)

The use of the 311 Triangular mark for Bulk Posted items

The Machine Canceller with 311 replacing the date plug.
Only used when a mail census was being taken

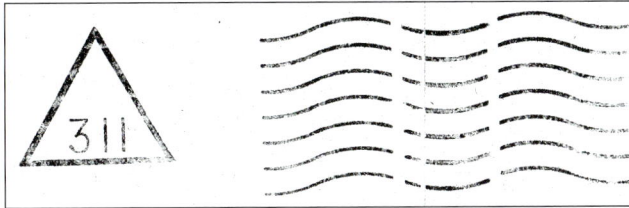

TO PAY marks with the Glastonbury 311 P.O. Number

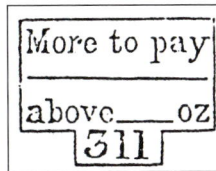

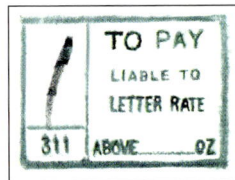

GLASTONBURY POSTMARKS (Cont.)

MACHINE CANCELLATIONS

The "KRAG" machine with continuous impressions.

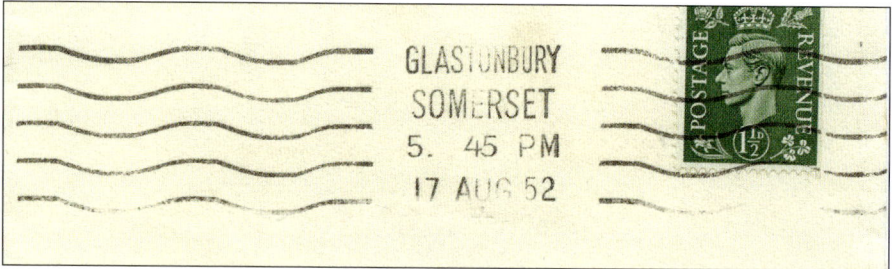

The "UNIVERSAL" machine with 6 bars broken into three sections
Earliest seen: 02-07-1954. Latest: 06-03-1962

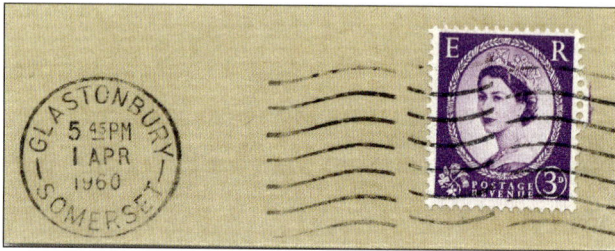

With Glastonbury - Gt. Britain die in red correctly used for Postage Paid letters

The Postage Paid Handtamp
used in 1944

GLASTONBURY POSTMARKS (Cont.)

The Glastonbury PARCEL POST handstamp

Mis-dated METER MARKS corrected.

GLASTONBURY POSTMARKS (Cont.)

*Wells Philatelic Society Exhibition
in Glastonbury Town Hall.
4th July 1970*

PRIVATELY SPONSORED
HANDSTAMPS.
Illustrations reduced to 80% of original

*Commemorating Glastonbury Abbey. 20th
November 1984*

*"Land of
Arthur"
Exhibition of
Celtic Legend.
3rd Sept. 1985.*

*The Christmas Stamp
depicting the Glastonbury
Holy Thorn.
18th November 1986*

GLASTONBURY and STREET POSTMARKS

With the closure of the Street Sorting Office in January 1958 and the work moved to Glastonbury, letters were still postmarked STREET until the Autumn of 1963 when new dies and handstamps were issued with GLASTONBURY and STREET, SOMERSET

HANDSTAMPS

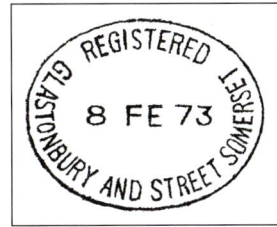

MACHINE CANCELLATIONS

The small lettered Glastonbury & Street date die. Seen 19.12.63 - 1971

The date die with larger letters. Seen 09.07.67 - 04.01.80

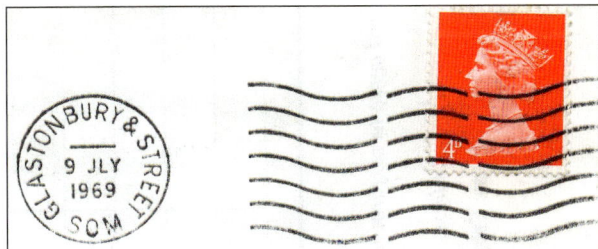

Machine Cancellations SLOGANS
with Small or Large Lettered Die

Small Die
MENTAL
HANDICAP
WEEK
June 1970

Small Die
Seen in Jan-Mar.
1971

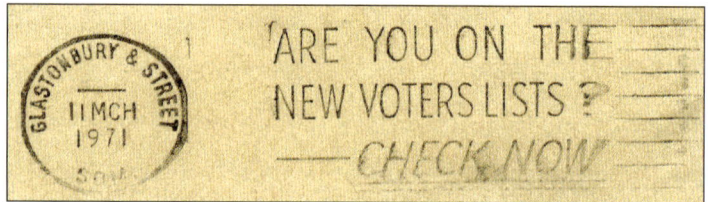

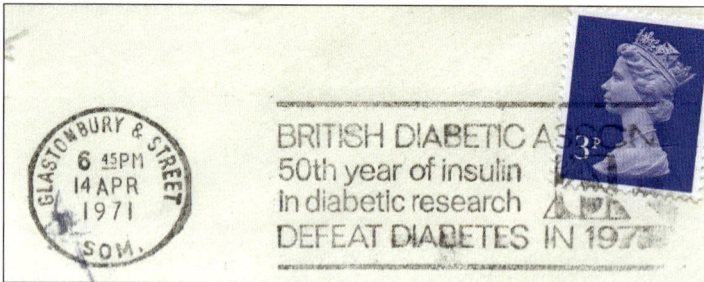

50th Anniversary
of Insulin.
Seen Apr-May
1971

Small Die placed
in the right.
Seen in 1974

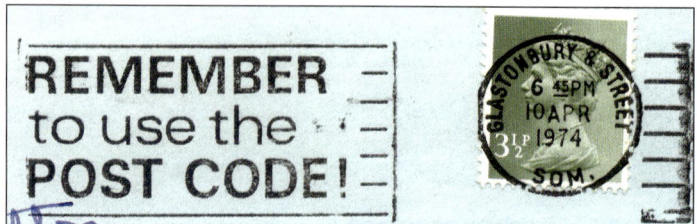

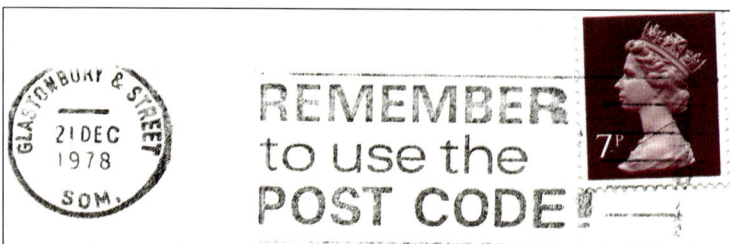

Small Die on
the left.
Seen 1978

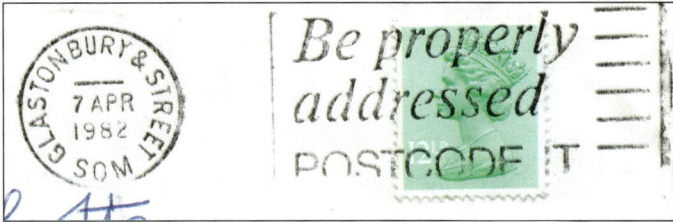

BE PROPERLY ADDRESSED.
Seen in use 1981 - 1985.
Resurrected December 2000-2002

Small Die.
BE PROPERLY ADDRESSED - POST CODE IT.

Large Die.
PASS ON YOUR POSTCODE.
1986

nd Mrs. A. W. Cotton,

Small Die placed on the right.
1972

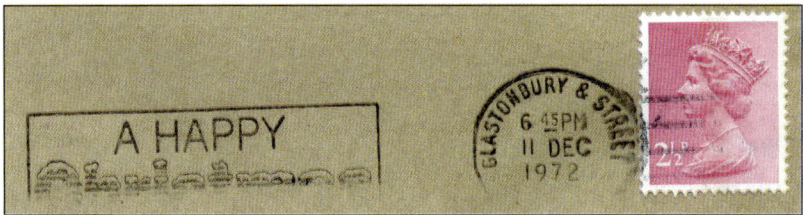

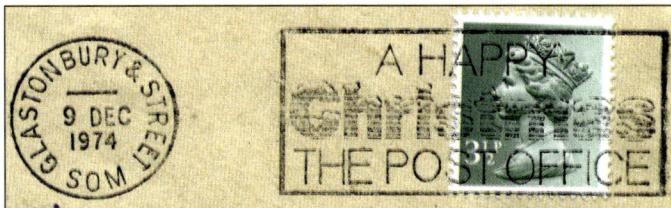

Large Die.
Seen in use at Christmas 1972 - 1989

GLASTONBURY and STREET POSTMARKS (Cont.)

Machine Cancellations - A Few Common Errors

The Date Plug inverted and to the right.

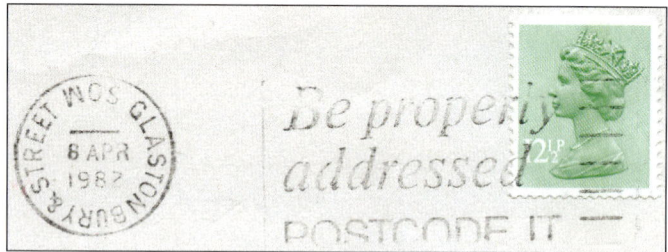

The Date Plug Inverted

Late useage of the machine. It was used at Christmas 2001 - 2003

Machine cancellations - POSTAGE PAID

Large Lettered Die used for Bulk Pre-Paid mail

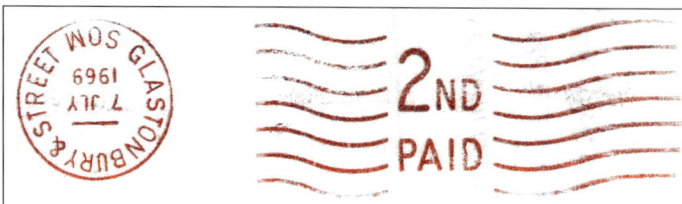

The Date Plug inverted

Ashcott

*A*SHCOTT, a parish in Bridgewater district, Somerset; near the Glastonbury railway, 5 miles WSW of Glastonbury. It has a station on the railway, and a post-office under Bath; and includes the hamlet of Pedwell. Acres, 2,272. Real property, £4,328. Pop., 817. Houses, 183. The manor belonged to Glastonbury abbey. The living is a vicarage, annexed to Shapwick, in the diocese of Bath and Wells. The church was restored in 1860. There are a Wesleyan chapel, and charities £70.

From:- *"The Imperial Gazetteer of England & Wales"* by John Marius Wilson.Pub. A. Fullarton & Co. 1872

ASHCOTT VILLAGE was on the Post Road from London, via Bath and Wells to Exeter. It presents a bit of a dilemma as to whether it should be included in this book as, although it was part of the Glastonbury Penny Post system before 1840, it very soon became a sub-office of Bridgwater.

In the Reports from Francis Freeling, the Secretary to the Postmaster General in London of 26th May 1826, Mr Louis the surveyor, recommends, amongst a reorganisation of the mails to Street, Walton and Shapwick, that a receiving house be set up at Ashcott at an annual cost of £7-7-0.

Ashcott is again mentioned in these reports on 4th July in the same year concerning the matter of a certain Mr Woodward to remain as the receiver of letters at the village but, due to objections from Mr Taylor, the Lord of the Manor at Shapwick, on no account should he be allowed to make deliveries. This does imply that there was a letter delivery in the two villages at that time. In *Bragg's Directory of Somerset* for 1840 a certain Miss Susan Woodward is named as the Post-mistress for Ashcott which lends support to the fact that the family retained the position. According to the 1841 census Susan Woodward was 66 years of age i.e. born around 1775.

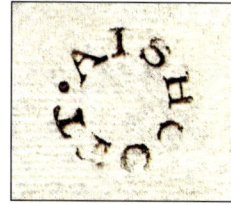

Letter of 6th May 1799
from Ashcott to Wiveliscombe
with postmark AISHCOTT,
a very old spelling of the village,
only ever seen before by the
author on the
"Protestation Returns &
Lay Subsidy Rolls"
of 1641-1642

We next see reference to Mr Louis' recommendations for the Ashcott mails when on 26th February 1835 he proposed that *"The present messenger shall start from Glastonbury to Street, Walton and Ashcott immediately after the arrival of the London mail....................."*

The *Bragg's Directory* of 1840 does list all the coaches, horse drawn in those days, which passed through Ashcott and providing both passenger and a parcel service. As the village was on the main road the service was fairly extensive as the following listing will show:

Bath. Mail coach daily at 3. White Hart Coach at 2. Union coach daily at a quarter before 1.

Bridgwater- Mail daily at Half-past 12. Swiftsure, Tuesdays, Thursdays & Saturdays at 8 in the evening.

Exeter. Mail daily at half past 2. White Hart Coach daily at 12.

London. Mail daily at 3. Swiftsure, Monday, Wednesday & Fridays at 9 in the morning.

Taunton. Mail daily at half-past 12, White Hart Coach daily at 12. Union Coach, daily at a quarter before 1.

In 1859 the *Somerset Directory* produced by *Messrs. Harrison-Harrad*, the Ashcott Post Office is listed as being run by George Chapman, receiver, with the

Straight line ASHCOTT. 1st August 1812.
Letter sent from Ashcott to Totnes charged 8d.

ASHCOTT

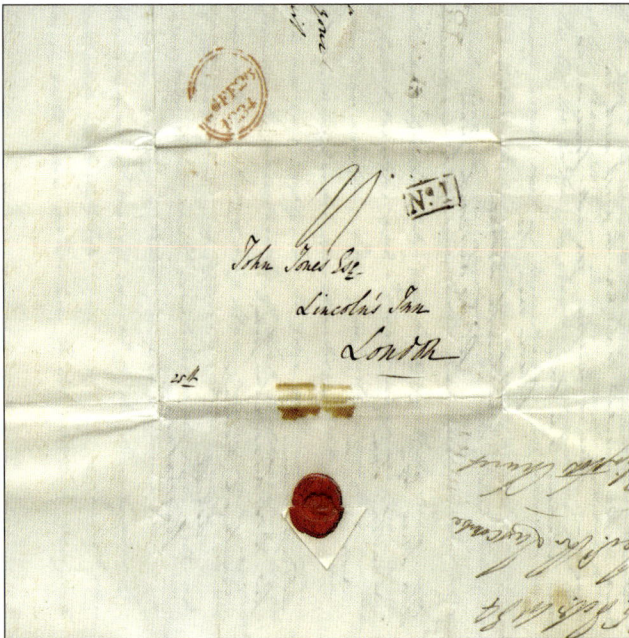

Letter to London, dated 23rd February 1824.
The Boxed No.1 indicates Ashcott was allocated the Number 1. of five
offices in the Glastonbury Penny Post system, established in 1823.

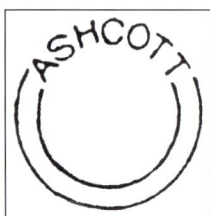

The Ashcott Undated Circular Postmark
issued to Glastonbury Post Office
8th January 1848

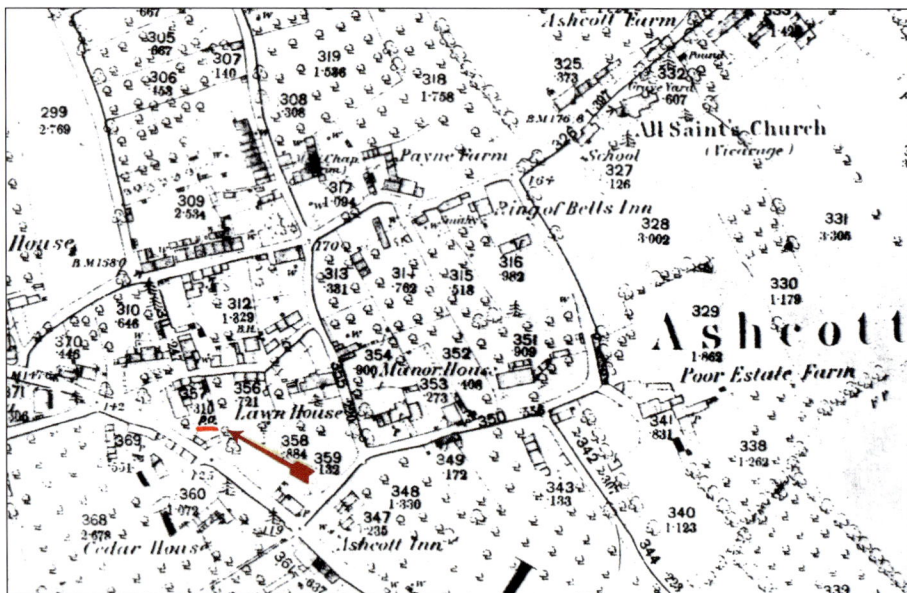

Ordnance Survey Map of Ashcott in 1885 showing the Post Office (P.O.) in the
same location as it is in 2014.

nearest Money-order office at Street. At that time there was a George Chapman living in Ashcott with his wife, Elizabeth, who carried out business as a butcher.

There is every possibility that they acted as letter receivers at the same time as in 1866 George Chapman had added beer retailer to his list of occupations.

Hugh Stone, aged 40 and born in Bourton, Dorset, & Martha, aged 33, his wife, had lived in the village since before 1851 and they were later to take over the Post Office. In both the census and *Kelly's Directory* of 1861 Hugh is described as a tailor and letter receiver. The census of that year, which carried much more detail than the one taken twenty years previously, lists Hugh & Martha now having nine children, all aged between 19 years and four days old, including two sets of twins, two girls aged 11 and mixed twins aged two, on the day the census was taken. From the information gleaned from the internet Hugh Stone died, aged 56, in the autumn of 1866. As we shall later see, his widow Martha, continued to run the business long after his death.

A Photograph of a young letter carrier taken by Mr A Carter, an Ashcott photographer, around the turn of the century

Around that time the letters were being sent out to the villages in the area from Bath, Glastonbury having been down-graded to that of a sub-office under that town in August 1853. Letters arrived at Ashcott at 7.45am; dispatched at 6pm. with the nearest Money Order office at Street.

By 1875 Martha Stone was still listed as the receiver but the hours of business had been extended, the first post still arrived at 7.45am., and the last mail did not leave until 8pm. By this time the Post Office at Shapwick must have been improved as it was named as the nearest office to obtain money orders.

Money Orders were a convenient means of sending cash by post long before the majority of people had bank accounts and even after the introduction of Postal Orders, which happened in January 1881, were still widely used, even for comparatively large sums of money.

Martha Stone, who had been born in the village in 1819, retired some time before 1883 but she continued to live in the district. There is a story, in the family, that after Hugh's death, Martha married a Mr Lock. This proved to be a bigamous marriage as he had a wife still living; for this offence he was tried and committed to prison with 4 months hard labour.

Martha Stone always lived in Ashcott and the following press cutting refers to her death in 1912:

ASHCOTT

DEATH OF THE OLDEST INHABITANT.

The death has recently occurred of the oldest inhabitant of the village in the person of Mrs. Martha Stone. The deceased, who was always proud of the fact that she was born in the same year as the late Queen Victoria, in 1819, was in her ninety-third year. She was always a strong, robust, and active woman, and retained her faculties to the last, being able to do sewing and also read and converse to within a few days of her death. She was born in the village, and it was interesting to hear her relate the many changes that had taken place during her lifetime. She once held the office of sub-postmistress for a number of years. She had been a widow about forty-five years, and had a family of thirteen children, one of her daughters being Mrs. H. Baker, of Summerland Avenue, Minehead, nine of whom are still living; she also has living thirty-seven grandchildren, thirty-nine great-grandchildren and two great-great-grandchildren.

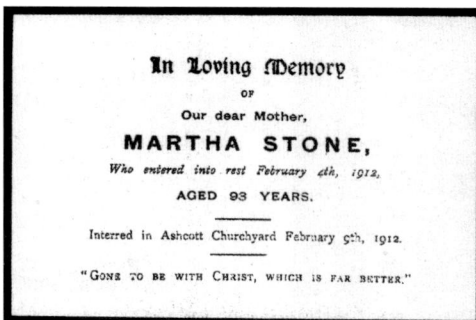

In Loving Memory
OF
Our dear Mother,
MARTHA STONE,
Who entered into rest February 4th, 1912,
AGED 93 YEARS.

Interred in Ashcott Churchyard February 5th, 1912.

"GONE TO BE WITH CHRIST, WHICH IS FAR BETTER."

We know that Martha had retired as the directory for 1883 lists Walter John Chapple and his wife, Anna, as shop-keepers and Walter as the receiver of letters. It is possible that they took over the Post Office duties rather earlier as we know that Walter was running a General Store in the village in 1881. By 1883 the hours of duty were very long as the first letters were arriving from Bridgwater at 5.04 am. and the latest dispatch was made at 8.10 pm. Glastonbury had been, once again, raised to the status of a head Office in 1872 but it seems that both Shapwick and Ashcott had both been transferred to the Head Post Office at Bridgwater before this happened.

Walter Chapple, was a man of many talents as the listing in *Kelly's Directory* of 1889 gives his occupation as *"Farmer, Grocer, Draper, Corn Factor & Provision Merchant, Post Office."* In the census return for 1891 Walter's nephew, James Sandy Chapple, is listed as a grocer's assistant and was obviously helping in the Post Office. By 1894 Walter had moved to Lawn Farm in the village and James, with his wife, Kate, had taken over the business as Grocers, Drapers and Post Office. Unusual for the times, Kate was not a local girl as she was born in Norwood, near London. By the 1890's running a village Post Office was by no means a part time occupation as not only were they dealing with two deliveries and dispatches of mail from Bridgwater a day but also offering many other services. The Post Office Savings Bank, Annuity Insurance, the Parcel Post service, the issuing of both dog (7s 6d a year) & carriage licences (15s a year) being amongst them. By this time Ashcott was still not connected to the telephone as Street is still given as the nearest Telegraph Office for sending of telegrams. This service was also available at Shapwick Railway Station on the Glastonbury to Bridgwater line.

*Ashcott Railway Station
and a Railway Letter
of 1905
to be put on a train
at Ashcott Station
and posted
at Glastonbury
for delivery
in London*

The Edward VII letter Box at Pipers Inn. March 2014

The General Post Office did not start a parcel delivery service until 1882 and carriers were still very important. You could get to Bridgwater daily on Thomas Cridland's Royal Mail 'bus as it came through from Glastonbury at 9.25 am, returning 5.30 pm. every day.

In 1906 we see mention of the wall letter box at Pedwell which was being cleared both early & late, but only on weekdays, i.e. not on Sundays. There is still a letter box on Pedwell Hill but no longer set in a wall as the above reference suggests. Before May 1910, the date of the death of the reigning monarch, a letter box was installed in the roadside wall of the Piper's Inn. It is one of the comparatively rare King Edward VII models and it is still in use in 2014. In 1906 this one was only cleared once a day, at 6.15 p.m. but, again, not on Sundays.

The afore-mentioned Chapple family were well established in the village and Walter is recorded as being at the Ashcott Vestry Meeting in 1895 and both he and his nephew, James, attended in 1898. In the Easter vestry meeting in 1906 James was elected to be a "Sidesman" in the church and continued in this role until at least 1914. A sidesman's duties were, amongst others, to greet people as they entered church on a Sunday. In 1909 James's uncle proposed him for the position of "Peoples Warden" . This was opposed and a village poll was called on the following Saturday; James being out-voted by 45 - 70 in favour of a Mr Francis.

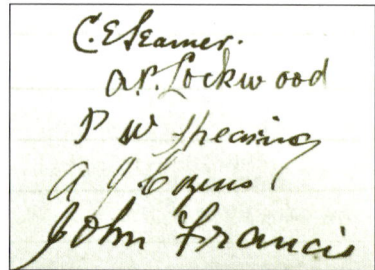

The signatories to the minutes

At the start of the first World War in 1914 James Chapple, whilst still described as the sub-postmaster, was also farming at Moses Barn Farm in the village. Some time before 1919 Albert Percy Lockwood had taken over the Post Office. Previously, in the 1911 census, Mr Lockwood had been at the Rush Hill Stores in Old Down, Bath, where he lived with his wife, Lucy, and their year old son who, incidentally, was born in Bristol. Obviously he only rented the premises as in the Ashcott *"Poor*

A Post Card circa. 1920 with the name Lockwood over the window

Rate book of the Bridgwater Union" for 1921 the Post Office is listed as occupied by him but the premises were still owned by J. S. Chapple. In the same document he was recorded as also renting two small paddocks amounting to just over 1½ acres from Walter Chapple. Often, before the general use of motor transport, shop-keepers kept a horse and cart for making deliveries; possibly the reason for renting the land.

Albert Lockwood was obviously popular in the village as the vicar, at the Vestry Meeting in April 1917 and at least for the next three years, proposed that he act as his church-warden. An excerpt from the minutes of the 1918 meeting is as follows:

"Mr Lockwwod made a statement in regard to the matter of the church roof & said that £101.7.0 had been raised up to date. A discussion ensued as to the best method of proceeding with the matter.

Mr S. Francis proposed a hearty vote of thanks to Mr Lockwood which was seconded by Mr A. J. Cozens & carried unanimously"

Ernest Richards, the Postman with Sid Baker in the village in the 1940's

The Lockwoods had already left the Post Office by 1924 as the entry in the *"Poor Rate"* book for that year, under the Post Office listing, a Mr Allcock not only as occupier but also owner of the property although he was still renting the paddocks in Middle Furlong. The change was confirmed by the entry in *Kelly's Directory* of 1927 with the entry *"Charles William Allcock, sub-postmaster"*. By this time, the Post Office was connected to the telephone as it was not only open for Money Orders but was also a Telegraph Office *"to which messages may be telephoned for treatment as express letters"*. In later directories the telephone number for the Post Office is listed as *"Ashcott No. 1"* and was, no doubt, manually operated from the shop.

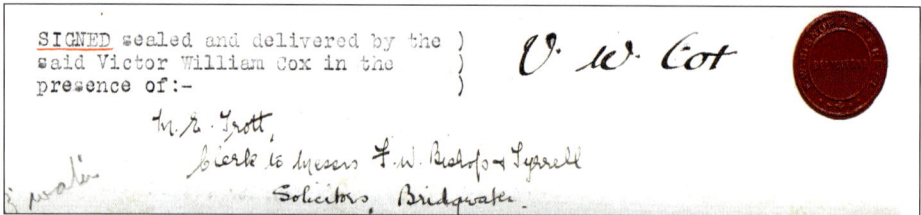

The deed acknowledging a mortgage for £65.00, signed in 1921

Victor William Cox and his wife, Annie Mabel, came from Edington Burtle, where, according to a deed he signed in 1921, they had been running a grocery business, and they were first listed as living at the Post Office in Ashcott in 1931. Victor's grandfather, Joseph, had lived in nearby Moorlinch in former days where he had been a Primitive Methodist Priest and a Peat Cutter. Victor, himself, was born in Street where his father, William Cox, worked in the shoe industry. Unfortunately William died fairly young and his widow, Mary, was left with 4 children ranging from Victor, at 19, to 5-year-old Olive. Victor and his younger brother, Cuthbert, aged 14 at the time of the 1901 census, both worked in the shoe factory. Victor's job description was *"Boot & Shoe Clicker"* whilst

Cuthbert's was "*Rough stuff cutter - boots*". By 1911 Victor was married to Annie Mabel and was obviously the main bread-winner with a 9-month-old son, Cecil.

He also had his widowed mother and a brother and sister living with him at 49 Cranhill Road, Street. It does appear that he had been a beneficiary in his uncle Jesse's will which probably enabled him to set up in business on his own. Uncle Jesse had been a farmer and did own some land at Burtle.

Trading as V. W. Cox & Sons they, as a family, started a long period of stability at Ashcott shop. By 1936 Cecil, the eldest son, together with his wife, Clara, were resident at the Post Office whilst Victor and Annie had moved to "Hill View" in the village. It seems that Cecil's stay in Ashcott was fairly short-lived as by 1938 he had moved to their shop in nearby Catcott whilst another son, Eric, together with his wife, Kathleen, had taken over at Ashcott.

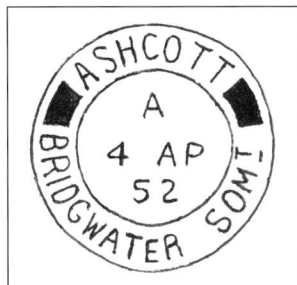

With the outbreak of the second World War, it seems that Eric was called up for the forces as Victor and Annie had returned to the Post Office and, in the Register of Electors for 1945, Eric is listed on the "Services Register". Four years later Eric and Kathleen were again back in charge and were to remain so until at least 1974, whilst his parents had moved back to "Hill View"

John Warman, who lived at Nythe Farm for most of his life, remembers a certain Noah Godwin making postal deliveries in the 1930s, also a Miss Forden, a doctor's

Reggie Bagg,
village Postman for 26 years
handing over the job to
Keith Cavill in 1972,
whose family had run
a grocery business in
the village for over 50 years.

Ashcott Post Office & Shop c. 1979 with J & M. KNIGHT
over the window.
The tree in "The Triangle" was reputedly planted to
Commemorate Queen Victoria's Golden Jubilee.

Photo from the *Somerset & West Magazine* of January 1979

daughter, acted as one of the two people doing the same job, the latter cycling to the outlying parts, until local sorting ceased and deliveries were made by mail van from Glastonbury.

John & Marie Knight came to the village in 1974 after Eric Cox left. Both John and Marie had been in the Royal Air Force, where John had been a Squadron Leader, whereas Marie had formerly been a midwife. From all the accounts I have heard about them, they were very popular in the village and were always willing to put themselves out to please the customers; if there was a product which they did not stock, they were always willing to make certain, on their next visit to the Cash & Carry, to purchase it. Whilst in Ashcott they extended the premises, both shop and domestic, as they were supplying not only groceries but other household products. Each morning, before the shop opened, John would drive to Othery to collect fresh bread and cakes from Maisies Bakery, the lardy cakes being a particular favourite with the staff at coffee time each morning. As part of the service available, John would make a local weekly grocery delivery round and Marie introduced the very popular "Home Cooked Ham" carved straight from the bone. They also had a room set apart for other wares such as knitting wool and paint together with the sale of cards. This room also housed the Post Office.

Pedwell Hill March 2014

It was during this time that Jenny Todman came to help out, on a part-time basis in the shop, initially doing 12½ hours a week. Jenny's husband had been promoted to a position in the radio station which was situated close to the Shapwick turning on the main Bridgwater road. For the next 31 years she continued with this work, the hours gradually increasing until she was doing 19 hours a week, only retiring in 2009. Because of her long service she has proved to be a mine of information about the different owners who have come and gone during her time. In the early days she remembers having to go up the garden to fill customer's paraffin cans, the fuel for their oil lamps and heaters. There were vegetables and hardware goods set up each morning outside the front of the shop. The only toilet available for the staff was in the dwelling house.

In October 1980 the Knights were to move to another similar business in Kingston St Mary, 4 miles north of Taunton on the edge of the Quantock hills, when Jim & Pamela Anderson came. Their stay in the village was only to last 3½ years and very little changed during their time. One memorable thing about this period was that, much to the surprise of the proprietors, a baby was born on the premises. The parents were on their way to hospital in Taunton but failed

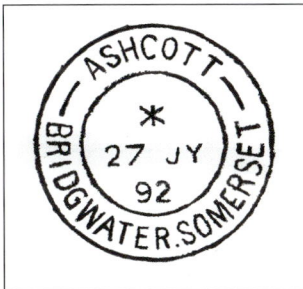

to make it in time; luckily the local nurse was able to be present to act as mid-wife. Customers also remember that each morning Pamela placed advertising rhymes in the shop window which always caused a degree of amusement. They left in 1983 when Mr & Mrs I J E Skudder, Ivor and Doreen, took over in partnership with their daughter and son-in law. Unfortunately this

Pam & Bruce Shilton

Graham Jesson

partnership did not work out and they quit after only 11 months although, during their time there, they introduced the idea of being associated with the "SPAR" group of suppliers.

Bruce & Pam Shilton with Pam's brother, Graham Jesson and his wife Olga, moved in to the Post Office on a memorable day, their wedding anniversary, the

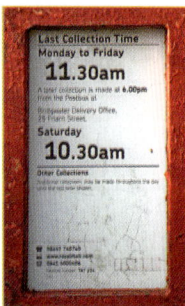

The Letter Box on the Ridgeway, March 2014.

27th July 1984. They had all lived in Leicestershire before coming down to Somerset; Bruce had worked as a tool-maker in an engineering works and later as a draughtsman for the local authority. Having been made redundant from that and with Graham having a difficult time as a builder, due to the recession, they, as a family unit, made the decision to find a suitable village shop and Post Office to run. The one in Ashcott particularly appealed to them as it had the advantage of having accommodation for two separate families, something that the previous owners, Mr & Mrs Skudder, had arranged. The only previous knowledge, between them, of the workings of the Post Office was the fact that Olga had worked on a part-time basis in the Post Office in their home village of Whetstone in the past.

Soon after taking over the shop they found that, under the "SPAR" banner it was difficult to comply with that company's wishes, particularly the requirement that they should keep the shop open every day "From 8 to late". This was the reason for the change and so the "LONDIS" name appeared over the shop window for the second time, it having been first tried when the Knights were involved. The logo originally stood for "London District Stores" and were owned by each retailer having shares in the business. They were later taken over by an Irish group and traded under the Budgen's banner, before a further take-over, finding them under the Booker Group of companies.

Although the Ashcott shop had joined the "LONDIS" franchise, much of the produce they sold came from local suppliers:- bread still from the bakery in Othery, cheese from Les Keen, the wholesaler in Meare, tea from Miles of Minehead and their meat could not have been much more local, it came from Fred Griffiths in the village. During their time at the shop they deliberately did not supply newspapers as there was already a delivery service operating in the village run by the Dean family; they did not wish to compromise its viability.

The Letter Box on Middle Street March 2014

They also altered the shop considerably, extending its size as well as taking down the external store. From the beginning Graham concentrated on running the Post Office whilst Bruce & Pam ran the shop. This they continued to do until 1991 when they sold the business to Ron and Linda Stevens. After their retirement Pam & Bruce continued to live in the village, celebrating their diamond wedding day in 2012. Graham & Olga moved to nearby East Lyng but also took over the running of the Post Office on East Reach in Taunton until their eventual retirement.

Ron Stevens had experience in the retail world as he had previously worked for BHS, (British Home Stores) and was also a very keen computer user and even shared a remote computer connection with his son, something unusual for that time. The couple always made a point of taking Mondays off, getting a relief in to run the Post Office while they were away. This was a task often undertaken by retired sub-postmasters in the district. Something that did not impress Jenny Todman or the other lady working behind the counter was Ron's insistence that the shop door should always be kept open, summer & winter, even on the coldest of days. He felt that a closed door discouraged people from entering the shop.

By 2002 Richard Stone & Michael Jones had come to Ashcott, the actual date when they took over the running of the shop was on 19th June in that year. Richard & Mike had met whilst they were both air-crew with British Airways and when that company was privatised in 1987 they decided to set up in business together in Sussex. Their cleaning company proved to be very successful; at one time they were employing over 70 part-time staff. Due to the pressure of work, the business having grown to such a degree, they decided in 2002 to sell and look for something a little less demanding. This was how they came to Somerset. Although unknown at the time of purchase, Richard, who runs the Post Office side of the business, discovered that some of his ancestors, Hugh and Martha Stone, had once owned and run the store way back in the mid-1800s. Also another connection he had with former owner's was when he discovered that the shop he often visited whilst at school in Rush Hill, when his family were living near Bath, was where the Lockwoods, owners of the Ashcott Post Office from around 1917, had come from before moving to the village, but obviously long after the Lockwoods had left.

With planning permission granted in 2013 to build a new flat above the shop and to separate the dwelling house from the business premises, the future of the Ashcott Post Office and Stores could see interesting developments.

Ashcott Shop &
Post Office.
March 2014

ACKNOWLEDGEMENTS
With grateful acknowledgements to the many people who have helped me fill in the details of the history of the Post Office in Ashcott, with especial thanks to Adrian Howe, Pam & Bruce Shilton, Bernard Stone, Richard Stone & Michael Jones, Jenny Todman, and John Warman.

Baltonsborough

*B*ALTONSBOROUGH, a parish in Wells district, Somerset, on the river *Brue, 4 miles SW of Glastonbury railway station. It includes the hamlet of Southwood and has a post-office under Glastonbury. Acres, 2,472. Real property, £6,934. Pop., 763. Houses, 166. The living is a perpetual curacy, annexed to Butleigh, in the diocese of Bath and Wells. The church is later English. There are Wesleyan and Moravian chapels, and two public schools.*

From:- *"The Imperial Gazetteer of England & Wales"* by John Marius Wilson.
Pub. A. Fullarton & Co. 1872

THE FIRST MENTION of Baltonsborough in the history of the Glastonbury post office is a reference in the archive copies of the *Freeling Index* to be found at the National Postal Archives in London when the Penny Post system was set up *(see also Butleigh)*. Another record in the archives casts further light on the rural delivery to the villages.

5th January 1838.

Allowances to deputy Postmasters & Salaries to Postmasters & their assistants.

For salaries to Sub Deputies & Receivers

Penny Post Foot Messenger for Glastonbury and Butleigh to serve that village & Battinsboro' twice daily. In the morning with the London & in the afternoon with the Western Letters 10/- per week

Also noted at this time was that the number of letters to London from Glastonbury in the week commencing 15th January 1838 was 98. Sometimes the person employed for the task was not quite up to the standard expected as in 1839 there is reference to a Confidential return in which the Glastonbury & Baltonsboro' messenger was cautioned, presumably for some misdemeanour.

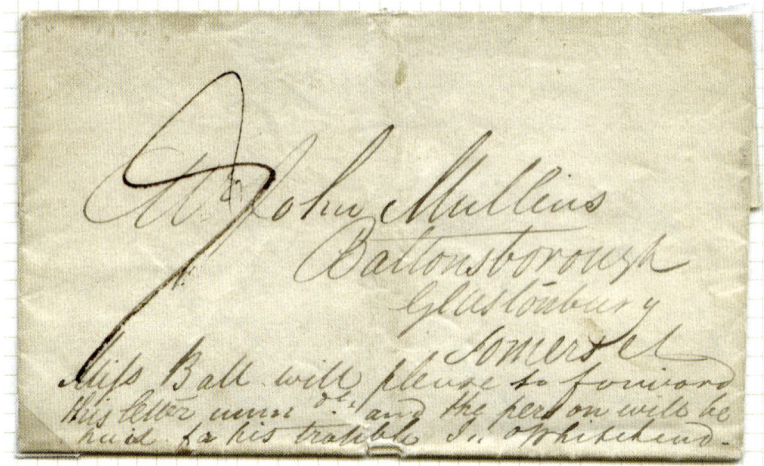

Certainly the holding back of the mail was considered a particularly serious offence and would most probably warranted more than just a caution.

The letter illustrated above was sent from Winchester on 20th February 1836 to Mr John Mullins at Baltonsborough at a cost of 7d. but obviously the sender, John Whitehead, wanted it delivered post haste so he inscribed it :

> "Miss Ball will please to forward this letter immediately and the person will be paid for his trouble,
>
> (Signed) Jn Whitehead

The 20th February that year fell on a Saturday so perhaps Mr Whitehead was trying to get a special Sunday delivery. Later on we find a letter from Ellen Ball to Mr Whitehead spelling out the rules. This also illustrates how business people who wished to get their mail early in the day were obliged to make their own arrangements:

Post Office, Glastonbury,
August 12th /40

Sir,

> *I am sorry that your letters have not been forwarded according to your directions but the boy was not here until ½ an hour or more after the men were dispatched, & I consequently supposed he was not coming.*
>
> *To prevent all mistakes I therefore write to say that the bag should be here by 10 o'clock at the latest every morning, that your bag should be furnished with 2 keys – one left with me, the other kept at Baltonsborough.*

The boy to come in & deliver his bag, when I will take out the letters sent in it, & put in those received here for Baltonsborough, & for the accommodation of this private bag or pouch, I claim £2.2.0 Pr An' according to the regulations of the office. This sum is paid me by Mr Grenville & he ascertained from the Surveyor that the charge was correct.

I do not know if you understand that this claim would be made, & I therefore write to you that no misunderstanding might arise on the subject.

I have the honour to be, Sir,

your Obdt. Servt

Ellen Ball

P.S. It would be more convenient for the bag to be hear(sic) at 10 minutes before 10 a.m.

Illustration of Penny Black Cover sent from Baltonsborough October 8th 1840 to London
As has been noted in the introduction, Uniform Penny Postage was introduced on 10th January
1840 and the Penny Black and Twopenny Blue stamps issued on 6th May in the same year

Obviously Ellen wished to supplement her salary and she could not be clearer; she did not want any mis-understanding about the charge.

All was not always sweetness and light in the Post Office world and the position of Postmaster was not without its problems; reliable staff being, as always, very important. This is illustrated from the entry in the *Postmaster General's minutes* of 10th June 1849, minute 8850, where we again find, under the heading of:

"Glastonbury to Baltinsboro' Messenger cautioned"

I submit that the Glastonbury & Baltinsboro' messenger may be reprimanded and cautioned for his improper behaviour in this instance and informed and be informed that if any thing of this sort is repeated the matter will be noticed much more seriously.

One does wonder just as to what the offender had done to annoy the authorities enough to reach the notice of the Postmaster General in London?

Living in Baltonsborough at the time of the 1851 census was Benjamin Cook, aged 72, described as a Postman. It is possible that he could have been responsible for the delivery round that took in Glastonbury, Butleigh and Baltonsborough, as illustrated in the following document, used in 1853.

Six of these very interesting documents, "Sub-Postmaster's or Messenger's Bills" came into my possession through the good offices of John Badman, a dealer in antiques and ephemera in Glastonbury. They were reputedly found stuffed into gaps in the walls of a house being refurbished at Havyatt, on the Glastonbury - Shepton Mallet road, which could well have been the home of the Post-Messenger. Unfortunately they are mostly in very poor condition but they do throw some light on the service to Baltonsborough and Butleigh at the time. The instructions at the base of the front of the form says:

> *"When this bill is used by a Post-Messenger, he is to present it at each Sub-Office along the road, at which no bag is made up, in order that the Sub-Postmaster may fill up one of the Forms at the back with the requisite particulars"*

> Also: *"No Sub-Postmaster must suffer his stock of Stamps on hand to fall below 10s. worth."*

The six forms cover a period from October 10th to October 27th 1853. The one for Monday, October 10th, contains the following information:-*"Time Outward" Despatched at -* by A. M. Vincent *Received at* 9.30 by M. A. Patten. *Total number of Letters sent out -* 21 *Letters sent in -* 60

On the reverse is a Butleigh postmark and the signature of John Wake.

> *1d. Labels on hand -* 14s. *Total number of Letters sent in -* 30

> *"Time Inwards: Despatched at* 3.40 by M. A . Patten *Received at -* by A. M. Vincent

Up until the end of 1852 the only external sign that a letter had emanated from Baltonsborough would have been the application of the No. 5 handstamp (as illustrated on the envelope with the 1d Black stamp). In December of that year it is recorded in the proof book, kept at P.O. headquarters and now in the archives, that a new undated BALTONSBOROUGH handstamp was issued to the Glastonbury office.

Illustration from the proof book in the Post Office Archives

BALTONSBOROUGH

12.1852

In the 1851 census return for the village we find the mention of Mary Ann Patten, aged 45, a Dressmaker, who was born in Baltonsborough living with her husband, Robert Patten, aged 41, a Master Carpenter, and she was obviously acting as Postmistress as the illustrated Sub-postmaster's Bill carried her signature.

In the 1861 *Kelly's Directory* under Baltonsborough the entry reads:-

> Post Office. Robert Patten, receiver. Letters arrive at 9 am; dispatched at 3.30pm. Nearest Money Order Office & Post Town, Glastonbury.

Although Robert is listed as the receiver of letters, there can be little doubt that the office was run by his wife, this being verified by the much later entry in *Kelly's Directory* of 1897 which states:

> Post, Money Order and Telegraph Office, T.M.O., Savings Bank and Express Delivery, Parcel & Annuity & Insurance Office - Mrs Mary Ann Patten.

The records over the period from 1861 to 1870 are rather sketchy. A lot was still happening in the development of the services offered but none of great note.

In 1871 Glastonbury Post Office was, once again, raised to the status of a Head Office and in 1874 Lottisham residents were served via Baltonsborough instead of Shepton Mallet (Minute 134. 5674)

It is very possible that by this time there was an established place to house the delivery wagon in the immediate area close to the Post Office in the village. We find an entry in the Postmaster General's minute book for 1880 which records that a delivery to Northwood was established and allowance was made to the Sub Postmaster to cover the extra expense. In 1881 the records state that the delivery for Baltonsborough and Northwood was to be more frequent and that an allowance was to be made for a Ham Street delivery.

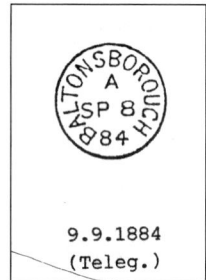

9.9.1884
(Teleg.)

Under district news in the *Central Somerset Gazette* of September 1897 was a short item under Baltonsborough stating - *Mr William Bartlett, the Rural Postman and mail-driver between this parish and Glastonbury, has recently received his fifth stripe and will soon be entitled to another. This is a very rare distinction, necessitating 30 years' service.* It is recorded that the Rural Letter Carrier was given an allowance for horse-keep in 1881. Inflation was not a great factor in those days as it was another 12 years before this allowance was raised. In 1887 the records state that not only were the Baltonsborough, Ham Street and Northwood deliveries revised but the Rural Post was accelerated as well - no wonder the horse needed extra feed!

In the 1891 census return Mary Patten was living in a residence called "Rockland" with her widowed daughter, Louisa M Bond, who was described as the Housekeeper (Domestic) and she had three other people living there; Mary Lamport aged 67, who was on Parish Relief, with a note beside the entry "Idiotic". Albert Hampherson, aged 18, from Bewdley, Worcester and also Gilbert Phillips, born in West Monkton, near Taunton, both of whom are described as Post Office Telephone Clerks.

Mrs Patten must have experienced tremendous changes over the 40 years she held the position of Postmistress, initially as receiver of posts carrying a small stock of labels, or stamps as we would now call them, right through to the coming of the telegraph and the telephone. Sadly, an entry in the *Central Somerset Gazette* for 15th January 1898, records:

BALTONSBOROUGH

DEATH OF THE POSTMISTRESS

On Saturday last, Mrs Patton (sic), who for over 40 years has held the important office of Postmistress, and for some years has had the distinction of being the oldest inhabitant, passed peacefully away at the patriarchal age of nearly 93 years.

The establishment of Post Boxes is attributed to Anthony Trollope the novelist, who was a Post Office surveyor at that time. They were not that common in the rural areas and in the *Central Somerset Gazette* of 12th February 1898 we find this reference under the heading of:

BALTONSBOROUGH POSTAL FACILITIES

"A letter box has been fixed at Southwood to be cleared every evening, which will be a real boon to the inhabitants."

The Letter Box at Southwood in 2012

Obviously Postal matters were exercising the minds of the public at this time as an entry in the same paper of March 26th under Baltonsborough news:

"Energetic efforts are being made to get a second delivery of letters in Butleigh and Baltonsborough and a memorial to this end is being designed by all the principal families and business houses in the parishes."

Left - No Address - Dead!

After the death of Mrs Patten a new appointment had to be made and in the 1901 census Mrs Louisa Mary Bond, Mary Patten's daughter, is given as holding the office. She had been living with her mother since at least 1881, although by this time she was about 75 but, no doubt, knew the business well. The clue as to who probably did the work can to be seen as the other resident in the house was Nellie F Somers aged 21 and described as *"Clerk, Postal & Telegraph"*.

The entry in *Kelly's Directory* of 1902 states that the wall letter box in Ham Street is cleared at 5.40pm. and Southwood, 4.45pm., Weekdays only. By 1906 these same boxes were also being cleared twice a day. The times of collection 7.55am. and 9.35am. were added but still only on weekdays.

A Post Card c. 1905 showing the Post Office on the Cross Roads

In 1905 the Postmaster General's minute book records that a Baltonsborough Day Mail was established and the delivery was extended to Solomon's Temple in Worms Lane (Teapot Lane) and the entry also records that a cycle was supplied together with a cleaning allowance, possibly not exclusively for the cycle.

Both in 1910 and again in 1914 the Sub-postmistress is recorded as Miss Charlotte Greedy and the Post Office was situated in the corner house on the cross opposite the Greyhound Inn but as the illustrated envelopes show, by July 1915 Arthur Roberts Brooks and Mrs Ellen Brooks had taken over the Post Office. The entry in the directory is quite intriguing in that not only was it a Money Order and Telegraph Office but also Telephone Call (**within limited distance**) Office. One has visions of the Postmistress answering the phone and then rushing round to find the intended recipient; or did *within limited distance* have another interpretation?

Redirected letters initialled by Arthur Roberts Brooks(ARB) and Ellen (Nellie) Brooks(EFB) and handstamped with the Baltonsborough postmark.

A Parcel Post label for Baltonsbor-ough, dated November 4th 1902. "BAS" was the telegraphic address of the village Post Office.

My father, who was living in the family home at Coxbridge on the outskirts of the village in the early years in the last century, once told me that they always had the daily newspaper delivered by post. This had a dual role: They were sure to get the paper but it also guaranteed that the postman delivered your letters every day. If there had only been one letter for delivery to an outlying farm there was a great temptation to pop it back in the bag for another day!

In Martin Street in a house called 'Clematis Cottage', lived a postal worker named Bill Hodges, with his mother and sister, probably the son of Frank Hodges who, in the 1901 Baltonsborough census, gave his occupation as that of a Postman who had a son called William aged 7 at the time. Bill was a First World War veteran and delivered all the village mail for Arthur Brooks. The G.P.O. Mail cart, which was horse drawn, was kept in a shed on the site of the former Wesleyan/Methodist Chapel with the horse living in the orchard behind. Bill collected the mail from Baltonsborough and surrounding villages, taking it to Glastonbury in the morning where he picked up the incoming mail and delivering it to different villages on the way back. Baltonsborough was the last on the circuit so that, when he arrived back, he would unhitch the horse and let it out into the orchard, push the mail van back into its shed and then sort the mail back at the Post Office. As the late Bill Dunkerton explained:

Bill Hodges, the Mail Cart and the shed behind the Methodist Chapel

He would then get on his bike and go around Lottisham and Southwood, delivering the mail, and then he would do half a day's work ploughing or acting as carter for my father. Then in later years they did away with the horse and cart and they had a motorised mail van. And the driver lived somewhere in the village - I can't remember who he was - he used to drive the mail van, and he used to go in and back every morning, take mail in and bring mail back.'

People can remember that in the 1930s the Brooks family were living in the Post Office on the corner of the cross roads with their son Cedric, but by this time Nellie (Ellen) was suffering from ill health. Mr Brooks, in addition to his Post Office duties, sold sweets and tobacco. On the corner of the shop was positioned a public telephone kiosk, an advance on the previous system whereby you had to go into the house to use the phone, presumably it not being available outside P.O. hours. In the illustration on the post card of about 1905 the letterbox can be seen inset into the right hand side of the front porch.

One of a set of four stamps issued for the Silver Jubilee of the reign of King George 5th. Postmarked with the date stamp of that period.

The telephone kiosk was mentioned in the minutes of the Parish Council on Nov. 4th 1935:

> *"The clerk was instructed to write to the District Manager, G.P.O. Telephones, Exeter and ask for the removal of the kiosk to a more private position as the users' conversation was usually overheard and also passing traffic made it difficult to hear."*

A second request was made nine months later, and as a result, it was moved to a position opposite the house now called Courtenays. Fourteen years later, in May 1949, the clerk again wrote: *"with reference to a telephone kiosk being fixed at the top of the village (Ham Street)"*. There was a follow-up request a year later that it should be *"situated at junction of Mulchney (sic) and Ham Street."*

As can be seen, the wheels of officialdom moved just as slowly then but the Parish Council's wish was eventually granted; a kiosk was still to be found on this site at the beginning of the 21st Century.

When Arthur Brooks retired, after 46 years of involvement with the Post Office, much of the time as Sub-Postmaster, he and his wife continued to live in the house on the corner, calling it "The Old Post Office." Before the end of 1949 the office was transferred for a time to The Old Parsonage in Teapot lane, run by Mary Broome (nee Richings) whose father was a past vicar of Baltonsborough. Whilst Mary ran the Post Office her husband, Don, continued with his agency with the Prudential Insurance company. It was during this period that Mrs Gladys Plumley took over part of the post delivery around the village.

The telephone Kiosk and Letter Box beside the Bus Stop at the junction of Ham Street and Muchelney Lane Photo: August 2013

From The Old Parsonage the village P.O. moved to the shop on the corner of Teapot Lane and Ham Street run by Mrs Joan Jenner until, she being left as a young widow, decided to retain the shop but not run the Post Office. So, once again, it returned to the site close to the crossroads. Gladys Plumley continued delivering the post for 27 years. Two others who acted as Postwomen during the time that "Glad" was carrying out these duties were Mrs Winnie Banbury and Mrs Rosie Higgins. One day, whilst Glad was pushing her bike up the hill by Orchard Neville House around Christmas time, the artist Richard Constable came out of his house on his way down to the school, dressed as Father Christmas "Have you got a present for me, then Richard?" says Glad. With that, he came across and gave her a big kiss, something she never forgot!

Glad Plumley's daughter, Gloria, could well remember the names of former Postwomen who made deliveries around the village by bicycle. These included both Mary Porter and Hazel Plumley, each knowing virtually every one who lived in the village at the time. When "Glad" retired in the year of the Queen's Silver Jubilee, 1977, the mail sorting and delivery reverted to Glastonbury and all the rural areas around were henceforth served by postal vans.

Previous to and throughout World War II, there had been a shop on what was later the site of the Post Office at the Crossroads. This was run by Edwin Gould and his son Arthur, who lived in a house on the opposite side of the road. They also had a newspaper delivery round as well as, in a wooden shed which is still to be seen on the right hand side of the driveway, a wireless (radio) accumulator charging service. This was long before mains electricity was available in the more remote rural areas and radios were run from a re-chargeable battery known as an accumulator. Generally the charge would last about a week of useage. Users owned two of these batteries; one in the radio and one being re-charged. Arthur Gould expanded the grocery business under the "SPAR" name and it seems that the Post Office became part of the business at this time.

Around about 1969 this he sold to a couple from Scotland, Geoffrey and Christian Watts, who took on the Post Office and shop but after only two years they moved on. They were followed, for a short time, by Robert and Marjery Griffin before Jim Everett and his wife came in 1977.

Unfortunately, shortly after coming to the village, Mrs Everett died of a brain tumour. Jim continued to maintain the business although he gradually relinquished control to Joan and Keith Birch. Joan had begun to work in the shop in 1980 and she eventually took over the business in 1997. Jim continued to

The Baltonsborough Post Office and Shop in October 2012.

Mrs Joan Birch

live in the village, taking a very active part in local affairs right up to the time of his death in early August 2000. The shop and Post Office continued to thrive with Dawn Gifford serving behind the Post Office counter and a number of local ladies helping out in the shop.

For various reasons, by 2014, Joan and Keith decided to retire, hoping to sell the shop as a going concern. Although being well situated for the passing traffic and, in spite of extensive advertising, unfortunately this was not to be. The decision to close by mid-April 2015 was eventually made.

It did appear likely that Baltonsborough could well have lost its Post Office and the many services it offered. Luckily Max & Maxine Cotton, incidentally no known relations to the author of this book, decided to take it on as an addition to their Farm Shop on Martin Street. And so it was that the last day of the Post Office at the crossroads shop was on Friday 17th April and the new one opened in the Farm Shop on Saturday 18th April 2015.

Local public consultation
Proposed branch move

POST OFFICE

What we're doing
We're proposing to move this branch to new premises. If the move goes ahead, the branch will change to one of our new local style branches.

What this would mean:
- Post Office services will be offered from a till on the retail counter in a modern open plan branch
- The majority of Post Office products and services will still be available
- Improved accessibility

What happens next
We're carrying out a local public consultation on the new location and we'd like you to let us have your views.

There's a leaflet available in this branch with more information, or if you have any questions or comments, please get in touch.

Items sent by FREEPOST take 2 working days to arrive. Therefore, responses by FREEPOST should be sent in sufficient time to arrive before the end of the consultation period. Working days do not include Saturdays or Sundays. Responses received after the deadline will not be considered.

Dates for the local public consultation on the proposed new location:
starts: 27/01/2015   ends: 10/03/2015

New location: Baltonsborough Post Office® branch, Baltonsborough Farm Shop, Martin Street, Baltonsborough, Glastonbury, BA6 8QU

An extract of the notice displayed in the Post Office in Baltonsborough in January 2015.

An impression from the Self-Inking date stamps, used on the last day of the Post Office being at The Cross, on the left.
On the right the new datestamp issued to the Farm Shop.

From the earliest times, when the village would have been virtually self-sufficient in most products, particularly food, there have been a number of retail outlets but over the last 50 years these have been gradually dwindling until there is now, in 2015, only one left, The Baltonsborough Farm Shop. As in former days, you can still buy your postage stamps but also, in addition, pay your telephone bill and even top-up your mobile phone account there; as well as collect your pension or buy a myriad number of items, many of which were unheard of when the postal service first came to the village.

Baltonsborough Farm Shop
Photo - 4th May 2015

ACKNOWLEDGEMENTS

With grateful acknowledgement to Joan Birch, Louise Clapp, the late Bill Dunkerton and Gloria Plumley. Also all the people of Baltonsborough who have added to this story.

Butleigh

*B*UTLEIGH, *a parish in Wells District, Somerset; on the river Brue, 4 miles SSE of Glastonbury railway station. It includes the hamlet of Butleigh-Wootton and has a post-office under Glastonbury. Acres, 4,467. Real property, £8,139. Pop., 1,038. Houses, 212. The property is divided among a few. Butleigh Court is the seat of R. Neville Grenville, Esq.; was recently rebuilt in part, from designs by Buckler; The living is a vicarage, united with the p. curacy of Baltonsborough, in the diocese of Bath and Wells. Value, £380. Patron, R. Neville Grenville, Esq.*

BUTLEIGH-WOOTTON, a hamlet in Butleigh parish, Somerset; 3 miles NE of Somerton. Pop., 212. Wootton House here is the seat of the Hon. A. Hood.

From:- *"The Imperial Gazetteer of England & Wales"* by John Marius Wilson.
Pub. A. Fullarton & Co. 1872

*A "Free" letter to Lord Glastonbury of Butleigh Court from his bailiff in
Butleigh dated 1822*

EARLY CORRESPONDENCE from Butleigh is very rarely seen as the nearest Post Office to the village was at Glastonbury and, even if it did emanate from the village, it is not easily discerned. Some correspondence from Lord Glastonbury to his bailiff at Butleigh Court is shown on the computer web-site maintained by Robert Senior, who resides in the modernised Court, does illustrate the use of the postal system. This was allowed free to the members of Parliament and the House of Lords although comparatively expensive to members of the public. A single sheet letter from London to Butleigh would have normally cost 7d.

A letter from a Mr Stow, the surveyor of Posts, to Sir Henry Freeling, the Secretary to the General Post Office gives an insight into the early posts in Butleigh.

Ilchester   August 30th 1836

Sir,

I stated in my Report of the 11th inst. that by taking off the Ride between Glastonbury and Langport and sending it from Taunton to Langport we should be inflicting great injury upon Butleigh situated about 4 miles from Glastonbury, and that I would take an early opportunity of seeing what arrangements could be made for serving that village. I yesterday in consequence of a Letter from The Hon. ble and Rev.d Neville Grenville proceeded to Butleigh and also to Glastonbury. Mr Grenville since he has resided at Butleigh Court has had a private Bag made up at Glastonbury for his Western Letters which has been dropped by the Langport Rider and has employed a special messenger to go daily to Glastonbury for his London letters...

Butleigh Court previous to the rebuilding in the 1850's.
The home of Lord Glastonbury, whose memorial tablet is to be found in Butleigh Church, and later his sucessors the Neville-Grenville family.
Print from the RIBA Library Photographs Collection.

Sir Henry Freeling's letter to the Postmaster General:

General Post Office   *1st September 1836*

My Lord,

In pursuance of the intention expressed in a former Report from Mr Stow, he now states in the enclosed, that he has considered the subject of serving the Village of Butleigh near Glastonbury which has sustained much inconvenience by the necessary alteration of the Ride from Glastonbury to Langport.

He has communicated with the Hon'ble. & Revd. Neville Grenville, who has much correspondence and readily acquiesces in the suggestion of a Penny Post. The surveyor therefore proposes it to include also the Village of Baltonsborough, both to be served from Glastonbury by a foot Messenger twice a day. He recommends an allowance of 10/- a week to the Messenger and £3.5/. a year for the Receiver at Butleigh being a total expense of £29.5/-. The Penny Postage on the letters now received would amount to £30.8s/4d and for the reasons stated by Mr Stow it will probably increase. There is therefore every encouragement to set up the Post and if the circumstances had been less favourable in regard to expense I should probably have advised Your Lordship to adopt the measure, recollecting that by other arrangements for the public benefit these villages have been deprived of a convenience they before possessed.

All which is humbly submitted by

H. Freeling

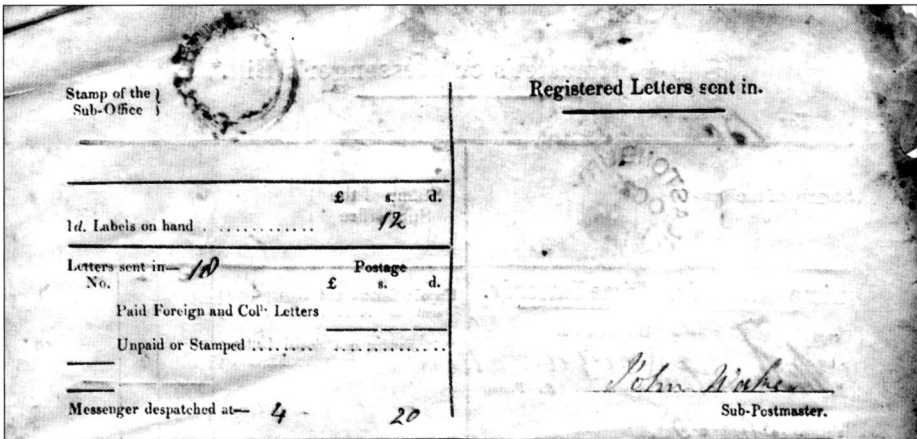

It is not certain as to who ran the postal services in the village before 1853 but in the census of 1841 William Britton is described as a Postman and in 1851 as both Postman and wood carver. It is recorded that some of his carved work was exhibited in the 1851 Great Exhibition. In the Glastonbury Rural Life Museum are copies of two of his poems concerning his occupation which are reproduced at the end of this chapter.

By October 1853 things had changed as John Wake signed a Messenger Bill as Sub-Postmaster; incidentally he also acted as the enumerator for the 1851 village Census. He was obviously a busy man as he was described as a stone-mason employing 6 men and living in Church Street. According to research carried out by Robert Senior, ten years earlier John, who was born in West Pennard, was living in No. 11 High Street with a servant, Elizabeth Hewlitt. They married in 1841 although she was only 16 and he was 45. According to the birthplace of their later children, they had at least 7 in all, they moved away from the village and in 1856 John was a miller and baker in West Quantoxhead.

In the same census of 1851 William Cannon, a Butleigh man and his wife, Mary, from Staffordshire, ran a lodging house at Parsonage House with 9 lodgers, all connected to the building trade, ranging from stone mason's labourer to carpenters and aged anything between 16 and 40. This, of course, was about the time that the new grand residence for the Neville-Grenville family, Butleigh Court, was being built where many tradesmen would have been employed.

We find that by 1859 in the *Harrison-Harrad Directory* William Cannon is named as "receiver" as confirmed in the 1861 census: *"The Post Office, Church*

A Post Card, c. 1905, of the re-built Butleigh Court.

Street, William Cannon, born in Butleigh, aged 63, Sub Postmaster," living with his wife, Mary, aged 55, and their daughter Mary aged 17 who was born at Wolford, Warwickshire. Glastonbury was named as the nearest Money-order Office and from which letters were received. William died in October 1862 and Mary then took over the business and in the 1871 census she was named as the Postmistress. I believe that she retained this position until the time of her death in 1872. That is when the Dyer family started their long association with the Butleigh Post Office.

The Dyer family had been saddlers and harness makers in the village for a long time, Charles Dyer (snr), who was born in Somerton in 1809, described as such in the 1841 census and he and his wife, Elizabeth Ann lived in No.17 High Street. The family ran their business from here, firstly as tenants of the Neville Grenville's and later as owners when their descendants bought the property from the estate in 1947. They had a number of children but by 1871 only Charles (jnr.) and William were living at home and were both listed as saddlers. So that when the directory entry of 1883 gives Charles Dyer as the Sub-Postmaster we are not certain as to which generation of the family this applied. William seems to have left the village after his marriage to a ladies maid from Butleigh Court and Charles senior and his wife continued to live with their son, Charles(jnr.), and their daughter in law until the old people died and both were buried on the same day in Butleigh on the 18th October 1894.

Charles Jnr. & Jane Dyer

By 1889 a number of things had changed and *Kelly's Directory* entry for that year shows that Baltonsborough was obviously connected to the telephone as it is named as the nearest Money Order and Telegraph office. It is interesting that as well as Money Orders, Postal Orders, which were first issued in January 1881, were mentioned as it said that they could be issued, but not paid, from here.

As the illustration from the proof book of postmarks in the Postal Archives shows the Post Office was issued a new handstamp for use on telegrams in February 1892 and this confirms the entry in the 1894 directory of the facilities available at the village Post Office which were listed as: *Post, M.O. & T.O.,(Money*

Order & Telegraph Office)S.B.(Savings Bank) & Annuity & Insurance Office with Charles Dyer remaining as sub-postmaster. Letters from Glastonbury, arrived at 6.35am. & were dispatched at 6.35pm. & there was also a service for letters posted on Sundays before 10.20am.

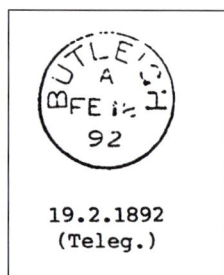

```
    ⌒‾‾‾‾⌒
   ⟋  U T L E  ⟍
  ⟋      A      ⟍
 ⎸ B  FE i≈ ⤳ ⎹
  ⟍     92      ⟋
   ⟍          ⟋
    ⌣_____⌣
```

19.2.1892
(Teleg.)

The Letter Box & Telephone Kiosk at Butleigh Wootton in 2010

The letter box at Butleigh Wootton, first mentioned in the 1882 directory, was probably called on by the postal worker taking the mail to Glastonbury as it was cleared 10 minutes later than the village office at 6.45 pm. daily and again this applied to a Sunday collection at 10.30 am.

By 1897 Express Delivery and Parcels were added to the list of services offered locally. The inclusion of parcels is rather surprising as, although the Post Office nationally had exclusively only handled letters until 1883, from that date they started a national parcel service although perhaps this had only applied to larger offices before this time.

Kelly's Directory recorded in 1906 that, as well as the letter box at Butleigh Wootton, there was also one at Butleigh Hospital which was cleared at 6.15pm. and 8.15am. on Sundays. The Hospital had been built in 1882 and it served the local community until its eventual closure in 2005 and the letter box was abandoned around this time. It was also noted that there were now two deliveries of letters from Glastonbury which arrived 6.35am. & 3.15pm. and dispatched at 12.25 & 6.35pm. daily & on Sundays at 10.20am. and the Saddlers and Harness makers were still trading as Charles Dyer & Son and Charles (Jnr) was the nominated Sub-Postmaster. By 1910 the Post Office was offering the service as a Telephone Call Office (available for calls within a limited distance).

In the 1891 census Charles' daughter, Annie, had "Telegraphist" down as her occupation and later her younger sisters, Edith and Mary, were also listed as Telegraphists so they had obviously been well trained

The Victorian Wall Letter Box at Butleigh Hospital December 2002

in this small office in Butleigh. Edith was later to be found boarding in Berkshire and working as a Post Office clerk. As all telephone exchanges were then operated manually and, before the telephone became almost universal, telegrams were a very important means of communication. Charles Dyer (Jnr) died rather suddenly in 1909 and the business was then taken over by his son, Wilfred, who was also the nominated Sub-postmaster and ran the Post Office as well as the harness and saddlery business at No. 17 High Street. He continued to live with his widowed mother at the house.

Wilfred Dyer

Wilfred's brother Charles, and his wife, also named Annie, who were married in 1911 and had sailed for Canada in the same year, returned to Butleigh before 1914 and they lived with his mother and brother before renting their own house

No. 17, High Street
with Wilfred standing nearest to the gate.
Notice the Post Office sign over the window on the left. Also the
poster on the wall.

in the village. Charles acted as a Postman in the village for a considerable time and a badge found in the garden of No.17 by Ann and David Heeley, who bought the house in 1969, could well have belonged to him. Annie is still remembered in the village as being a tall, happy person.

Charles Dyer (3),
brother to Wilfred

Wilfred's mother, Annie, no doubt ran the Post Office and it was not until after her death in 1926, when he was aged 45, that he married Sylvia Fox and they subsequently had a daughter, Edna born in 1930. They continued to run the Post Office and saddlery business until about 1953. Because the public telephone was positioned inside the saddlery shop the outside door was always kept open, much to the consternation of Sylvia, running the Post Office in the next room.

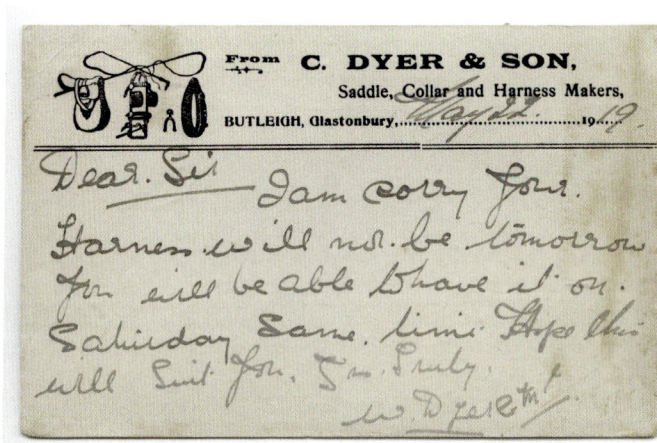

A Post Card from
Wilfred Dyer
to
Mr Allen
of West Bradley

In the electoral roll for 1932 Wilfred and Sylvia Georgina Dyer are still listed as living at the Post Office and the directory entry gives Wilfred, as well as being a Saddler & Harness Maker, as clerk to the Parish Council with the telephone number given as Butleigh No. 1. By 1938 the new automatic telephone exchange at Baltonsborough had been built and the business was then given the a new number, Baltonsborough 29.

The major event that took place in the village in 1947 was when the Butleigh Court estate was put up for sale.

SOMERSETSHIRE

IN THE PARISHES OF
BUTLEIGH, BALTONSBOROUGH, STREET, COMPTON DUNDON, GLASTONBURY, KINGWESTON, SOMERTON and BABCARY.

PARTICULARS, PLAN AND CONDITIONS OF SALE OF A
HIGHLY IMPORTANT, FREEHOLD, RESIDENTAL, SPORTING AND AGRICULTURAL

LANDED PROPERTY

KNOWN AS

THE BUTLEIGH COURT ESTATE

Nr. GLASTONBURY

comprising the Commodious and Substantially Built Country Mansion known as

"BUTLEIGH COURT"

THREE ATTRACTIVE RESIDENTIAL PROPERTIES.
TWELVE EXCELLENT DAIRY AND MIXED FARMS, SMALL HOLDINGS, etc.
100 COTTAGES AND GARDENS, SHOPS AND BUSINESS PROPERTIES.
ENCLOSURES OF RICH MEADOW AND ORCHARD LAND.
WOODS AND PLANTATIONS OF APPROXIMATELY 709 ACRES.

The Whole embracing an area of approximately

3,258 ACRES

TO BE SOLD BY AUCTION IN LOTS
(unless previously disposed of by private Treaty)

=== BY ===

WYNDHAM LAVER, A.A.I.

AT THE TOWN HALL, GLASTONBURY
TUESDAY, 25th FEBRUARY, 1947

COMMENCING AT 10.30 a.m. PRECISELY WITH INTERVAL FROM 1.30 to 2 p.m.

Copies of Particulars with Plan and Conditions of Sale may be obtained from :

THE LAND AGENTS—Messrs. WAINWRIGHTS & HEARD, Shepton Mallet, Somerset
THE SOLICITORS—Messrs. GOULD & SWAYNE, High Street, Glastonbury, or
THE AUCTIONEER—WYNDHAM LAVER, A.A.I., Shepton Mallet.

This entailed the majority of the properties in the village. In the sale catalogue No.17 The High Street, was assigned Lot Number 11. Also included in the sale was the orchard opposite, known as Dyer's Orchard, Lot 67. We are unable to see what the Dyer family paid for the properties as they were, as with so many of the other lots, withdrawn from the auction previous to the sale.

In the 1951 electoral roll Wilfred and Sylvia are still at No. 17 and their daughter Edna is noted as a young voter; she would have reached the voting age of 21 in that year.

We know that sometime before 1955 Reginald Biggs and his wife, Florence, bought the Post Office business. Reginald was about 50 and they had been married for 28 years when they came so one would anticipate that this was a change in life-style for them but they only stayed for a short while. Henry and Gwen Cottle came in 1956 and they stayed until at least 1962. Henry had been born at the end of the 19th century in Bristol whilst Gwen was born in Axbridge, so they were both Somerset people. Gwen is still remembered by Nora Woolley, a long-time resident in the village, as carrying out hairdressing locally. At that time the Post Office only transacted P.O. business with just a few other lines on sale.

With the arrival of Henry & Betty Davey things began to change as they realised that to be a viable business the Post Office needed to start selling more things. To achieve this they bought the Butleigh Co-operative across the road, whose new shop had been built in 1962. They then built the house next door to it, "Arlington" and sold the original house, No. 17, to David and Ann Heeley. Henry & Betty were known to be very generous people and they took a deep interest in village affairs, especially the church and Betty also sang in the Wells Oratorio. They are also remembered by the fact that their son, Andrew, was very tall at over 6' 4".

No.17, High Street, in 2011

Arthur Sharley and his wife, Catherine came from Lyme Regis in 1972 to Butleigh but were of a shy nature and did not really like meeting people so they did not stay long in the village. Their son, Alan, delivered the mail in Butleigh for a short while but by 1973 Ernest & Georgina Phelps were living at the Post Office Stores. They ran the business until 1982 when they sold out to a Mr Williams. This was a time when few proprietors stayed long as shortly afterwards Roger and Jean Tripp moved in. This couple had both been University tutors and found the long hours needed to run the Post Office rather arduous and were not really suited to shop life.

It was only in the summer of 1982 that a period of stability began for the Butleigh Post Office. That was when Mike and Anne Green arrived from Torquay where they had previously run a confectionery/tobacconists shop. They needed to take a business with a Post Office attached in order to give them some security by way of salary. Mike's family had been in the wholesale sweet business when he was a boy so he knew the trade well.

In talking to Mike and Anne one learnt a lot about the running of the village Post Office and shop and also the changes that took place between the summer of 1982 and 1996 when they decided to retire, firstly to live in Wells and then Glastonbury.

The opening hours of the Post Office were restricted as the insurance was only valid for the prescribed hours of opening. These ran from 9.00am. to 5.30pm. with an hour off for lunch although the shop was open from 7.00am. daily

Mike and Anne Green in the Butleigh Shop

especially for the sale of newspapers. When they first came, there was a sorting office in the back of the Post Office for the mail and Joan Davis, who lived on the Kingweston Road, was employed full time and Margaret Jeffries part time on the postal work, their salary being paid from the General Post Office headquarters.

In those days there were two collections and deliveries every weekday and one on Saturdays, when the Post Office closed at mid-day, the shop at 1.00pm. Although there was a local tradition of early closing on one day a week during their time there they remained open throughout the week. Nora Woolley came in on Wednesday afternoons and a relief worker, Sandra, for the Post Office to allow Mike & Anne to have time off together. Sandra also stood in at holiday time.

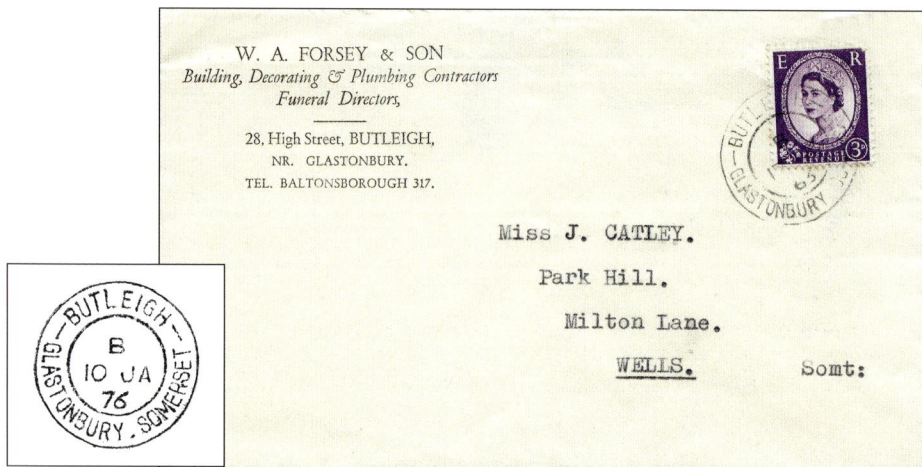

W. A. FORSEY & SON
Building, Decorating & Plumbing Contractors
Funeral Directors,

28, High Street, BUTLEIGH.
NR. GLASTONBURY.
TEL. BALTONSBOROUGH 317.

Miss J. CATLEY.

Park Hill.

Milton Lane.

WELLS.   Somt:

The Post Office was administered from the Bath Head Office, who also provided training for Anne when they first came. They actually had very little communication with Glastonbury, their local head office. One thing that Anne remembers very well was the balancing of the books every four weeks on a Friday evening when all the stamps, postal orders, pension slips and other financial transactions had to be checked and a return made.

In January 1989 both mail sorting and local delivery were removed from village Post Offices and this was then carried by van from a central sorting office based at Glastonbury. Joan Davis, who had been carrying out these duties in all weathers as well as delivering newspapers to many of the houses in the village, then retired after 20 years of service and the *Central Somerset Gazette* carried an appreciation of her work in their edition of 26th January of that year.

*Joan Davis
on the day of her retirement
as Post Lady in Butleigh
after 20 years.
January 1989*

One of the local farmers was very annoyed with Anne & Mike as he believed that they were responsible for this rather retrograde move but, of course, it was a decision made by management at a much higher level.

After the retirement of Mike and Anne, Paul & Glynis Harwood came to Butleigh and they are continuing to run the shop and Post Office in 2015. Paul, who was born in 1957 in Kingston upon Thames, got married to Glynis in 1980, and had worked for Barclays Bank for nearly 20 years before they both decided that they needed a change of life style. They had in mind that country idyll of a small village shop with roses around the door and surrounded by a friendly neighbourhood.

It was whilst on a visit to Paul's parents, who lived in Devon, and, having a long list of businesses for sale in their hands, they saw that a village shop and Post Office in a place called Butleigh was for sale; but they had no idea where Butleigh was other than in the West Country! So they decided to check it out and, having found it decided, there and then, that this was for them. And so it was that they came to Butleigh, taking over officially in September 1996.

The Post Office Letter Box November 2011

Paul as the designated Sub-Postmaster and the hours of the opening of the Post Office differ from those of the shop as before. In 2015 the shop is currently open from 7.30am. to 7.00pm. on weekdays, the official business of the Post Office counter is only from 9.00am–1.00 and 2.00–5.30pm except on Wednesdays and Saturdays when it is only available until lunchtime. Unlike the Greens, Paul and Glynis decided that as only approved personnel can work at the Post Office counter, rather than bring in outside staff, they would close on a mid-week afternoon but stay open for longer at the end of other days.

Paul's remuneration is through a basic salary, which is laid down for Sub-Postmasters depending on the office size, and there is a variable element in as much as each transaction made goes towards an enhancement of this sum, therefore the busier the counter the more it is worth to the proprietor.

As time goes on, it appears that the Post Office management are trying to reduce the number of

Paul Harwood behind the counter of Butleigh Post Office in 2012

The Butleigh Self-Inking Date Stamp used for counterwork
August 2012

salaried sub-offices and either close them altogether or make them totally dependant on turnover commission. Without the basic salary many of the village stores, such as the one at Butleigh, would become unviable.

Butleigh Post Office and Shop in July 2012
The year of the Diamond Jubilee of the Queen's Coronation

Lines written to paste on WILLIAM BRITTON's Christmas Box

1841

The dank and dark season of winter has come
When the Englishman's fireside is dear
And the Britton below (your Postman you know)
Waits to wish you a Happy New Year.
And whilst you're enjoying your Christmas with glee
In my box put your gift, and happy I'll be.
There's my donkey, my wife, my brats too beside
To depend on your generous gift.
Your Postman is poor, but yet he is sure
You will give a poor Britton a lift
And whilst you're enjoying your feasting and cheer
His joy is the same, without cider or beer.
(His song is teetotal – find fault those who can –
With the movement of Britton, your Butleigh Postman)

1842

And I hope for us all, it's a prosperous one.
Whilst sad we look back on the ills of the last
Let its blessings be treasured although they are past,
For the heart that is grateful knows a happier thrill
Than the heart that commands everything at its will.
Receive then my thanks, they are warm and sincere
For the favours you've shown me throughout last year.
If my efforts to please you be crowned with success
No language as true as this box will express.
In return for your kindness I'll do all that I can
That no fault can be found in your Butleigh Postman

Rural Life Museum, Glastonbury
Donated by Mr E J Chapman 1993

ACKNOWLEDGEMENTS

With grateful acknowledgement to Mike & Anne Green,
Paul & Glynis Harwood, Ann Heeley, Robert Senior, Nora Woolley.
Also all the people of Butleigh who have added to this story.

Meare

*M*EARE, *a village and a parish in Wells district, Somerset. The village stands on a quondam (i.e. former) island, near the river Brue, and near the Highbridge and Glastonbury railway, 2½ miles WNW of Glastonbury; dates from ancient times; was long approachable only by water; could be approached, so late as about 1808, only by a horse-path; and has a post-office under Glastonbury.*

From:- *"The Imperial Gazetteer of England & Wales"* by John Marius Wilson. Pub. A. Fullarton & Co. 1872

IT IS INTERESTING that the first reference to Meare Postal service is when the new double arc canceller was issued to Wells Post Office in December 1853. The Post Office in the village was obviously considered to be a sub-office of that city, in spite of the fact that Glastonbury had been up-rated to being a Post-Town earlier that year.

12.1853

In a list of Somerset Post Towns in 1855, as quoted in the Somerset & Dorset Postal History group journal and taken from the Post Office archives in London, Meare is still listed as a sub-office of Wells but by 1861 the entry in Kelly's directory for that year is as follows:

Post Office. Mrs Sarah Wilkins, Receiver. Letters arrive at 8.30 am. Dispatched at 5pm. The nearest Money Order Office is at Glastonbury, Population 1640

In the 1861 census, Mrs Sarah Wilkins was aged 60 and described as a Washerwoman, born in Minehead, with a 13 year old house servant, a 19 year old groom and a pupil teacher, aged 19, born in Devonshire, all in her household.

The reference in 1866 was very similar to the previous one but by 1871, in the census return, Sarah Wilkins had become a "laundress" with her unmarried carpenter son, George, living with her together with Mary Ann Nutt, 36, a laundress, and

Elizabeth S Nutt, grand-daughter aged eight, each of whom were born in Meare, and the population had actually dropped to 1631 persons.

As so often happened the Post Office remained within a family over a very long period of time and the position was combined with another totally unrelated occupation as is shown in the 1881 census.

Post Office, George Wilkins aged 51, Carpenter and Sub-Postmaster with *Jane Wilkins, his wife, aged 39, Dressmaker and Sub Postmistress.*

In many cases the husband is noted as the sub-postmaster but it was most likely that the wife actually ran that side of the business. In the 1883 edition of *Kelly's Directory* the entry reads:

.Post Office. George Wilkins, Receiver. Letters through Glastonbury arrive at 8.30 am.; Dispatched at 5.15 pm. The nearest Money Order & Telegraph Office is at Glastonbury. Letters for Godney received through Wells.

It is interesting that there is, once again, designation to that of "Receiver" rather than sub-postmaster but it obviously referred to the same duties and in 1884 in the Postmaster General's Minutes. Vol. 271, Minute 6643, it states that the Meare delivery extended to Westhay and makes reference to the Westhay Rural Postman's wages. Obviously Westhay did not have its own Post Office at that time and was served from Meare.

The Railway Inn, Meare.
The station, situated between Ashcott & Meare served both villages equally.
Photo: May 2011

Also the railway, established between Glastonbury & Highbridge in 1854 and not initially much used by the Post Office, was making an important contribution to the speeding up of the mails as in 1887 in the Postmaster General Minutes. Vol. 327. Minute 3152. an item reads: *Meare to Ashcott Station delivery established.*

By 1889 *Kelly's Directory* still names George Wilkins as Receiver with letters arriving through Glastonbury at 8.30am. and dispatched at 5.40pm. The nearest Money Order & Telegraph Office is at Glastonbury. Postal Orders are issued here but not paid and George Wilkins, in the index, is listed as Carpenter & Post Office.

Obviously the next door village of Godney was still considered to be under the Meare office as the entry also states:

Wall letter boxes, Upper Godney, cleared at 5 pm. & Lower Godney at 4.40pm.

By 1894 Meare Post Office was uprated to deal with Post & Money Orders, Savings Bank & Annuity & Insurance Office. The nearest Telegraph office is still at Glastonbury. This was important as the telephone was not universally available and anyone wishing to get a message transmitted quickly used the telegram. To make this available to as many people as possible a service was introduced in 1872 whereby you could buy a preprinted card for one shilling on which you could write in up to 20 words, put this in the nearest letter box and, bearing in mind the frequency of the collection times especially in the towns, the message would then be sent as a telegram from the nearest Telegraph office.

Very little changed until one finds a reference in the *Freeling Index* in the postal archives which states that in 1900: *Glastonbury & Meare. Rural Post revised* and also that *Westhay transferred to Bridgwater* so obviously servicing the latter village was now removed from Meare

although this does not seem to have been noted in later editions of the directory

In the 1901 Census George Wilkins, aged 70, was still described as a Carpenter but his wife, Jane, then aged 59, was described as the Postmistress. At that time the position of Postmaster carried a higher salary than that of Postmistress so,

*Meare Post Office on the left hand side. Then known as
"Vicarage Cottage", later renamed as Nos. 1 & 2 Church Path
From a postcard dated December 30th 1905.
Postcard in the collection of Alan Difford*

no doubt, the postal authorities would have been only too quick to note the change of status. It is interesting that in the same census they had visiting them a Samuel Whiting, aged 23 and born in Reading, Railway Signalman and his wife, Mary, aged 21 who was born in Bristol, Gloucestershire. It begins to show the effect of the advent of the railway and also, in the case of Meare, better road communication, allowing much greater freedom of movement and bringing in new families to the area.

Also to be noted in the same census was that at the Crown Inn, John Baker, aged 29, described as Publican & (Black)Smith with Thurza,(sic) his wife, aged 24, and their two children, Hilda aged two and John of 10 days, as this family was to play an important part in the story of the village Post Office later on.

The entries in the 1902 edition of *Kelly's Directory* were virtually unchanged and George Wilkins was still the Sub-Postmaster and letters were still arriving and being dispatched once a day and it still stated that:

> *The wall letter box at Westhay was cleared at 5.10 pm. & Stileway 5.50 pm.*
>
> *Letters through Glastonbury arrive at 8.20 am. dispatched at 5.40 pm. The nearest Telegraph Office is at Glastonbury, 3 miles distant.*

Letters should be addressed: Westhay, Shapwick, Bridgwater.

It is interesting that the village of Godney was not declared as a separate parish until a civil order was made, dated April 1st. 1904, it being part of Meare parish until that time.

The entry for 1906 was virtually identical but there was a Wall Letter Box, in addition to the one at Westhay, at Oxenpilll which was cleared at 5.25pm.

It is noticeable that the directory entry for 1910 shows a change in that it reads:

Stileway Letter Box in 2010

Post, Telegraph & Money Order Office. John Baker, Sub-Postmaster.

Letters through Glastonbury arrive at 7.30 am. & 2.30 pm.; dispatched at 11.10 am. & 6.5 pm. No delivery on Sunday.

One of the changes to note is that there are now two deliveries and dispatches a day. John Baker jnr. listed as smith and beer retailer & also at the Post Office. As he was also running both the village blacksmith's shop and the public house it is not surprising that by 1914 Mrs Thirza Baker, John's wife, is noted as the sub-Postmistress. She continued in this role until after 1927. Over this time

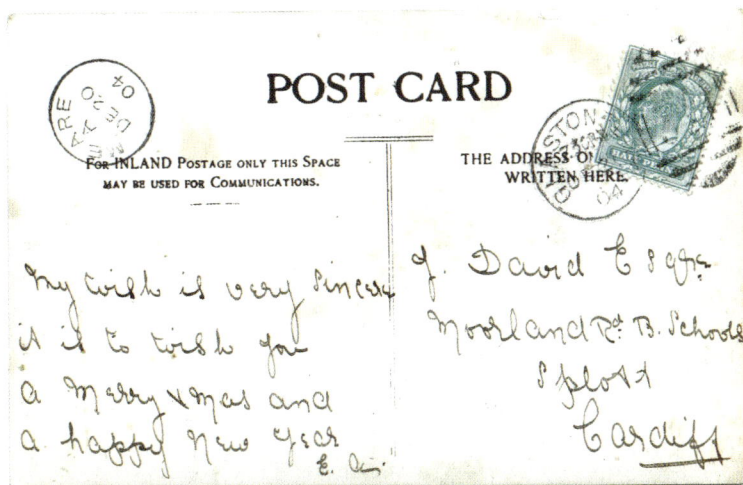

Postcard correctly showing the Meare postmark as a receiving mark rather than cancelling the stamp, as per the Post Office regulations in force at the time December 20th 1904

she must have noted the major changes in the services that were offered by the village Post Office, let alone the strain on everyone due to the First World War. They had moved back to the village from High Ham, a nearby village, where John had already been working as a blacksmith. Their grand-daughter, Ida Allman, has been able to give me a lot of information about the couple. In 2015 Ida is still lives in the village and owns the original property.

Thirza & John (Jack) Baker on their Golden Wedding day. 14th April 1948
Thirza Baker (Nee Wride) was born in 1877 in Mark and at one point their son
Leonard delivered letters around the village as well as helping his father in the
smithy. Photo loaned by Ida Allman

The *Directory* entries subsequent to 1931 were much less informative than in previous editions as far as details of the local Post Office services, probably because they had become almost universal to all rural offices. By this time Harold Luke Baker was listed as Postmaster and also Dairyman with Telephone Number No. 1 and also running the Telephonic Express Delivery Office, presumably the name for the Telegram service. The telephone address for the village was "Meare Heath", probably to differentiate it from the other identical sounding Mere in Wiltshire although, as noted later, they did get mixed at times. Harold had first started work in the Post Office in Glastonbury as a "Learner" and progressed through his career from there. He was working in Weston-s-Mare in 1914 before coming back to Meare where, in the 1939 *Kelly's Directory*, he is listed as a confectioner and also running the Post Office.

The House, formerly "The Crown" inn from where, behind and to the left, Jack ran the forge. In the front room on the left is where Thirza ran the Post Office. Set in the road can still be seen the cast iron circular disc, known as a bonding stone, used for heating the steel rims before they are put on the wooden cart wheels.

Alan Difford tells the story:

During the second World War, when Harold Baker was running the Post Office and had one of the few telephones in the village, he was also responsible for delivering telegrams. Both Post and Telegrams could bring both good news and bad in those difficult times, especially when many servicemen were in mortal danger in campaigns in foreign parts. A certain Mrs Wilkins was delighted to receive a scrap of paper, apparently brought into the country via the Red Cross, with only her address on it but she immediately recognised the writing as that of her son, Fred. This was the first she had heard of him since he was reported missing after the Dunkirk evacuation and it proved to her that he was a survivor.

One fact that people still living in the village can remember about the Baker family is that they had twin daughters, Dorothy and Marion, both born during their time at the Post Office.

During this period the mail for the village was delivered by Billy Barker who reputedly only had one arm. He

No.7 Church Path, Meare
from where Harold Baker the Post Office.
Photo taken in 2002

cycled out from Glastonbury daily in all weathers and is remembered for wearing a very distinctive cap. Speaking to his nephew, Hugh Barker and his niece, Mrs Carroll, who both still live in Glastonbury, a few more details have emerged. Uncle Bill, as he was known to them both, was one of five children whose mother, living in Somerton, was widowed when her husband died of a water-borne disease whilst serving in the army during the Boer war in South Africa. Threatened with having the children put into an orphanage, she walked the family across to Glastonbury where she had found accommodation and settled there. Billy left school at 12 and worked in the "India & China Stores" before joining the army during the First World War. He was seriously injured in the trenches and received a "Blighty" i.e. was unable to rejoin the front line troops again. Although he did not actually lose his arm it was badly withered and hence the local impression that he had lost it.

Billy Barker

Some time before 1954 Trevor Lewis and his wife, Beryl, took over the running of the Post Office in the village. Trevor, sometimes known as Brian, was a great supporter of the local football club, as can be seen in the picture; during his time

Trevor Lewis in the centre, back row
Picture from the book "Meare, Its place in History"

in the village the team had great success. The couple came to Meare from Wales and in conjunction with the Post Office they also ran a small library for the benefit of the villagers.

In 1958 Reginald Charles and Mary Nelder were the proprietors of the village shop and a report in the local paper showed that the village was not immune to some petty crime and small Post Offices are considered to be very vulnerable as they handle comparatively large sums of money.

In the *Central Somerset Gazette,* in February 1960, there was an item concerning a raid on the village shop when it was reported that the contents of the stores were strewn about and the sum of £3 was taken from the Post Office. No mention was made of any subsequent arrests for this crime.

From 1963 Harold Robinson and his wife, Joan, were in charge. Unfortunately Mrs Robinson suffered from severe arthritis and died whilst Harold was the postmaster. It is remembered that he later married Barbara Cook-Fox, the widow of the late head-master of the village school.

Another local person, Gloria McClurg, editor of the book on Meare brought out to celebrate the new millennium in early 2001, *"Meare. Its place in history."* worked for Harold & Joan, on a part-time basis, in the shop during 1973-74

The predecessors to Peter & Margaret Haworth taking over the running of the business in 1988 were a Mr & Mrs Taylor but their stay was only brief. Peter and Margaret originally came from Hertfordshire.

Oxenpill Letter Box, December 2002. In the background is The Countryman Inn where Sidney Whitcombe was the publican when it was called The New Inn. c.1961.

When Peter was working in Wiltshire he was made redundant from his job. They then decided to take a small village Post Office/stores somewhere in the area. Meare P.O./village store became available when the Taylors decided to move. Mrs Taylor had, at that time, four children and was expecting her fifth and was finding the work and the family responsibility far too much to manage.

Peter Haworth came down for a week before taking over in order to learn the system, together with a further week with a trainer employed by the Post Office, who lived locally. The mail in 1988 was delivered to the Post Office by van from Glastonbury and then sorted for delivery by local Post Lady, Margaret, who did her rounds in all weathers by bicycle. It was in the early 1990s that this all changed; she was then retired as all the mail for the village was firstly sorted in Glastonbury Post Office and then delivered by motor van

Margaret Haworth has told me about the times when the cash, intended for Mere in Wiltshire was, on more than one occasion, mis-directed to their office. In order that the Mere Post Office were able to pay their pension, child allowance, etc. on time she had to drive up and personally deliver the, not inconsiderable, sum of money.

Peter and Margaret joined in with the local activities and Peter was the President of the Meare & Westhay Drama Group. They usually used the loft of their house for rehearsals. In 1994 they decided to retire and then moved to Ashcott.

Peter Haworth

Robert & Julie Elkin took over from the Haworths. Bob Elkin originated from Ireland and he was instrumental in making many changes to the Post Office, especially enlarging the Car Park.

In the late 1990s I am told that a Mr Chesterman came to run the business but did not stay long.

In June 2002 Paul and Sandra Hillson took over the running of the shop and Post Office. Whilst Paul took work away from home to supplement their income, Sandra ran the business single-handed. In 2010, Post Office Counters Ltd., in order to reduce their trading deficit, decided that many of the smaller rural Post Offices should be closed. So, by mutual agreement, Westhay lost the Post Office but retained its general store and Meare retained its Post Office but relinquished the grocery and general trade. In 2015 Meare still had the Post Office serving pensioners, issuing licences, selling stamps and greetings cards with limited banking facilities also being available.

No.7 Church Path in April 2011.

ACKNOWLEDGEMENTS

With grateful acknowledgements to the many people who have helped me fill in the details of the history of the Post Office in Meare, with especial thanks to Ida Allman, Alan Difford, Margaret Haworth and Gloria McClurg amongst others.

Middle Leigh and West End, Street

Middle Leigh, Street. Post Office.
19 Middle Leigh.

A Town Sub-Office. T.S.O.

The first sub-Postmaster of the Post Office in Middle Leigh was Arthur Goodland. Arthur was born in Sherborne, Dorset in 1878 where his parents ran a market garden as had grandfather's family before him. In 1901 Arthur was living in Andover where he was working as a grocer's assistant as was the description of his occupation in the census of 1911 when he was staying with his parents at North Road, Sherborne, just before his marriage to Emma in Bristol. After that it is difficult to follow their progress but in the *Kelly's Directory* of 1931 they are listed as running the Sub Post Office at Middle Leigh in Street with a telephone number of 30. This is the first reference found to the establishment of a Post Office here in any of the local publications. Arthur and Emma continued to run the Post Office together until, unfortunately, Emma died in late 1938 aged 65. Their daughter, Joan, who first appeared on the register of electors in

A letter registered at the Post Office in Middle Leigh on
26th February 1972

1937, was living with them and she and her father continued the business until 1952 when they retired.

That is when Frederick & Beryl Jones arrived at what was then numbered No. 26 Middle Leigh. They are remembered for the fact that they had two daughters living with them. Interestingly, still on the wall when the Davies family moved in, in 1981, was record of the girls heights as they grew. The Jones' were to remain at the shop, subsequently re-numbered No. 19, until the arrival of Arthur and Ethel Fullbrook sometime before 1975.

The Fullbrooks stayed for under two years as in 1976, John Champion, Ex RAF. & his wife, Joan, an ex Police-woman, came to Middle Leigh and ran the small shop and the "Town Sub-Office", referred to as a "T.S.O." in all Post Office official papers, for five years. John Champion came from a farming family as his father had a small holding which he continued to run until a great age. He is said to have been still buying cattle at market at 90 years of age. The Champions owned one of the chalets on Dunster Beach and on one weekend the key holders of the Post Office, John & Mary Hecks from the nearly cider factory, heard the burglar alarm going off. They went to investigate only to find an old gentleman in the shop choosing a birthday card, quite oblivious to the alarm. He had quite innocently entered the shop as the door was unlocked and did not realise that the owners had gone away for the weekend. John thought Joan had locked up and vice-versa. In this instance the key-holders

The broken bracket on the top of the box originally held a direction sign to the Post Office as illustrated.

This Pillar Box was originally outside the Middle Leigh Post Office before this office closed. It was then moved to a position outside the Ivythorn Stores in a nearby road.
Photo: December 2012

were told that someone would come down from London to attend to it!

The Champions had a reputation as connoisseurs of home-brewed beer, a hobby that was very much in vogue at the time. When they decided to retire they then moved to Wiltshire and John & Janice Davies took over. John, who was born in South Wales, first came to Somerset, Creech St Michael near Taunton, with his parents at the age of six weeks in 1931. Janice (nee Sanders) and he first met when they both went to schools in Taunton, one to Richard Huish's and the other to Bishop Fox's Schools.

John, having completed his compulsory two years National Service in the Royal Air Force, where he had qualified as a navigator, signed up to remain in the service where he was to remain for the

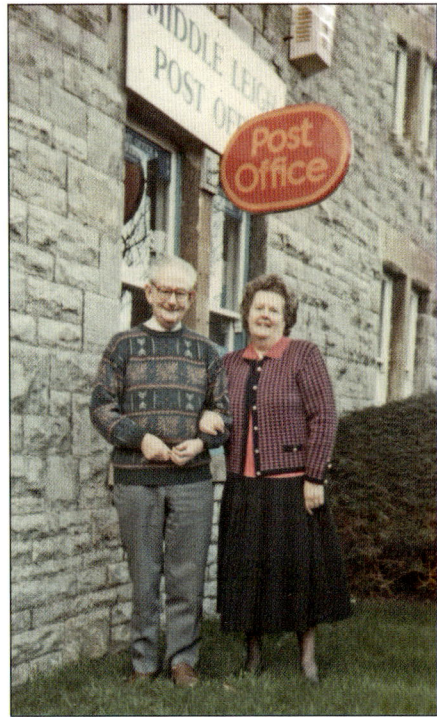

John & Janice Davies outside the Post Office in Middle Leigh

next 15 years. Undeterred by the prospect of the service lifestyle, John and Janice were married in the church of the village where she was born, Thornfalcon, in early 1955, As John was stationed all over the world they had many homes, both abroad and in this country. The first of their children, Kathryn, was born in Taunton whilst their son, Stephen, in Malaysia.

On leaving the services in 1969 they decided to take a grocery and off-licence shop in Wiveliscombe where they stayed for 12 years until coming to live in Street. Here they took over the small Sub-Post Office in Middle Leigh on 21st February 1981.

During the next 14 years there they got to know all their regular customers well and gradually increased the turnover of the business, operating not only the Post Office but also offering cards and stationery as well as a good selection of sweets. Janice did not take kindly to interference from Post Office officials from on high and, if they rang and she answered it, she told them that she was only the "Postmasters mistress" before handing the call over to John. They well

An Aerial photo of the Middle Leigh Post Office showing the canopy over the entrance. The Pillar Box can be seen on the roadside

remember the occasion when, for some unknown reason, the burglar alarm was set off and when this happened, as the Hecks family had found out before, it could only be re-set remotely by someone from head office. Due to the noise upsetting the neighbourhood, the local constabulary became involved but, in spite of trying desperate measures which only made matters worse, nothing could be done until the following day and, by all accounts, the officer's management had to, eventually, pay compensation to repair the damage done to the equipment.

The business had virtually out-grown the small room from which they operated by 1994 and the Post Office wanted to install a second computer which would have taken up most of the counter space. This was a step too far for John & Janice so they made the decision to retire. The Post Office was then taken over by Simon & Denise Johansson.

Simon and Denise had met at a very early age, both living in Hereford from the age of about three and so it was that they were married, at a comparatively young age by the standard set in more recent years, when they were both 22.

In 1986 Simon, a qualified accountant with the Ministry of Defence, was transferred to the E.M.I. factory at Wells

and when their daughter, Natalie, was only just three months old they came to live in this part of the country, finding a house in Street. Their son, Ben, was born three years later in 1989.

Denise had experience of the workings of the Post Office as she had been employed in the Main Post Office in Hereford before their marriage. She had even undertaken 7 weeks training at the industry training centre at Rhyll in order to take a more responsible position. When that Office opened a Philatelic Counter she also spent a week of training at the Philatelic Bureau in Edinburgh.

After coming to Street, Denise, using her Post Office training, helped out on a part-time basis at the Middle Leigh Post Office being run by John & Janice Davies, even acting as relief when they went on holiday. With John & Janice wishing to retire in 1994 their first thought was to offer the Post Office to Simon and Denise and, after much heart searching, this couple decided to take it.

The Johansson's first day was not without its drama; they were having central heating installed in the house at No.19. and ten minutes before opening time there was a loud shout; with the floor boards up, Simon had put his foot through the ceiling of the living room, luckily not over the shop!

This Middle Leigh Post Office could be very busy as they were paying out somewhere in the region of £65,000 a week in pensions and benefit as well as acting as banker for three local shops, one of which was run by Royston Maddaford whose brother, Preston, ran the Post Office at Windmill Hill in Glastonbury. They also sold cards and stationery as well as a selection of sweets

Denise Johansson

and toys but the shop, in the front part of the semi-detached property, was too small to sell other products.

On occasions, keepers of small Post Offices had trouble with the time-locked safe as, when the clocks changed in the spring, unless they had remembered to change the setting the night before, they would be unable to gain access to the cash for an hour after opening, much to the annoyance of the waiting customers.

Three part-time staff were employed at Middle Leigh to help out and Simon was occasionally brought in to take charge on a Saturday morning. He did complain that Denise gave her other staff training but ignored him! As can be seen from the illustration of the opening hours on the following page, Wednesdays were early closing day and that is when the weekly audit was undertaken although Denise, with her years of practice, never had any trouble with this side of the business.

After five years Denise and Simon decided the time had come to give up the Post Office. Rather than the business being run as before, from No.19 Middle Leigh, this shop closed for good on Friday 14th April 2000. The Post Office was then transferred to the West End shop being run, at that time, by a local group of mini-supermarkets trading as "Smile"; to be later taken over by McColls.

West End Post Office and Shop. September 2011

POST OFFICE

MIDDLE LEIGH POST OFFICE
19 MIDDLE LEIGH
STREET
SOMERSET
BA16 0LB

Name and
Address of
Sub-Office

MIDDLE LEIGH STREET
J
14 AP
00
SOMERSET

OPENING HOURS

Monday	9.00 AM - 1.00 PM	2.00 PM - 5.30 PM
Tuesday	9.00 AM - 1.00 PM	2.00 PM - 5.30 PM
Wednesday	9.00 AM - 1.00 PM	CLOSED
Thursday	9.00 AM - 1.00 PM	2.00 PM - 5.30 PM
Friday	9.00 AM - 1.00 PM	2.00 PM - 5.30 PM
Saturday	9.00 AM - 12.30 PM	CLOSED

Closed on Sundays, Public and Bank Holidays

ROYAL MAIL COLLECTIONS

FROM POST OFFICE COUNTER. PLEASE SEE PILLAR BOX FOR
ADDITIONAL COLLECTIONS.

Monday	2.00 PM	5.30 PM
Tuesday	2.00 PM	5.30 PM
Wednesday	1.00 PM	CLOSED
Thursday	2.00 PM	5.30 PM
Friday	2.00 PM	5.30 PM
Saturday	11.30 AM	NOON

Registered letters and overseas insured items
If intended to connect with a particular collection please could these items
be handed in at least 10 minutes before the advertised time of collection.

The Opening Hours of the Middle Leigh Post Office.
The postmark is dated with the last day of business on the premises.

The West End Post Office Pillar Box BA16 312
Photo - September 2011

The internal layout of the West End store before it was re-modelled in 2014.
The Post Office counter then moved across to become an extension of regular
sales counter on the left.

The closure of one office and the opening of another in this part of Street after a weekends break meant that no-one was deprived of the services offered, so very important when so many were dependent on receiving their pension from their nominated Post Office on a very regular basis.

In order to help the smooth change over, Denise Johansson continued to work in the Post Office at "Smile" for the first six months after the move, Cathy Williams then became manager of this side of the business, the position she still holds in 2014. Nick Roberts, whose parents live locally, is not only the overall manager of the store but acts as relief in the Post Office when needed. Nick started his career with Tesco Stores, in stock control, before moving to McColls. His first position with them was when they took over the Windmill Hill shop and Post Office in Glastonbury. After a short period working in North Petherton, he was promoted to manage the West End Stores.

A report in the local paper *The Central Somerset Gazette* dated 27th March 2008, following reports of problems at the main office and rumours about the future of this office, headed:

The Self-Inking Date Stamp used in the Post Office

Nick Roberts in West End Post Office November 2014

POST OFFICE WALK.

Campaigners wanting to save a central Somerset Post Office are to take to the streets tomorrow at 10.30am.

Protesters will march from West End Post Office, which Royal Mail officials are proposing to close, to the main Post Office in Street, timing how long it takes.

They hope to demonstrate how difficult it will be for local people to get to the counter situated at Martins, (in the High Street. Ed.) particularly those with mobility difficulties and parents with pushchairs and buggies.

This public outcry was obviously effective as the Post Office in West End, Street is still operating and serving the public in 2014.

ACKNOWLEDGEMENTS

With grateful acknowledgement to John and Janice Davies, Ken and Diana Dunthorn, Denise and Simon Johansson, John and Mary Hecks and all the people of Street who have added to this story.

Parbrook,
West Bradley

*WEST BRADLEY, a parish in the Wells district, Somerset; on the
Somerset & Dorset railway, near West Pennard station, 4 miles E.
by S. of Glastonbury. It includes the hamlet of Parbrook; and its post-town is
East Pennard, under Shepton Mallet. Acres 625. Real property £1,183. Pop. 136
Houses 31. The living is a perpetual curacy, annexed to the vicarage of East
Pennard, in the diocese of Bath & Wells.*

Parbrook, A hamlet in West Bradley parish, Somerset.5½ miles N.W. of Castle Cary.

From:- *"The Imperial Gazetteer of England & Wales"* by John Marius Wilson.
Pub. A. Fullarton & Co. 1872

PARBROOK is a small hamlet on the boundaries of East Pennard and West
Bradley which also incorporates the hamlet of Lottisham, situated in a valley
with a stream passing through which occasionally floods. The actual hamlet
consists of some 30 houses but the Post Office catered for a much larger area, the
nearest other Post Offices were at Baltonsborough, in East Pennard village or at
West Pennard. The population in 1851 was 265 and by 1881, it was 280.

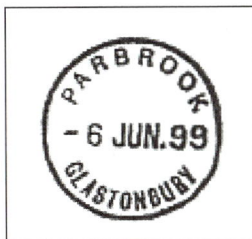

*The First Parbrook
Postmark used
when the Post Office was
opened in 1899*

It was the centre of the community and in the
1940's it had a village school, which doubled as
the village hall, with two classrooms opened in the
late 1870's serving the surrounding inhabitant's
children. A Young Men's Institute with its own small
corrugated iron clad meeting place, built just after
the First World War, adjoining the school playing
field. There was a village shop selling small goods;
it had a cobbler, George Gilbert; its own slaughter
house and butchers shop run by Ernest Reakes and
employing Charlie Porter to deliver meat by bicycle
around the area; a small shop run by Mrs Flagg and

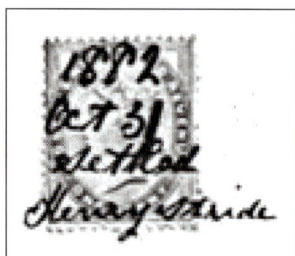

Henry Stride's signature on a receipt stamp. Stamps were designated for use for both Postage and Revenue use after 1881

The Shop, Parbrook in 2005

men's barber (only open in the evening after working time) run by Reuben Flagg, her husband, who had also built the bungalow they lived in; and, of course, the village Post Office run by Minnie Griffin.

Gleaning information from both *Morris's* and *Kelly's Directories*, it stated that in 1866 letters for the village came through Shepton Mallet. By 1883 Glastonbury was the main office which was also the nearest Money Order office, a very important service before the days of almost universal banking facilities and cheque books. By 1889, it is stated that letters arrive at 10.00am. and the wall box is cleared at 5.00pm. By 1897 a wall box at Lottisham was cleared at 5.25pm. as well.

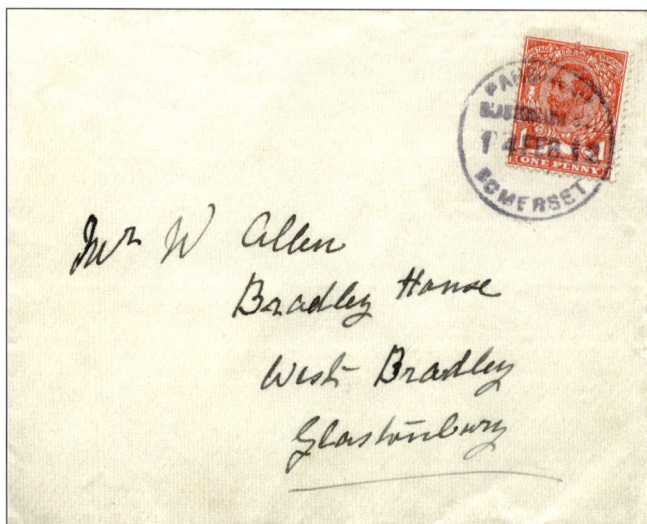

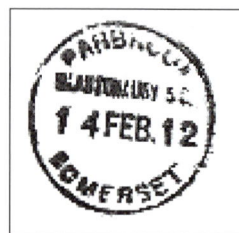

A letter posted in Parbrook on Valentine's Day 1912 with the new hand-stamp with Glastonbury S.O. (sub-office) incorporated

The Victorian Wall Letter Box at Lottisham House in 1996

In both the 1902 and the 1906 *Kelly's Directories,* Henry Stride, who lived in the house known as The Shop, opposite Brook Farm, was noted as the Sub-Postmaster.

Henry Stride was a builder, as was his father before him, and the house next door is called Stride House after them although it was originally called "Laureldene".

In the *Kelly's Directory* entry for 1902 under the heading: *Post Office. Henry Stride, Sub-Postmaster. Letters through Glastonbury arrive at 9 am. Dispatched at 4.45pm. No arrival or dispatch on Sunday. Postal Orders are issued here but not paid. The nearest Money Order & Telegraph Office is at West Pennard, 1.5 miles distant.*

Again in 1906:

Henry Stride,, Sub-Postmaster. Letters through Glastonbury arrive at 8.30 am & 4.15 pm for callers only. Dispatched at 9 am, & 4.45 pm. No arrival or dispatch on Sunday. Postal Orders are issued here but not paid. The nearest Money Order & Telegraph Office is at West Pennard, Wall letter box cleared at Lottisham at 8.25 am, & 5.25 pm. & at West Bradley at 9.10 am.,& 5 pm.

By 1914 the entry in *Kelly's Directory* read:

Post Office, Parbrook Mrs Minnie Griffin, Sub Postmistress. Letters through Glastonbury arrive at 8.05 am. & 4.15 pm; dispatched at 8.45 am & 4.55 pm. Wall letter boxes at Lottisham cleared at 8.25 am. & 5.25 pm. & at West Bradley at 9.10 am. & 5 pm.

Although, as we can see from the Certificate of Posting illustrated, Minnie was in office as early as 1910.

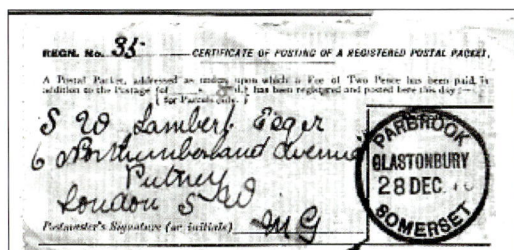

A Certificate of Posting initialled by Minnie Griffin in 1910

Minnie Griffin

The Postmark without S.O. was introduced prior to 1914

Although West Bradley did not have a Parish Council, they did have a Parish Meeting that met about once a year and matters pertaining to the postal service occasionally get a mention in the minute book;

March 26th 1912. Mr James Pearce proposed that the delivery of letters should be made throughout the parish on Sundays, which was seconded by Mr W. T. Allen and carried.

March 28th 1925. A letter was read, received from Bridgwater Postmaster, suggesting half holidays for Postmen on Saturday afternoons in each week,. The Parish Meeting unanimously agreed in favour of this.

May 26th 1929. A letter was read by the Chairman, received from Bridgwater Postmaster asking the Parish Meeting for their approval of an earlier delivery of letters on Saturday afternoons and the letter boxes to be cleared also earlier. The Parish Meeting unanimously agreed to this & also it was proposed & carried to

Batch Cottage, Stone Lane Parbrook The home of Joe & Minnie Griffin

ask the Postmaster of Bridgwater if the letter box at Lottisham Corner could be cleared on Sundays for the convenience of Lottisham

April 1st 1938. The Chairman requested to ask the Postmaster to change the name of the Post Office to "Parbrook, West Bradley", instead of only Parbrook.

March 29th 1939. The letter from the Postmaster was read as to changing the name of the Post Office from "Parbrook, Nr. Glastonbury" to "West Bradley, Glastonbury" & his reply was not agreeable to altering the name.

The Wall Letter Box at the entrance to Dials Green Farm in 2002

The entry in *Kelly's Directory* of 1919 reads:

Post Office, Parbrook   Mrs Minnie Griffin, Sub-postmistress, letters through Glastonbury. West Pennard, 1.5 miles distant is the nearest M.O. & T.Office. Wall letter boxes. Lottisham, opposite the church, Lower Lottisham & West Bradley (near Church)

There was also a note to say that letters for Lottisham should have "Baltonsborough" included in their address as the delivery for the further part of the village came from that office whereas the rest of the West Bradley letters were delivered from West Pennard. No sorting or deliveries were carried out from Parbrook although there were two postal deliveries a day being made at this time.

Joe Griffin

I have seen a postcard sent from one lady in West Bradley letting her friend, who also lived in the village, know that she would be unable to come to tea that afternoon! No telephones in those days.

When Minnie died 1957 aged 80, her widower, Joe, became the Postmaster but only on the understanding that Leila, his niece, would do the weekly book-keeping for him (see below). One week she could not find the pension counterfoils to prove that Joe had paid out the money and she had to go around the village

One of the many envelopes collected by the late John Worrall, a noted collector of Somerset Postal History. He endeavoured to have a Registered letter posted from every Post Office in Somerset.

checking each ones pension book before realising that the envelope with them in must have been stolen, the thieves obviously thinking the envelope contained money. Joe knew the lads who were most likely to be responsible and the counterfoils were eventually found behind a loose stone in a wall at Lottisham.

One very memorable pensioner in Parbrook was Miss Whitehead who lived in a bungalow in Stone Lane. She invariably collected her pension between 1.00 and 2.00pm carrying a paper bag in which she concealed her handbag containing her pension book. If there was anyone around at the time she would dart back indoors and wait until the road was clear. One day she came in and asked if she could have her pension in £5 notes; Joe queried as to why, as she invariably took £1 notes, to which she replied that she had just been listening to the news and had heard that the pound had just been de-valued!

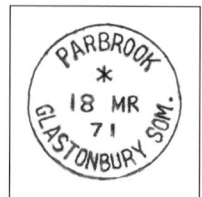

I did have the opportunity to visit to Leila and Fred Chinn at their home, Pembroke House, Parbrook, on 27th August 2005 when I heard more about their background story.

Leila Chinn, (nee Higdon,) was one of six children of Leonard and Margaret Higdon who were married in 1916. Leonard worked for the cider maker, Mr

Pembroke House, Stone Lane, Parbrook.
Fred & Leila Chinn's home

This house is reputedly one of those in the village built by the the Stride family.

W. T. Allen at West Bradley House, for most of his working life taking barrels of cider across to West Pennard Station 6 days a week with a horse and flat-bed wagon. He could be relied on not to get drunk as he was strictly teetotal. Leonard was obviously called up for the services in the First World War. In the parliamentary election list of absent voters in 1918, at the end of the war, he was listed as a private in the 18th Wing Aeroplane Repair Section, R A F.

Leonard's sister, Minnie, was married to Joe Griffin and lived in the first house on the right on The Batch, Stone Lane. She was well known for always wearing a black hat pinned on and was never seen without it. It was said that the first thing she did in the morning was to put it on, and the last thing at night was to remove it!

Leila, born in 1923, started work at the age of 14 at the grocery shop of Colliholes, in Glastonbury. It was during World War II when she first worked at the Aeroplane Company in Bridgwater, before being transferred to work at Taunton Railway Station. It was here that she met a young military policeman who was on duty at the station. Fred, from nearby Westonzoyland,. They were later to be married in the Methodist Chapel in Parbrook before coming to live in the village. Later

Leila worked in the Post Office at West Pennard when Mr Downing, a retired school-master from Weston super Mare, was the Postmaster. At that time May Phelps was one of the post ladies who cycled around the villages delivering letters and is well remembered by some of the older residents in West Bradley.

When Fred came back from war service, he went bus driving as he was unable to follow his first choice which was to become an A.A. (Automobile Association) man. The A.A. had to first wait to see how many of their former employees wished to take up their previous positions again before they could recruit new staff. After one year, in 1947, he was able to join the A.A. and spent six years with them. He then joined Clarks shoes as a lorry driver, driving to their factory at Barnstaple and back every day of the week. After being made redundant in 1967 he then became a postman based in Glastonbury for the following 5 years. His day then started at 4.00am. and his duties rotated with other Postmen over three or four different rounds on a weekly basis. Following that time he rejoined Clarks Shoes and remained with them until his retirement.

Shortly before Joe Griffin died in 1962 aged 83, Leila, had taken over the Post Office and ran it from their home, Pembroke House. This was in that part of the house which is now the sitting room, on the right hand side of the front entrance, and she continued to do so until the spring of 1985.

Leila Chinn working in the Post Office on the last day before it shut

The village finally lost its Post Office for good after 86 years of which members of one family had run it for more than 70 years. Leila regretted the fact that as she had only been in charge for 23½ years, she did not qualify for the gold watch given by the Post Office for 25 years service.

To mark her retirement and in recognition of her many years of service to the village a surprise party was organised at which she was presented with a large bunch of flowers and a cheque by the villagers. Leila and Fred continued to live in Parbrook until Leila sadly passed away in March 2011 after 65 years of marriage.

The Wall Letter Box at West Bradley, opposite the church

The Letter Box in Stone Lane, Parbrook in 2002

ACKNOWLEDGEMENTS

In grateful thanks to Leila & Fred Chinn and their daughter, Judith, for all their help and their local knowledge of the Parbrook Post Office.

Shapwick

*S*HAPWICK, a village and a parish in Bridgewater district, Somerset. The
village stands under Polden Hill, 2 miles S of the Glastonbury railway, and
5½ W by S of Glastonbury; and has a post-office under Bath, and a railway
station. The parish includes a detached portion, and comprises 3,781 acres. Real
property, £4,644. Pop. 407. Houses, 88. The manor, with Shapwick House,
belongs to G. Warry, Esq. The living is a vicarage, united with Ashcott, in the
diocese of Bath and Wells. Value, £350.* Patron, Sir G. Montgomery, Bart. The
church was restored in 1861. There is a national school. Charities, £8.

From:- *"The Imperial Gazetteer of England & Wales"* by John Marius Wilson.
Pub. A. Fullarton & Co. 1872

AS IS THE CASE of Ashcott, Shapwick was part of the Glastonbury Penny
Post system from 1826 but to later come under the Bridgwater Head Office.

In the *"Freeling Reports"* written by Francis Freeling, the secretary to the General
Post Office, to the Postmasters General, now in the Post Office Archives. In Volume 57, Page 131, is the following entry:-

16th November 1832.

My Lord

    *I presume your Grace will readily authorise
the proposition in the enclosed Report from Mr.
Louis (The Post Office surveyor for the district), to
open a receiving house at Shapwick, a village in the
Glastonbury Penny Post, where many respectable
inhabitants reside. He states that it will be a great
accommodation and the expense will only be a salary
of £2 - 2- 0 to the receiver, which the produce of this
Penny Post (about £30 per annum) will well afford.*

*The Undated Circular
Postmark issued to
Glastonbury before
being sent out to Shapwick.
8th January 1848*

A letter posted in February 1837 from Shapwick to Bruton, Somerset, charged at 5d.
The No. 3 Receiving House mark denotes Shapwick within the
Glastonbury Penny Post System

Another reference, this time in the Postmasters Minute Book in the Postal Archives, dated 15th February 1855, is an intriguing entry which reads:- *"I submit that the 4/- claimed by the Postmistress of Glastonbury for her journey to Shapwick, under Mr Cresswell's recommendation, be allowed"* One does wonder as to what required her to make the journey?

In the *Harrison-Harrad Directories*. Robert Martin, is given as the "receiver" i.e. in charge of the post, with the nearest Money-order Offices being at Glastonbury and in Street. In any research, the census returns are exceedingly useful, and in the one dated 1861 we find that Robert Martin was born in Shapwick and described as Carpenter & Joiner employing 2 men. His wife, Mary Ann, a year older than him at 54, was born at Kingsteignton in Devon. Of their three children living with them, two were daughters, Elizabeth was a dress-maker and Maria, a miliner (sic) whilst their son, George at 22, was, like his father, a carpenter. They also

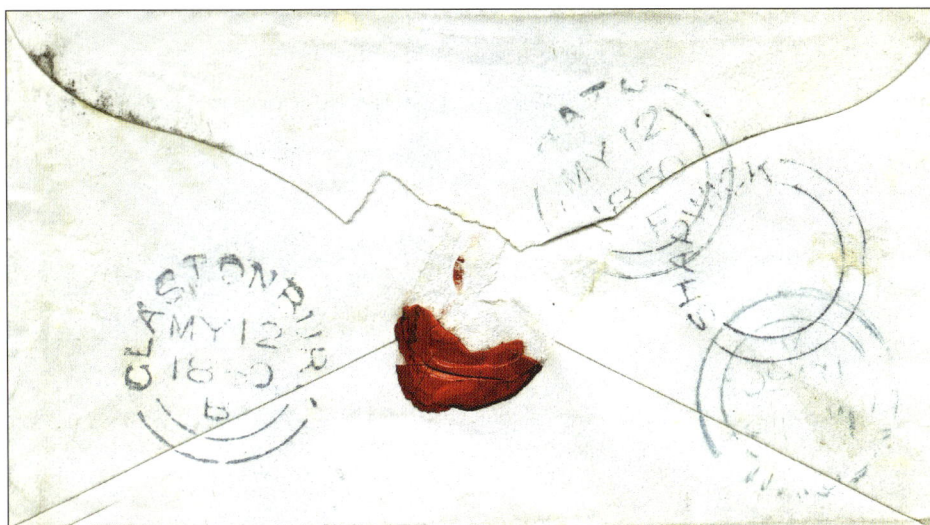

A letter from Shapwick to East Chinnock, near Yeovil. 12th May 1850.
The SHAPWICK receiving mark, the date stamp of the local head office, GLASTONBURY.
Date stamp of BATH on the same day and the receiving mark of YEOVIL

had, living with them, two apprentice carpenters, aged 18 and 15, coming from further afield. By 1861 the *Kelly's Directory* also says that *"Letters were arriving from Bath at 7.16 am. and being dispatched at 5,50 pm."*

By 1872 *Morris's Directory* had raised Robert Martin to the status of Sub-Postmaster with Street is the nearest M.O. Office, but by 1875 the status of the Post Office had been raised as they could now deal not only with the post but also Money Orders and Savings Bank transactions themselves.

Gradually the opening hours had been increasing as by 1875 it is stated that letters were arriving from Bridgwater at 7.00am and the last post went out at 8.20pm. Eight years later, still with Robert Martin acting as sub-postmaster, the first post was arriving from Bridgwater at 4.48am. and the evening mail was going out just a bit later at 8.37pm.

In 1889 we find the first mention of Thomas Crossman Harvey, the Post Office now transacted Money Orders, Savings Bank, Annuity and Insurance and a Telegraph Office was to be found at the railway station. This

The Postmarker issued to Shapwick on the 30th August 1873, primarily for use on Post Office Savings Bank pass books

The Shapwick Post Office from a Post Card dated July 21st 1907.
Possibly Thomas Harvey standing outside

station was about a mile north of the village on the Somerset & Dorset Joint line which ran from Evercreech via Glastonbury to Highbridge, and later to Burnham on Sea, first opened in 1854.

People only rarely moved very far in those days: Thomas Harvey was born in Shapwick c. 1838 and was married in Ashcott, in early 1858, to Ellen Elizabeth Sawtell (born c.1836). Ellen was the daughter of George & Jemima Sawtell of Ashcott, one of 3 girls living at home in 1861. In 1851 George Sawtell gave his occupation as "Saddler" but by 1861 he was farming 110 acres while his wife, Jemima, was a shopkeeper so, obviously Ellen had experience of retailing.

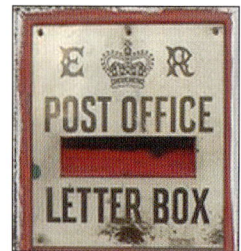

By 1894 there were now two arrivals and despatches of mail a day, the extra times coinciding with Thomas Cridland's Royal Mail Bus passing through to Glastonbury at 9.45am; returning to Bridgwater at 5.00pm, daily. Therefore mail was taken to either Glastonbury or Bridgwater Head Offices depending on the time of day. There was even a despatch at 5.00pm. on Sundays and, if you called at the office on weekdays you could collect your post at 5.00pm. By

An Edward VII
"Ludlow" type
Letter Box, as set in the
window of the shop

Nos. 1 & 2, Station Road, Shapwick in March 2014

1902 two deliveries a day became the normal service although the Post Office still did not have the telephone installed, you had to go to Ashcott, 1½ miles away, for the nearest Telegraph Office.

Thomas Harvey died in early 1909, aged 71 and the Post Office was then run by the daughter, Violetta, now nominated as the sub-postmistress, and her mother, from their house on Station Road in the centre of the village, opposite the church.

Violetta Harvey appears to be the youngest child of Thomas & Ellen and she was born in Ashcott in 1881, as was her eldest brother, William, and was then aged 18 They obviously had lived in West Harptree around 1883 as their second son, Victor, was born there although, according to the census returns, Thomas was carrying on trade as a haulier in Ashcott in 1881.

Violetta and her parents outside the shop prior to 1909.

Whilst No.1 Station Road was solely the Post Office, by 1911 Frederick & Emily Wren were running a grocers and drapery business at No.5 Northbrook Road where, much later, the Post Office was to be situated. The

Wrens came from Luton, Bedfordshire; Frederick's father had been a general porter but both his mother and two sisters were involved in the straw hat trade. By 1891 Frederick was a grocer's assistant but later, having married Emily, from Colville in Leicestershire in about 1897, he was running his own grocer's shop in Luton with his wife looking after two small children, Edith Emily aged 3 and 5 week old Kenneth Costin but by 1911 they had moved to Shapwick. As can be seen from the signature on the minutes of the Vestry Meeting held on 14th April 1914 Frederick Wren was not only present but also a member.

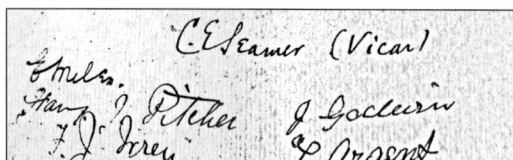

The Signatures of those present at the Vestry Meeting.

According to these minutes:- Mr Wren then asked that the Churchwardens should allot his family in Church a definite seat in order to save inconvenience. This the Churchwardens promised to do.

Emily Wren later taught in the village school and had a reputation as strict disciplinarian.

An extract from the book *"The Wrong Side of the Track"* by Fred & Trish Jennings, published by Trish Jennings and produced by Noodle Books in 2012.

Fred Jennings, born in August 1908, wrote:

The only postman I remember at Shapwick until about 1924/5 was Johnnie Godwin (nicknamed 'Tit-Pont'), and he lived in the house adjoining the village hall. He wore uniform with the flat-topped helmet of the time and he walked. He had a very wide area which took in the outlying farms such as Northbrook, Manor and Kent, each up to a mile distant from the post office. He also covered the Griffin's Head pub at Shapwick Station and the two farms which lay off the main station road. He was a bit curt in manner and was not the most liked of Shapwick's citizens. The story used to be told of how Cecil Davys of Kent Farm was at Shapwick Station one day with a horse and cart when he offered Johnnie a lift, which met with the reply that he didn't want a lift in his so-and-so cart, Cecil repeated the offer later when it was raining heavily, and this time Johnnie said thanks very much, whereupon Cecil said not likely and you can bloody well walk. This was said to be quite true, and I never heard it doubted. ....

When the Misses Harvey ran the post office they had a horrible little terrier dog which sat inside the shop on top of the letterbox and snarled every time a letter was posted. One day, when I was about six years old and living at the Albion

Inn, I was going home from school, and he planted his teeth in my seat without any provocation. Miss Harvey apologised and scolded 'Fido', who was still going when I had left school. I often threatened what I would do to him if I ever caught him alone but the chance never came.

George Williams left our employ about 1924/25 to take over Johnnie Godwin's job as village postman.

I do think that the mention of the Misses Harvey is incorrect, probably referring to Violetta and her mother, Ellen, the latter living until after the end of the World War II.

The telephone service had been run by the General Post Office since the early1870s, but Shapwick did not seem to run a telegram service much before the mid 1920s as it was not until the 1927 directory was issued that one finds that Shapwick Post Office could deal with Telegraphs and Telegraph Express Deliveries *"to which messages may be telephoned for treatment as express letters"*

Dora Watkins, aged 87 living on Station Road in the village in 2014, still remembers Miss Harvey being known to her as "Auntie Lottie". Around 1939, whilst Violetta Harvey, now aged 60, was still running the Post Office there was a serious fire on the premises but luckily most of the furniture and the things of value were able to be salvaged. The contents of the Post Office were carried across the churchyard, under the supervision of a man from the head Post Office in Bridgwater, to Church Farm where he was lodging. This was the home of Joan and William Marsh.

Joan & William Marsh at Church Farm. Easter 1948

William Marsh was the farm bailiff for Miss Strangways, having taken over this position from his father, John, prior to 1919 and Joan (nee Melhuish) had, before her marriage, worked in the Post Office in Dunster. She was the youngest of a large family of a tenant farmer from Luckwell Cross on Exmoor and, before her marriage, used to cycle the 8 miles down to Dunster, where she lodged all the week, to work in the shop.

Because of her previous Post Office experience the decision was made that Church Farm was to become the village Post Office from that date. With some minor adaptations to the house the sitting room on the right of the front door became the public area and where the mail was sorted on a large table in the corner. Mary Watts, their daughter, remembers the Postman, Ernie Fear who was living in a cottage on the Tully's Home Farm, sorting the post there.

According to the document illustrated, the grand-mother of Adrian Howe, who lives in Ashcott in 2014, was taken on in 1940 as a "Temporary Post_man_" (sic) as well.

Church Farm   May 2014

Joan continued to run the Post Office up until the time that William retired in 1950. No doubt the farmhouse was occupied as a "Tied" property and was included as part of his remuneration whilst he worked for Miss Strangways so, on giving up his job, he was obliged to vacate the property. A move to the next door village of Ashcott followed where they enjoyed their retirement.

I, *Bertha May Howe*, a natural born British subject, the child of a person who ~~is~~ was at the time of death a British subject, having been selected for employment as § * *Temporary Postwar* at *Shapwick Post Office*, am fully aware that my services may be **discontinued without notice ;** and that this employment, however long it may continue, will not give me any claim to an Appointment, or entitle me to Promotion, to Compensation under the Superannuation Acts for loss of office ; or to Pension.

I understand that I shall not be entitled to receive any pay from the Post Office during absence from duty owing to illness, except any sick pay which I may be allowed under the rules of the Department for the time being in force if my employment qualifies me for the allowance of sick pay.

I also understand that employment as substitute on other duties, established or unestablished, or alterations in duty or pay, involving no change in rank, will not affect these terms of employment.

I fully understand and agree to these terms of employment and I acknowledge the receipt of a copy of this form.

Witnessed by *J. Marsh*   Signature *B M. Howe*

Rank *Sub Postmistress*   *Feb 13th*   19 *40*

In the register of electors in 1945 Percy and Jessie Ings were keeping the General Supply Stores, Emily & Frederick Wren, having retired, were now living at Lawn Cottage in the village. Percy Ings was born at Lawn Farm, Foddington, which is near Babcary in Somerset, into a farming family. He had married Jessie Ellen (nee Hoddinott) in December 1906 when he was 23 and she was 24. Although they were married in Horsington Parish Church Jessie's family had lived in South Cheriton when she was born. The wedding certificate was witnessed by John & Phyllis Myra Hoddinott, her brother and sister as by then her father, George Hoddinott, had died. According to the family, Percy was quite a character although, by all accounts, he was not too much help to his wife in the shop, largely leaving her to run the business

Percy Ings outside the shop.

By August 1945, Percy aged 62, had died. So Jessie, with her son Leonard who had done army service in India during the war, ran the Supply Stores. This they continued to do even after Leonard's marriage to Ivy (nee Bull) from the nearby village of Moorlinch. When Joan & William Marsh retired from the Post Office in 1950 the Ings family

Printed in England

TUCK'S POST CARD
CARTE POSTALE
For Address Only

Regd.d Trade & Exam. Lab.

Mrs Cotton
West Brook
N

SHAPWICK
B
23 DE
38
BRIDGWATER. SOM.

"FORSTERS" SHAPWICK   SPWK 5

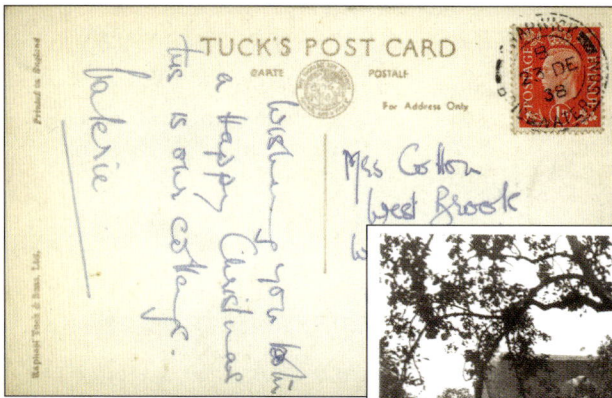

took it over and ran it in conjunction with their General Store from 5 Northbrook Road, Shapwick. With the Post Office duties to attend to Ivy always got up early in the morning and had the post sorted for Leonard who then acted as Postman around the village. One incident that Geoffrey, their youngest son, remembers is the occasion when they were opening a box of Fyffe's bananas in the store when a snake crawled out. With the door on to the road open they chased it only for it to slither up into the engine compartment of their van which was parked on the roadside. He is not quite certain as to what happened after that but he believes it came to a rather sad end after giving them all a nasty shock.

The young Leonard & Ivy Ings at Shapwick

When the two estates that owned most of the village were sold to the Vestey family in 1954 Leonard had to sign a new lease on the premises and to "*personally to live in the dwelling house and to carry on the business of Grocer and Draper on the premises*" for a consideration of £100 a year , the lease to run for 7 years. They were later to buy the freehold from the estate and Leonard & Ivy retired in 1978 when John and Margaret Motum took over the business on the same premises. Ivy, who was born in 1922, continued to help out in the Post Office,

particularly when the new owners wished to take a holiday. Having managed, after some delay, to obtain planning permission to build on the orchard behind the shop both Ivy and her daughter, initially, each had a property there and Ivy, now 92, was still living in the village in 2014 in her retirement home.

Both John and Margaret came from the north of England but they met in Bristol. John had been an apprentice with the Bristol Aeroplane Company and had joined the Royal Air Force at the beginning of the war whereas Margaret's family had moved to the area in the early 1930s in search of work during the depression years. They were married in Bristol in early 1945, when John was 22, and on his leaving the R.A.F. in 1947 they decided to try their hand at farming and market gardening. This was not too successful and John's love of aviation called him back so in the late 1950's he joined Vickers, the company making the famous VC-10 civil airliner. This job came to an end in the 1970s and a short spell at The Air League in London followed, living in Guildford, after which John and Margaret decided that they would like to return to the West Country.

And so it came about that, having visited a business agency in Bridgwater, it was suggested that they should call in on Leonard & Ivy Ings at the shop and Post Office in Shapwick, on their way home, as their business was on the market. The asking price was a total of £26,000 which not only bought the property but also the goodwill, fixtures and fittings and equipment; the shop stock to be taken over at valuation. In the sale particulars it gives a figure of £1,625.00 as the Post Office salary. They were at once taken by, not only the suitability of the business, but also the surroundings and the house that went with the it.

Margaret & John Motum at the Post Office

No. 5 Northbrook Road. circa 1980
Again note the "Ludlow" type letter box set in the window of the shop. These letter boxes were made especially for sub Post Offices by James Ludlow & Co of Birmingham. They were made mostly of wood with a cast iron front and could be opened from both inside and out

And so it was that in 1978 they came to the village and were to stay looking after the Post Office and shop until they retired in April 1984. Even then they only moved to The Home Farm on Station Road, where their son, Michael in 2014, is living and later to a smaller cottage in the village where their daughter now resides. Michael recalls that his father often drove to Bristol to get stock for the shop and that East end of the house was used as a store as well as acting as the sorting office for the mail.

One memorable episode occurred in August 1982 when Shapwick Post Office hit the local as well as the national press. There had been a spate of petty vandalism; tyre valve caps being removed from nearly every car in the village. John Motum decided that enough was enough so he banned all children under 18 from his shop: no ice creams, sweets, crisps, etc. until someone owned up or the missing items were returned. In the event the ban only lasted for five days and most of the valve caps were either returned or were found thrown into a garden on Station Road.

Even after selling the business to Mr & Mrs Brian Perrett, Margaret continued to act as the Post lady for the area, driving around in her small car and visiting all the outlying farms as well as delivering in the village.

The Perrett family only stayed for a short time and in 1985 Ralph & Maureen Packer with their son, Simon, came to No.5 Northbrook Road. Ralph had an important job in the insurance industry and continued to work in Bristol, a job that had brought the family, in 1972, to the West Country in the first place.

Maureen was the nominated Post-mistress whilst Simon dealt with the general stores and the collection and delivery of the various commodities they, as a village store, provided. Bread from Maisey's Bakery in Othery, for instance, was collected and on the way home a delivery was made to Shapwick School based on the old Manor House in the village. The school, which specialises in educating children with dyslexia and associated problems, was an important customer of the business either directly or indirectly. A local girl from the village, Jaqui Palfrey, seen in the accompanying picture, helped Maureen in the shop and, later, when she left to go to college, her sister, Karen, took her place. They reckoned to stock a very wide variety of goods but, due to the nature of the newspaper business, they were unable to supply the national dailies although they were allowed to stock the Bristol Evening Post.

During the time the Packer family ran the shop, Keith Cavill, who had taken over the cycle round in Ashcott from Reggie Bagg earlier, drove the post van starting out from Bridgwater each day. Local sorting and delivery of the mail

Maureen Packer on the right, with Jaqui Palfrey.

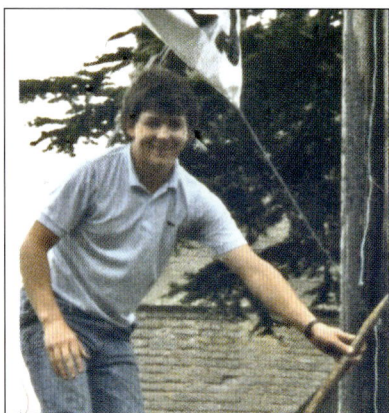

Simon Packer erecting the banner across the road for the Shapwick "Fun Run"

had long ceased but Simon recalls the fact that the large sorting rack, together with the associated table, was still to be found in the room at the end of the house when they first came. In common with most of the retail shops in the area, Wednesday was early closing day, the shop hours being from 9.00am. to 1.00pm. on that day giving the opportunity to visit the cash & carry grocery suppliers, Nurdin & Peacock, in Bristol. These suppliers were later to become part of the nation-wide Booker group of companies. On other days the shop and Post Office was open from 9.00am. to 5.00pm. with an hour for lunch other than on Saturdays when they closed at 1.00pm. They did deal many other local suppliers, Simon particularly remembers the source of the shop's fancy goods from a small wholesaler in the nearby village of Westonzoyland. Ultimately the development that really made the business unprofitable was the scourge of the out-of-town retailer: Safeways Supermarket started to provide a free bus service on one day a week to their new store in Glastonbury and, to add insult to injury, the pick-up point for the village was just outside the Post Office. And so it was that in 1988 they decided to sell the business.

The Post Box in High Lane.
March 2014

*The very
delapidated
Post Box near the
A39 Main Road
March 2014*

In October 1988 Angela & Simon Howden came to the village. Simon was a very keen animal man who actually kept some milking goats on a bit of land close to the Post Office whilst Angela usually ran the business. After less than four years they also moved on and that was when Steven & Janice Newe came.

Janice Newe was the nominated Sub-Postmistress but she had a connection with an opticians business in Street and left the Post Office and shop in the hands of untrained local girls. This did not satisfy the postal authorities and, at very short notice, on a Saturday morning, they closed the Post Office in Shapwick.

Although the Newe family continued to keep the shop open for a while; without the Post Office to draw customers in, the business ran down and was soon closed, although the family continued to live in the house until at least 2010.

*The replacement Pillar Box and Telephone Kiosk on the corner of the playing field
after the closure of the village Post Office.
Photo - November 2013*

The former shop at No. 5 Northbrook Road, Shapwick, in November 2013. Converted to two private dwellings.

ACKNOWLEDGEMENTS

With grateful acknowledgement to Catherine Groves, Ray Hilburn, Geoffrey Ings & Pat Lanham, Trish Jennings, Michael Motum, Ralph, Simon & Maureen Packer, Dora Watkins and Mary Watts. Also all the people of Shapwick who have added to this story.

Street

STREET, a parish, with a village, in Wells district, Somerset; 1½ mile SSW of Glastonbury railway station. It has a post-office under Bath. Acres, 2,913. Real property, £7,970. Pop. in 1851, 1,647; in 1861, 1,898. Houses, 381. There is a large sheepskin, rug, and shoe manufactory. The church is later English and good. There are four dissenting chapels and two public schools.

From:- *"The Imperial Gazetteer of England & Wales"* by John Marius Wilson.
Pub. A. Fullarton & Co. 1872

FRANCIS FREELING, later Sir Francis, was secretary to the Post Office from 1798 until his death in 1836 and during his time in office he kept very comprehensive records of all his correspondence with the Postmasters General, called, in philatelic circles, the *"The Freeling Index"* ; these are now kept in the Post Office Archives. In Vol. 26, Page 65 of 1806 we find:

General Post Office   *June 19th 1806*

My Lords

I have the honour to enclose a report from Mr Lott,(the Post Office Western District Surveyor) *stating that when he lately carried into effect an alteration ordered in the route of the Mail to Somerton... he found it necessary to establish a receiving house at a village called Street, situated on the junction of the Somerton road with the Bridgewater & Wells road. It is not an uncommon thing for a surveyor to be under the necessity of setting some small point of this sort not foreseen in the first planning of an alteration.*

I presume your Lordships will readily sanction the salary of £4 per annum to the Receiver.

All which..........

F. Freeling

In 1821 Glastonbury had been raised to the status of a Main office and it is stated that *"Letters are delivered at 8 a.m. and are despatched to all parts, via Glastonbury, at 5.50 pm."*

In *Pigot's Directory* of 1830 we also find a reference to the Post Office being at the Street Inn with James Sherrin as Postmaster.

> *"Letters from GLASTONBURY arrive every afternoon at one and three, and are despatched every forenoon at ten and eleven. – Letters from ASHCOTT and SHAPWICK arrive every forenoon at a quarter before eleven, and are despatched every day at half-past twelve. – Letters from SOMERTON and LANGPORT arrive every morning at a quarter before eleven, and are despatched every afternoon at three."*

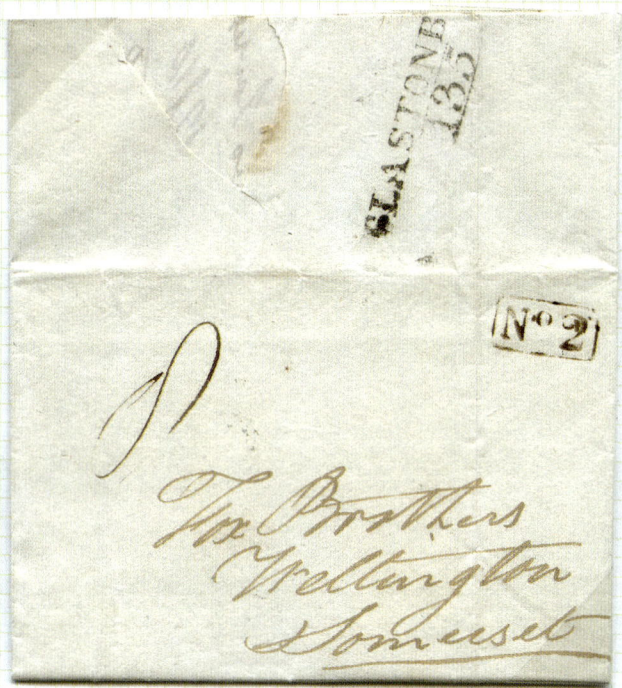

Street was allocated "No.2" in the Glastonbury Penny Post system which was originally established in 1823.

The 135 below Glastonbury denotes its distance from London and was the basis for charging postage

The business section also names James Sherrin being at the Street Inn and Posting House. The same directory is rather less than flattering about the village as it says:

> *Street is an inconsiderable village, ... Nothing worthy of notice is attached to the place. The population of the parish, by the last census, was 791.*

Again in the *Freeling Index* dated 7th April 1835 another reference to Street is found:

My Lord

I have before had occasion to remark to your Lordship, that there are few of our arrangements, which however beneficial generally, do not create some partial dissatisfaction. He (Mr Louis, the surveyor) took great pains a short time ago to effect some material improvements in the Penny Post from Glastonbury to Street, Shapwick, etc., and which he now describes.

Messrs C & J Clark, a respectable firm at Street, complain that these arrangements are unsatisfactory, because they do not happen to benefit the particular correspondence in which they are interested, losing sight altogether of the advantages that have been in other respects conferred, a proof that the department is judged, not by what it may have effected for the public convenience, but what it may have left unaccomplished.

With respect to the proposition to alter the new plan, it is not only opposed by Lord John Thynne and others residing in that neighbourhood, but Mr Louis has shown that it would be detrimental in many respects. I presume therefore the interests of the many cannot be sacrificed to the few, and the remaining question for your Lordship's decision is whether, as the inconvenience with the Bristol, North and Irish letters, of which Messrs. Clarks complain, can be remedied by a further expenditure of 1/- a day, to be appropriated to Messengers from Glastonbury to Street, and from Ashcott to Shapwick, and as the total expense

8.1.1848

This Undated Circular handstamp was usually found in Black, although the Post Office did experiment by using Blue or Grey-Blue ink between 1849 and 1857.

Street Inn. Circa 1900

will even then be covered by the Penny Post revenue, it may be right to make this further arrangement in order to remove all cause for complaint and place these Posts on a complete footing.

In 1840, according to *Bragg's Directory,* the Post Office was being run by a grocer, George White, who, in the census of 1841 was living in Street with his wife, Mary, both of whom were stated to be 30 years of age at the time. *Pigot's Directory* of 1842 also names George White as in charge of the Post Office and states that

"Letters from Glastonbury arrive every morning at half-past seven, and are despatched thereto every evening at half-past six.- Letters from Wells &c. arrive every evening at half-past six and are despatched thereto every morning at half-past seven"

This information does agree with what was written in a booklet reprinted by the Somerset County library service entitled:

Reminiscences of Life in the Parish of Street, Somersetshire, from the year 1844 by an Old Inhabitant (W. Pursey) 1909

"The convenient and easy arrangement of postal service of to-day is the very opposite of that existing at the time of which I write. Instead of the mail cart which now travels

from Glastonbury to Bridgwater, all letters were then conveyed on horse back, the rider fixing himself in the saddle, with bags thrown across his shoulders, one hanging in the front, the other behind, travelling morning and night from Shepton Mallet to Shapwick. This was the task assigned William Hiscox, who employed and delegated this duty to Smith, who journeyed thus on a blind horse. The Street postmaster at this early time was George White, whose residence was near Street Cross, the letter box of the post office being easy of access to all requiring its use."

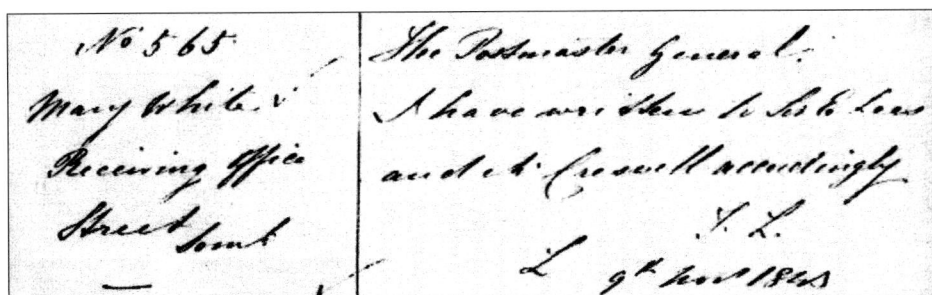

In a list of Post Office appointments is to found this entry dated 9th November 1843 appointing Mary White as the Receiving Officer for Street:-

This Mary White was probably the widow of George White, the previous holder of the post, and she ran the office from her grocery and sundries shop.

In *Hunt's Directory* of 1848 there is a brief description of Street:

Several good houses have lately been built, and others are in the course of erection, as is also a spacious meeting house for the Society of Friends; in the neighbourhood are some extremely rich and excellent quarries of Blue Lias stone, and near here embedded in the strata, has been found perfect specimens of animals in a fossil state.

By 1851 another Mary White, born at Brewham in 1798, was the Inn-keeper of the Street Inn and also the "Post Mistress". Mary was widow of Robert, described as a yeoman in the 1841 census, with seven children, six boys and one girl ranging in age from ten up to twenty nine, the eldest of whom was Charles. This again ties in with a passage in Pursey's reminiscences:

"Another notable feature of the life in Street at this early date was that of the so-called public-houses, which numbered then as many as now. The most conspicuous and notable was "Street" inn, already mentioned in connection with the Stage Coach. This inn at the time of which I write had a great quantity of farm land which was farmed by the proprietor or occupier, Mr. George Fry. The land then attached to this inn has long been sold, and the inn to-day, now in the occupation

of Mr. Hicks, is run absolutely as an inn. After Mr. George Fry's decease, the inn for very many years was in the occupation of Mrs. White, widow, and her sons; this is another family of which not a member is left"

Charles was later to marry a local girl, Caroline Talbot. Caroline was born in about 1830, and was living at Townsend, Street, and already described as a grocer in the 1851 census. She was living with her mother and father, Charlotte and Robert Talbot; father being a master stone-cutter employing four men at that time. In the *Harrison-Harrad Directory* of 1859 Charles had become the postmaster. The Post Office in Street by this time was becoming more important as the note says *"Money-orders are granted and paid at this office".*

It seems that Charles must have died soon after the directory was issued as in the 1861 Census, Caroline is described as a widow, aged 30, Grocer and Post Mistress, living with her infant son, Charles aged 11 months, a man-servant and three of the Reynolds family from Butleigh boarding and working in the shoe factory. She later re-married, this time to William Boyce, who was born in Oxfordshire but

The Street Post Office Staff 1895:
Back row: Postman Stag, Miss Thomas, Postman Mortimer, Emily Griffin?, Postman Arthur Griffin. Mrs Caroline Boyce sat in the centre. The three lads were probably telegram boys.

It is believed that Miss Thomas later became Mrs Alfred Templeman and Emily Griffin progressed to being Postmistress at Glastonbury

had been working as a draper's shopman in Bath in 1861, and they, together, ran the Post Office and Grocers in Street for the next 28 years until his untimely death in 1890. His obituary (*see page 174*) in the local paper describes the many changes that took place during this time. The first arrival of letters in the morning was now coming in at 5.30am. and a further delivery at 10.30am. whilst the last despatch of mail from the office was at 7.25pm.; quite a long day by any standard. This did not seem to interfere with their family life as by 1871 they had produced three children, Harriet, seven, Annie five, and Alice one, as well as having Caroline's son, Charles White, living with them. No doubt, Caroline was having help from her widowed mother as we see that in the census of 1881 Annie Boyce, now aged 15, although she was acting as a Post Office assistant was, together with her sister Alice who was still at school, living with their 80 year old grand-mother, Charlotte Talbot. Charlotte was then living, in what appears to be the next door property to the girl's parents, at No.68 on the High Street.

In the *Kelly's Directory* of 1889 the Post Office provided Money Orders and was a Telegraph Office, also transacted Savings Bank business and was an Insurance & Annuity Office. The Parcel mail also gets a mention in that it is despatched at the same time as the last mail of the day, 7.40pm. Although the Telegraph Office was open from 8.00am. to 8.00pm, Money Order business could only be transacted between 9.00am. to 6.00pm. which was probably because of the need for more senior staff to be present. In order to differentiate Street from other similar sounding destinations there were also instructions, for correspondents, to the effect that letters should have *"S.O. Somerset added to the address."* The S.O. standing for sub-office.

A Parcel Post Label of 1899
issued to Street, then under Bridgwater. As much of the wrapping paper at the time was of a very
course nature the Post Office used these gummed labels to attach the stamps to parcels.
The initials SUG were the Telegraphic address for Street

THE LATE MR WILLIAM BOYCE.

Central Somerset Gazette.   20th December 1890.

DEATH OF THE POSTMASTER.

The inhabitants of this town and neighbourhood were much grieved on Saturday on hearing of the sudden death of our esteemed postmaster Mr Boyce. He was in his usual health on Friday morning and quite cheerful, but early in the afternoon he was seized with paralysis and rendered speechless. When this was known, but little hope was entertained for his recovery. Some few months ago he had a somewhat similar seizure. From this he had, however, fully recovered, and has done since then a vast amount of useful public labour. Great regret is felt and expressed at the loss of this useful public servant. The duties of postmaster, which he discharged for 28 years, were faithfully and accurately discharged, and, we have scarcely ever heard of errors or mistakes. In this department his obliging manner was much appreciated, as the numerous details are understood by very few, and therefore his large fund of information had to be frequently drawn upon by every class of enquirers from the most ignorant to the most intelligent. He has been able to adapt himself to the new and varied developments of this important branch of the public service. A mere handful of letters served the purposes of Street when he commenced operations; now three deliveries are required daily. The money order, the savings bank, the telegraph and the parcel post have come into operation during his period of service, and he has been fully equal to all their requirements. The youngest child, as well as the highest forms of manhood, alike obtained, his courteous and careful attention. He has held the office of Local Board and Poor Rate collector for over twenty years, and the day previous to his death attended the audit at Wells, and the auditor (Mr H. D. Gordon) complimented him upon the way in which his books were kept, and the clerk (Mr Russ) said he was the most regular in his payments. The same methodical habits are also apparent in his work as postmaster, and though called away so suddenly, and in the midst of his work, yet everything is in perfect order. Few men have crowded into a life-time of fifty three years a larger amount of public service. It is very remarkable that three of our most useful public men should have ended their days suddenly - the late Mr Aubrey Clark, Mr Talbot, and Mr Boyce ~ all within the brief space of six months. Much sympathy is felt for his widow and family. He leaves three daughters, two of whom are married, and one step-son. The funeral took place on Wednesday afternoon, the remains being interred in the parish churchyard. The coffin was covered with several beautiful wreaths contributed by members and friends of the family. The chief mourners were Mrs Boyce (Widow), Mr C. J. White, Mr & Mrs Freak Healls, Mr & Mrs Thomas Pitt, Miss A Boyce, Mr E. Petvin, Mr & Mrs Frank Petvin, Mr Edward Talbot, Mrs Robert Talbot, Misses K.& F. Petvin, Messrs W. S. Clark, F. J. Clark, S. T. Clothier (representatives of the Street Local Board) and Mr A. D. Porter

With the passing of William Boyce, his wife, Caroline, became the sub-postmistress, a position she held until well after her 70th birthday.

A report in the *Central Somerset Gazette* dated April 4th 1891 gives an insight into the hazards of travel even in those days:

ACCIDENT

The mail-cart, which runs from Glastonbury to Bridgwater, when going through Street came into a collision with a baker's cart (Mr. Classey's, of Butleigh), one of the horses fell and broke the shaft of the mail cart. The driver was thrown out on his back, and taken into a neighbouring house in an unconscious state, where he remained for a considerable time. Dr Eglington was soon on the spot, who carefully examined him, and applied a plaster to the back of his neck, which had a good effect. After about an hour the man was removed to Glastonbury. Fortunately no delay was occasioned to the mail service, as Mr. Pursey's driver and waggonette were at once engaged and Bridgwater was reached in good time. It was also fortunate that an employee at the Street post-office was present, who accompanied the new driver on his journey, so that all the bags at the sub-offices were delivered and received. Mr. Aplin, jobmaster, of Bridgwater, visited Street the next day and made every enquiry. It is gratifying to know that the driver of the mail cart was able to proceed from Glastonbury to Bridgwater the next day, who stated that he was very stiff and sore, but it is hoped no serious damage was done. It is also gratifying to know that no injury was done to Mr. Classey's cart, with which the collision was made. The accident occurred in one of the darkest parts of the village, but the mail cart ought to have been provided with lamps.

Although the General Post Office held the monopoly for the carrying of letters this did not apply to parcel traffic. In fact, the Post Office did not offer a parcel service until 1882. For this reason the business directories issued in the 19th century were very good about listing the times of the various coach services available. These not only carried passengers but parcels and sometimes, as in the case of the one following, the mail carrier to Bridgwater: *"Thomas Cridland, Royal Mail omnibus, through from Glastonbury 8.45 a.m. daily, returning same day 6.00 p.m. with frequent buses to Glastonbury daily"*; no doubt all being horse drawn at that time.

By 1900 a series of Wall Letter Boxes had been provided around the town and it is noted that the one at Tanyard was cleared three times a day, at 10 am. & 2.15 & 7.10 pm, as was the one on the Cross. The one at West End was only cleared twice a day, at 2.50 and 6.55 pm. and then on week-days only. By 1902 Middle Leigh had been added to the list and Cranhill Road was added by 1906.

The name of Alfred Herbert Templeman now came to prominence as he and his wife were to take over the Post Office and shop after Mrs Boyce retired. Alfred was born around about 1873 in Street, the son of a shoemaker called Joseph Templeman. He was working as a grocer's assistant in 1891 and had his first shop further along the High Street at No. 50 where he was living with his wife, Alice, in 1901. Alice, came from Pontypridd in South Wales and they were married in 1897. They then moved to the Post Office and stores at Nos.66-68 where the family lived for the next 30 years or so.

By 1906 *Kelly's Directory* entry shows that not only was Mrs Alice Templeman now the sub-postmistress but also how much the business of the Post Office had increased. Not only did it deal in postal items but also was a Money Order and Telegraphic office (M. O. & T. O.) Telegraphic money orders, (T. M. O.) Savings Bank (S. B.) & Annuity and Insurance (A. & I.) Office as well as having four postal deliveries a day ranging from the first at 7.00am. until the last at 6.20pm. There were also six mail dispatches ranging from 6.30am. through to 7.40pm. Even parcels were dispatched at 7.30 pm. every day of the week including Sundays and the telegraph office was open and money orders issued twelve hours a day, from 8.00am. till 8.00pm. Even most of the wall letter boxes were cleared three times a day but only on weekdays. At that time weekdays meant six days a week as Saturdays were considered to be a normal working day.

The Templeman's Shop and Post Office, Nos. 66-68 High Street, on a Post Card.
The Postman is William Mortimer. Probably taken c. 1907.
Lloyds Bank occupied No.70 on the left hand side of the building..

Alfred Templeman is listed as grocer & fruiterer trading in the High Street so it seems that the two premises, the Post Office and the shop were kept as separate businesses. Not much changed right up until the outbreak of war in 1914 although it did seem that by then there were only four mail dispatches a day as opposed to the six previously. Telephonic Express Delivery Office had, by then, been added to the list of facilities available. Was this another name for telegrams one wonders?

A H Templeman outside No. 50.

Working for the Post Office was a secure occupation, although not particularly well paid, but you did have a smart uniform and when you retired it carried a pension. William Mortimer, the great-grandfather of Ken Nicholls who still lives in Street in 2015, came from Chippenham in Wiltshire and is featured as a younger man in the photograph of Mrs Caroline Boyce and her staff taken in about 1895. He was obviously proud of his position as he wore his uniform when he had his studio portrait taken.

Immediately after the war, in 1919 when the next directory was issued, it was noticeable that the telegraph office hours had been reduced considerably, not opening before 9.00am. and closing again at 7.00pm. although the service was now available on Sundays from 8.30 to 10.00 in the morning.

A studio portrait of William Mortimer in his Postman's uniform.

Alice Templeman continued to run the Post Office until her death, aged 49, on June 24th 1923 as a result of a motorcycle accident. Her son was driving with his six year old sister, Margaret, as a pillion passenger with mother in the side-car. Not only did mother lose her life but Margaret also lost a leg. The accident occurred at what was always a notorious black spot before the round-about was constructed, at the cross roads at Podimore, near Ilchester.

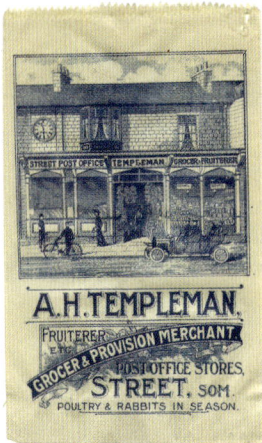

A paper bag as used in the Templeman shop.
The car depicted reputedly belonged to Major Blandie of Ivythorn Manor and the Telegraph Boy was Alfie Hole.

By 1927 Alfred was listed as the sub-postmaster and the 1929 electoral roll lists, the first after universal suffrage allowing women full voting rights, Alfred, Elizabeth and Herbert Templeman were listed as living at No.66 in the High Street. In 1937 Herbert's wife, Doris, was added and his sister, Margaret, was living with them. As a result of the previously mentioned accident Margaret had one prosthetic leg. This fact was known particularly to the Nicholls shoe repair shop as she came to them, on occasion, to replace the leather straps that kept the false leg in place.

The traditions of the Post Office had been built up over a very long period of time and there was a reluctance within this public service to make changes. Even from the days of Queen Victoria it was normal to appoint a Medical Officer to the Post Office and we do find that one of the doctors practicing in the town, Dr John Henry Cox Eglington L.M.S.S.A. physician & surgeon, being appointed to the position of Medical officer to the Post Office & he also acted as the official doctor the Board of Education. Was this a descendant of the Dr Eglington who attended the accident in Street in 1891 and was the Medical Officer of Health who reported to the Street Council in 1915? In this report he stated that there had been 94 births and 45 deaths in the village in the past year.

Not much information is available about the Post Office in Street during and after the second world war but we do know that the Templeman family were still on the electoral roll as living in No.66 High Street in 1938 & '39. It is reported that Alfred Templeman died, aged 75, in 1948.

In the register of electors in 1945/46 the names of Alfred and Sarah Little are listed at this address. The following year Alfred Little's name disappeared but later the names of Maureen, James and Terrance Little appear.

According to the daughter of Albert and Thelma Sheppard, her family were living at No.66 in 1956 as her mother was the night telephonist in the manual telephone exchange at the rear of the building. At that time George Polkinghorne was the postmaster but was living away from the premises. It is believed that

George started his career in the Post Office at Weston-s-Mare in 1919 and came to Street in 1938. There is an entry in the electoral roll for that year of George and Dorothy Polkinghorne living at 26 Grange Avenue, Street.

After 1964 the Templeman shop and the former Post Office at Nos. 66 - 68 were not listed in the Register of Electors as they had probably been replaced by the new Lloyds Bank building before that time.

A major change was envisaged in the running of the Street Post Office and the preparatory work for the transfer of all Street inward mail to Glastonbury Post Office was being planned as early as June 1949 but, after protracted negotiation with the unions involved, was eventually fixed for 6th January 1958. Prior to the transfer not only was Street Post Office the base for the town Postmen but there was also one rural round by bicycle to Ivythorn, Marshalls Elm, etc. operating on a twice a day basis. In Appendix 1, at the end of this chapter, the arrangements are listed concerning the actual change-over.

A list of Post Boxes around Street in 1949 had appeared in the proposed re-organisation papers. These were:

West End	*Overleigh*	*Elmhurst*
Middle Leigh	*Cranhill Road*	*Grange Avenue*
Stonehill	*The Cross*	*Ivythorn*

Nos. 66-70 completely rebuilt and occupied by
Lloyds Bank plc. Photo in 2014

At the time of the change-over the Street Postmaster was Alfred G Winter. On a search of the Post Office records it seems that Alfred started his career in the service of the G.P.O. in Southampton in August 1917 as an assistant postman; he would have been 16 at the time. By 1919 he had qualified as a Sorting Clerk and Telegraphist and was posted to Salisbury. His next move was to Weston-s-Mare in April 1927 with the same qualifications but obviously gaining experience all the time. Alfred was married in the spring of 1931 to Dorothy May Pople who was born in the nearby village of Puriton, near Highbridge in Somerset. A search of the electoral rolls for Street, finds them, in 1954/55, with their two children, Brian and Sheila, living at No.35 Orchard Road.

It is very possible that Alfred's last posting before retirement was at Street as the final reference to them living there was in 1970 when he would have just had his 60th birthday.

The Post Office was not immune to attacks by the local council. A report in the *Central Somerset Gazette* of 25th March 1960 reads:

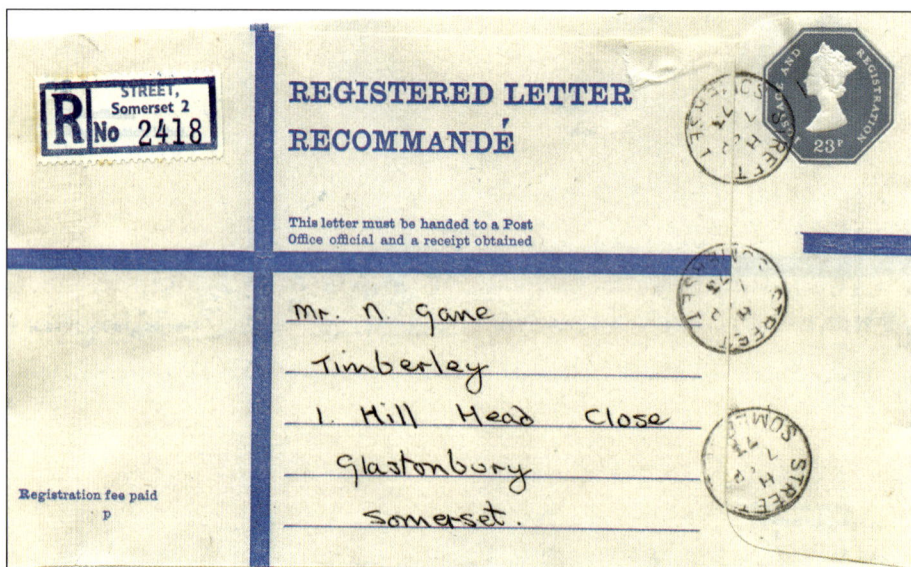

A Registered Envelope
posted at Street
on
September 7th 1973

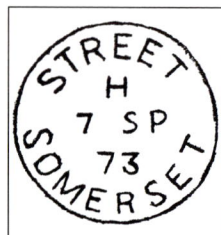

"Plans for a new Post Office and telephone exchange at Street were mentioned at Monday's meeting of the Urban District Council.

The plans were mentioned in the report of the Health & Housing Committee. The Committee having resolved to comment (1) that the size of the public office appears to be too small; and (2) that the Council would like to be told what kind of rendering was proposed for the outside treatment of the building."

Again, in 1961, they criticised the inefficient postal deliveries, especially of registered letters and parcels. At the same meeting another resolution *"Deplored the decision of the General Post Office not to have a sorting office in the new proposed Street Post Office".* Councillors were obviously unhappy with the sorting office being removed to Glastonbury.

The new building was completed in 1962 and the Post Office was open for business on Monday 3rd December of that year. A release to this effect was sent out to the local press by the Head Postmaster of Bridgwater, Mr F R Prichard.

Later, after some delay, on 8th January 1964, the new Automatic Telephone Exchange, housed in the upper storey, was officially opened with a large gathering of people from the local council, business, trade and the press. Amongst these were both the Chairman of the Urban District Council, Mr Ralph Clark, Mr N A Bird, Manager of the Street branch of the National Westminster Bank and President of the Chamber of Trade at the time, as well as the local Member of Parliament.

The old manual exchange had continued to operate, until the new one was completed in late 1963, behind the former Post Office on the High Street. One of the telephonists, was Margaret Templeman who, it is said, ran a very personal and helpful service. This is borne out by reference to the following account in the *Central Somerset Gazette* of 9th January 1964 with the headline:

"GOODBYE TO HELLO GIRLS"

Street's association with a manually operated telephone exchange ended yesterday, in a mixed mood of sentimentality and relief.

As the new £32,000 Subscriber trunk Dialling exchange took over, the obsolete "hello-girls" in the old exchange made 600 calls to say goodbye to local subscribers.

"Many people said that they would miss the personal service" said one of the girls in between calls. "One elderly lady asked if she could come and see us if she became muddled"

The golden-voiced girls of the Street exchange pictured during their last day

The Picture in the Central Somerset Gazette

*The former Post Office in December 2002 with
JAMES BARRY, Clothing retailers, on the ground floor and the
Telephone Exchange above.*

Among the guests for the opening ceremony was Lieut.-Cmdr. Lynch Maydon, the M.P. for the Wells Constituency. He thought it all so marvellous that he, personally, rang the Postmaster General, Mr Bevins, to tell him so.

Margaret Templeman was later to find employment in the Street branch of what was then called the "Labour Exchange", one of the nation-wide state funded employment bureau founded following an act of Parliament in 1909.

As forewarned in a leading article in the local paper in September 1993, Post Office Counters moved their operation out of the purpose built offices in 1994, moving to Martins Stores, part of the McColl's group, in the High Street. The clothing retailers, James Barry, subsequently moved in to the redundant building but the Telephone Exchange continued and continues to operate from the upper storey.

Martins Stores in the High Street, December 2002

Initially the Post Office moving to the stationers shop had not been popular and the service was considered to be very slow in comparison with the former office. An article in the *Central Somerset Gazette* dated August 10th 2000 headed:

"POST OFFICE ROW"

A row over the Post Office services at Street looks set to intensify. For months complaints have been made about the services at the village's main Post Office counter in the Martins Store.

Individuals, the Parish Council, Street Chamber of Trade and Neighbourhood Watch have all written about the length of time it takes to queue, as well as security and access problems.

After months of repeatedly requesting a meeting, representatives of the Post Office and Martins have now agreed to meet with the Parish Council at their meeting on August 23rd. Campaigners against the level of service are expected to attend the meeting.

Martins Stores in Street was transferred to the W H Smith group of companies, and the store re-named, sometime before June 2008. The level of complaint seems to have dropped in more recent times.

The shop was re-named W H Smith
by 2nd June 2008
Photo - September 2014

ACKNOWLEDGMENTS

With grateful acknowledgement to Ken Gane, John & Mary Hecks, Ken Nicholls and Angela Sweet. Also all the people of Street who have added to this story.

THE POST BOXES OF STREET

High Street
Double Pillar Box
BA16 15
September 2011

West End Post Office. BA16 312
September 2011

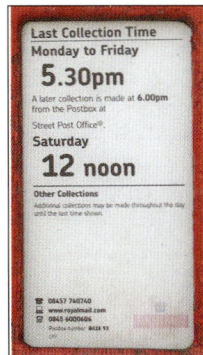

West End - Brook-
leigh Road
BA16 93
February 2011

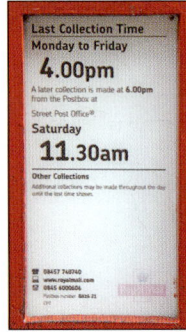

Clark's Village
BA16 21
July 2014

Street Inn
BA16 62
September 2011

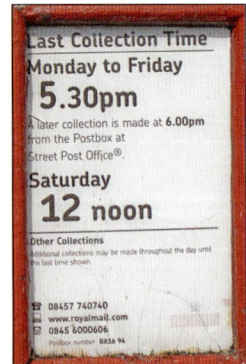

Leigh Road BA16 94 July 2014

ERRATA

24.11.2015

Page 32 & 176. Dr Eglinton, Not Eglington

Pages 97-98. Please read as Joan & **Graham** Birch, not Joan & **Keith** Birch

Pages 208 - 215. Vera Ridout, not Vera Rideout.

Page 184. Leigh Road Postbox. Incorrect picture. Please see below.

The author sincerely apologises to all the parties concerned over the above errors.

Goss Drive BA16 100
July 2014

Cranhill Road
BA16 101
February 2011

Ivythorn Road -
Glanvill Road
BA16 108
July 2014

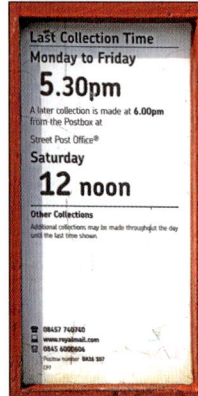

Stonehill
BA16 107
July 2014

Strode - Westfield Road BA16 126
July 2014

Southleaze Orchard   BA16 127 July 2014

Grange Avenue BA16 230   July 2014

Green Lane Avenue
BA16 265
July 2014

Somerton Road
BA16 236
February 2011

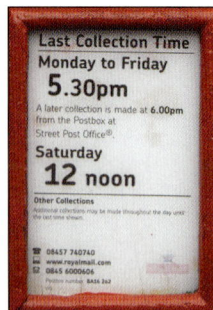

Portland Road
BA16 262
November 2011

Ivythorn. Wall Letter Box.
Marshalls Elm cross roads

The letter box at Marshalls Elm Farm
was destroyed when a car swept it off the wall of the garden c.2011 and it was not replaced.

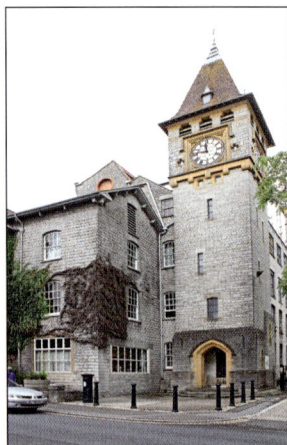

Placed close to the Main
Entrance to Clark's
Factory.
A Private Box

The type of Direction sign originally on the Pillar Box

Ivythorn Road
BA16 3
Post Box Panel
October 2011

This box was outside the Middle Leigh Post Office until it closed in 2000.

Ivythorn Road Shop
December 2002

Sainsbury's Supermarket
BA16 109
February 2011
Removed before 2015.

SOME OF THE POSTMARKS OF STREET

A copy of an entry from the Proof Book of Handstamps kept in the National Postal Museum.

This page illustrates Proof Book Impressions as recorded by Mike Welch in The *Somerset and Dorset Postal History Group* Publication. 1995

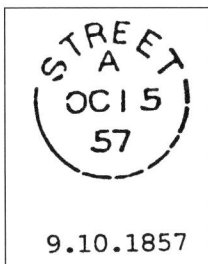

8.1.1848

9.10.1857

12.4.1864

8.6.1872

18.2.1876

8.7.1882

18.6.1886

Street Postmarks (cont.)

Sorting Office and Counter Handstamps

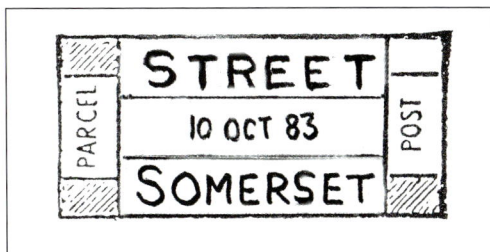

Parcel Post Cancellation

NOT KNOWN
STREET, SOMERSET

Only seen on an envelope
dated 30th June 1983.

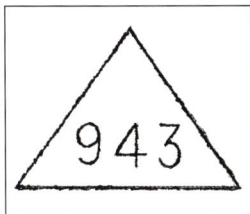

No. 943 was as-
signed to Street in
1936. Previously,
in 1844, allotted to
Beaminster, Dorset.

An excerpt from the instructions relating to the transfer of the sorting office from Street to Glastonbury:

> *"Correspondence which was formerly date-stamped at Street Post Office should be date-stamped with a Street postmark at Glastonbury. Arrangements are being made for a Street die with complete set of type for date-stamping machines to be issued to the Postmaster, Glastonbury." See Appendix 1.*

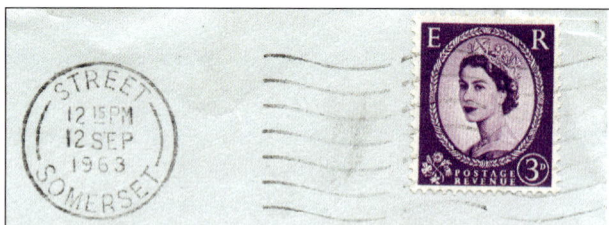

This arrangement lasted for nearly five years. At some point between September and December 1963 a new die was introduced which combined Glastonbury and Street in the title.

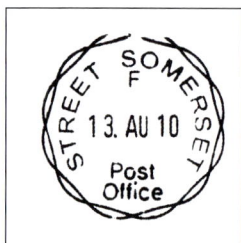

The Self-Inking Hand-stamp as used at the Post Office counter.
2010

APPENDIX 1.

To Glastonbury & Street

BRIDGWATER

2nd January, 1958

Arrangements for transfer of Street postal services to Glastonbury

Date of Commencement

The date of commencement will be Monday, 6th January, 1958.

Duties.

Schedules are being prepared and will be forwarded to the Postmaster of Glastonbury as early as possible.

Supervision.

A new Assistant Inspector Post will be created to commence on the 6th January, 1958. Details of the duty are attached for the information of the Postmaster of Glastonbury. No doubt the question of dealing with posting sheets from Messrs. Clarks will be considered with a view of the Assistant Inspector giving assistance in this work. Mr. Hembery, P.H.G.,(Postman Higher Grade) will be temporarily promoted as from 6th January for a period of one month. The question of an officer being given a trial on the duty after one month will be considered in the meantime

Travelling to and from duty by Street staff

Travelling time at single rate will be allowed to existing Street staff under the usual conditions. It will be necessary to ascertain the time to be allowed either from Street office or the officer's home whichever is the shorter distance. The time to be allowed is under consideration.

Rotation of P.H.G.'s   (Postmen Higher Grade.)

This question has yet to be resolved. For the first week of the transfer Messrs. Jones and Edwards will perform the

P.H.G. duties at Glastonbury. Mr Withers, P.H.G., Street, will
have one week's training at Glastonbury to make himself familiar
with the P.H.G. duties of this office. He will also be available
to help with the Street despatches and give any information
to the Glastonbury staff as regards Street deliveries and
collections. He will work under the direction of the Postmaster,
Glastonbury, and the Assistant Inspector.

Cycles.

It will be seen from the duty arrangements that on the
first delivery postmen will be conveyed to Street by official
van. One cycle will be conveyed in the van to be used by one
of the officers to return to Glastonbury. At the completion
of their duties the Street officers may have permission to
take the official cycles home but if they do not wish to do
this the cycles can be locked in the garage at Street Post
Office. Arrangements should be made between the Postmaster,
Glastonbury, and the Postmaster, Street, for the issue of keys
for this purpose. Additional keys should be obtained locally if
necessary.

Pouching Off   (Reporting off duty. Ed.)

The rules for pouching off are contained in Rg. 13, Rules
for Postmen, III 19 and 194. The office for pouching off will be
Street Post Office. If the staff are not clear on the rules for
pouching off and any further information is required, the Head
Postmaster should be informed.

Parking of official vehicle at Street

The official vehicle used for the conveyance of postmen to
Street for the first delivery should be parked at the rear of the
British Legion. Permission has been obtained for this.

Collections in Street

Correspondence which was formerly date-stamped at Street
Post Office should be date-stamped with a Street postmark at
Glastonbury. It will be necessary, therefore, to keep this
correspondence separate and any instructions necessary for this
purpose should be issued to the staff. The collections from the
Street Post Office will be unsealed and T.S.O. bills will be
used. Registered bags should be made up where this is warranted

on numbers. Sealed bags should be made up for H.V.P.'s and the Postmaster, Glastonbury advised of the sealed despatch. If, in practice, this arrangement causes any difficulty, the Head Postmaster should be advised. The Postmaster of Street will transfer any obliterating date-stamps used in the Sorting Office to the Postmaster, Glastonbury. Arrangements are being made for a Street die with complete set of type for date-stamping machines to be issued to the Postmaster, Glastonbury.

Callers

Despatches of callers from Glastonbury to Street will be at 8.15a.m. and 11.0a.m. If other despatches are considered necessary the Head Postmaster should be advised.

Messrs. Clarks delivery arrangements

Letters

First delivery 7.0a.m. by postman to the Commissionaire at the entrance.(6.45a.m. despatch)

Second delivery 11.10a.m. as above. 11.0a.m. despatch)

Registered letters to be called for at Street Post Office at 8.30a.m.

Business reply correspondence will be delivered by the first delivery and tied up in a separate bundle.

Parcels

First delivery - to be collected by Messrs, Clarks at 7.30a.m.

The parcels should be divided as follows:-

Guarantee Department

Repair Department

Cowmead

Avalon

Miscellaneous

Second delivery, - to all departments at 11.0a.m

Third delivery. - Any parcels on hand at 3.45p.m. to be
delivered to all departments by the collecting services.

Telegrams

With the transfer of postal force it will be necessary
for telegrams for Street area to be delivered from Glastonbury.
The best possible arrangements should be made. No doubt it will
be possible to effect some delivery by collecting services
or the Postmaster, Street, may be able to co-operate with any
casual messenger available at any difficult times.

Window Notice

The first collection at Street for delivery purposes will
cease. This will require an amendment to the Street window
notice. The particulars of delivery times and despatch times
should remain on the window notice but if there is an alteration
in times of despatch this will, of course, require amendment on
the window notice.

Accommodation at Glastonbury.

This will be taxed to the limit by the new arrangements.
It would appear that the most difficult period will be between
9.0a.m. and 11.0a.m. when there will be a large number of bags
of outward and inward mail on hand. The best arrangements for
providing for inward and outward parcels should be made under
the supervision of the officer in charge. A close watch should be
made particularly at the commencement of the new working to see
what is the best method of handling the parcel mail.

General

Any points not covered by this memorandum which are not
clear to the Postmasters should be referred to the Head Office.

Bridgwater

2nd January 1958

Mr A. G. Winter

Street

Please transfer to Mr Southgate on Saturday (or before if convenient) all sorting office instructions, redirection records, special delivery instructions, etc. etc.

The following should also be transferred:-

Current business reply accounts

Private Box and Bag service records

Coin Box clearance schedules and coin box keys

Forms P.760W and Rural Post details should also be transferred

It would seem proper to transfer the present arrivals list to Glastonbury.

A sealed mail arrival from Glastonbury will be due at 8.25am and it is proposed that your 11.40 am despatch to Glastonbury should be retained as a sealed despatch

H J Green

H/Postmaster

P.S. Postman's Lockers will also need transferring

Walton

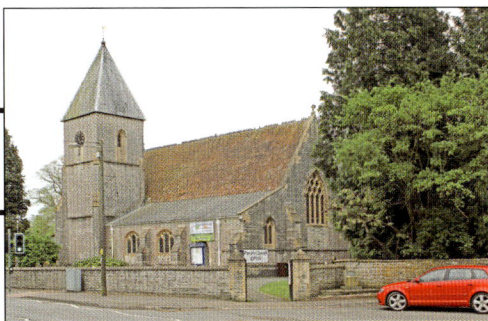

*W*ALTON, a parish, with a village, in Wells district, Somerset; 3½ miles SW of Glastonbury railway station. It has a post-office under Bath. Acres, 2,502. Real property, £4,259. Pop., 731. Houses, 164. The manor belongs to the Marquis of Bath. The living is a perpetual curacy, annexed to Street. The church is decorated English. There are a Wesleyan chapel and a national school.

From *"The Imperial Gazetteer of England & Wales"* by John Marius Wilson. Pub. A. Fullarton & Co. 1872.

WALTON WAS ONE of the early villages to get a mention in the Postmaster General's minute book when, on the 26th May 1826, it states: *"A Penny Post to Ashcott, Street, Walton, Shapwick from Glastonbury established."* Walton was allocated the number "4" in the system. After many years of searching, the No.4 mark, illustrated, is the only example ever seen by me.

A "Free Front" letter with the WALTON No.4 posted Jan 1st 1840 from the Earl of Doncaster whose brother in law was Rev. Lord John Thynne, who lived at the rectory.
Parliamentary Free postage ended on January 10th 1840.
This illustration comes from a private collection.

In the *Freeling Reports* we find the following:-

My Lord.   *26th February 1835*

     The two enc.d reports from Mr Louis upon applications from Lord John Thynne & the Rev.d Mr Luscombe both refer to the Posts established to the several villages intermediate of Bridgewater & Glastonbury. His Lordship is desirous of some arrangement to expedite the receipt of the London & Eastern letters at Shapwick, & other places in the neighbourhood where he resides,& Mr Luscombe prays that the Villages of Greinton & Moorlinch may be included in the official delivery. It will be seen that it has required some ingenuity to meet the wishes of the Parties without sacrificing other material objects. In result Mr Louis has proposed the following arrangements, viz. that the present messenger shall start from Glastonbury to Street, Walton & Ashcott immediately after the arrival of the London Mail- that £6.8.0 be allowed for a receiver at Walton to deliver the London letters there, & proceed twice daily to Street (one mile distant) to meet the Langport Ride with letters for the West in the morning, & to bring those from the West in the afternoon............

The total expense would be £18.9.4 per ann: but Mr Louis calculates that the additional facilities will produce a sufficient increase in the correspondence to meet this charge-your Lordship will therefore probably be pleased to sanction the arrangement.-

                                          F. F.

                                   (Francis Freeling)

A note at the side reads: *"approved Maryborough.   27 Feb 1835"*

Note: Lord Maryborough was an elder brother of the Duke of Wellington.

*The Mail Bag Seal
for WALTON*

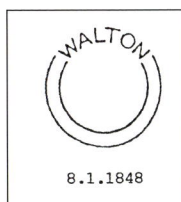

The receiver at Walton was not to keep this income for long as the following appears in the reports of the following year:-

Ilchester   *August 31st 1836*

Sir,   In my report of the 16th Inst, I pointed out the inconvenience that the alteration in the time of the Bath & Devonport; and the Bristol & Barnstaple mails making through Bridgewater would inflict on the Villages of Shapwick and Ashcott situate between Glastonbury and Bridgewater .... To obviate the inconvenience which the inhabitants of these places feel by the loss of the Western letters, I would venture to submit the following arrangement for serving them.

The Receiver at Shapwick who is also the messenger to Glastonbury reaches Glastonbury with the London, etc. letters in time for the Up mail - here his duty ceases - but I would recommend that in future he should be detained at Glastonbury 'till after the Up Mail arrives, and take back the letters for Ashcott and Shapwick brought from the West.............it would however make an addition to his journey of 8 miles a day, and for this I would venture to recommend that his wages be increased from 12/- to 15/- a week.

I am however happy to be able to report a saving which will nearly cover this extra expenditure. Under the late arrangement of 6d. a day or £9-2-8 per year was granted to the Receiver at Walton for conveying the letters daily from Walton and Street to Glastonbury in time to be forwarded by the Ride to Old Down – This ride having been abolished, and the Northern Letters now being conveyed by the Mail Coach to Old Down. The Messenger from Shapwick takes them into Glastonbury and the allowance to the Walton Receiver has consequently ceased. If therefore His Lordship should be pleased to approve this proposition, the additional expenditure will be in fact only £1-6-0 a year

I am, Sir,   *Your most obedient servant*

Geo: Stow

The gentlemen who had made representation, Lord John Thynne and Rev. Richard Luscombe were respectively vicar of Street and Walton, a combined parish until 1886, and the vicar of Moorlinch and Greinton. Lord John Thynne was the 3rd son of the 2nd Marquess of Bath and, until the sale of the Walton estate in July 1939, his family, from Longleat in Wiltshire, had owned almost the entire village since the Reformation in the 16th century. Lord John lived in the rectory at Walton where he and his wife had a total of 10 children, not all of whom survived childhood. Not only was he the vicar of the two villages but he also was appointed Sub-Dean of Westminster Abbey in 1835. When he died in 1850 a large marble memorial to him was placed there.

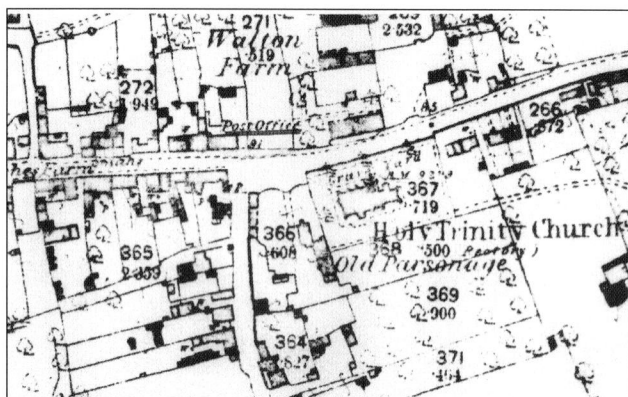

Ordnance Survey Map of 1871 showing the site of the Post Office

In 1859 we find the next reference to the village in the *Harrison-Harrad Directory* where the entry reads- *"Post Office - William Lester, receiver. Letters are received through Street, which is also the nearest Money Order Office".*
William Lester seems to have only been in the village for a short time as there is no reference to him in either the 1851 or the 1861 census returns and little is known about him. We do find that by 1866 *Kelly's Directory* reflects the downgrading of Glastonbury Post Office to the status of a sub-office in that the entry reads *"Letters through Bath, etc."*

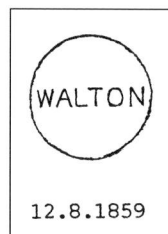

WALTON

12.8.1859

In the 1871 census the Post Office and Grocery store were facing the Main Street on the opposite side of the road to the church. George Westlake, aged 55, and his wife, Sarah aged 58, were in partnership as grocers, both being born in the village. Their son, Henry G. Westlake, then aged 23 was the nominated Sub-postmaster. Also living with them was their dressmaker daughter, Elizabeth, then aged 21. This is supported by the entry in *Morris' Directory* of 1872 with Henry George Westlake named as the sub-postmaster with the addition of *"Letters through Bridgwater arrive at 7 am.; dispatched at 7.40 pm. The nearest Money Order Office is at Street".*

Walton Post Office with H. G. WESTLAKE over the window

It does not seem as if times were too good for the family as by 1881 George was a widower and classed as a "General Labourer" whilst Henry , still unmarried, was now a "Warehouseman" as well as "Postmaster."

The Post Office hours were rapidly extending as in 1883 letters were arriving from Bridgwater at 5.30am. and being dispatched later, at 7.55pm.. The only change by 1889 was that the latest despatch was now " *at 8.05pm.*" with Henry Westlake being designated as Shop-Keeper & Post Office.

Elizabeth Westlake had married Charles Phillips from East Lydford in the mid-summer of 1873 and by 1881 they were living in Walton with their two young daughters, Mabel, six, and Blanche aged eleven months. In 1871 when he was 22, Charles had been working under a master baker employing four people in Langport named James Cable, He was described as a "Journeyman Baker" at that time.

Above: A Post Card from around 1900 showing the shop at No. 48 High Street and the water pump.
Right: 2015

By the time of the 1881 census they had obviously started up their own business in Walton as Charles was described as a Baker & Grocer and head of the household. By 1891 the couple had four daughters, the eldest of whom, Mabel, was helping in the shop as a grocer's assistant. On the other hand, Henry Westlake was then living with his father in another property where his description was that of "Clerk". Also living with the Westlakes was a boarder, Alfred Labdon, a nephew working as a baker's assistant, presumably working for Henry's brother-in-law.

The *Kelly's Directory* of 1894 still lists Henry Westlake as the Sub-postmaster. Letters were coming through Bridgwater and arriving at 5.30am. & 5.45pm.; dispatched at 9.00am. & 8.50pm. By this time the nearest Money Order & Telegraph Office was still at Street but Postal Orders, which first came into use in 1881, could now be issued but not paid here. The two extra letter arrivals coincided

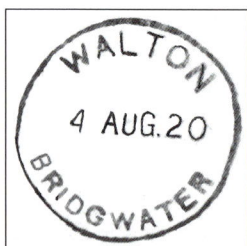

with the other information included in the directory which was:- *"Royal Mail Omnibus to Bridgwater, Thomas Cridland, through from Glastonbury daily at 9 am.; returning 5.45 pm."*

The census information for 1901 tells us that by this time Charles and Elizabeth's second daughter, Blanche at 20, was now head of the household at No. 48 High Street and was an assistant in the shop and the Post Office with her Uncle, Henry G. Westlake, as the sub-postmaster. Her sister, Gertrude, 15, a dressmaker, was also living there together with Adeline Perry, a cousin aged 35, described as a "Letter Carrier". Blanche married Henry Cavill, listed as a grocer in the directory entry, in the spring of 1911 and she continued to run the Post Office in Walton until at least 1914. Another shop-keeper in the village was Frank Fleetwood whose premises were in No. 42 South Street. He was later to take over the Post Office, reputedly in 1916, certainly before 1919, the next time that *Kelly's Directory* was issued following the Great War.

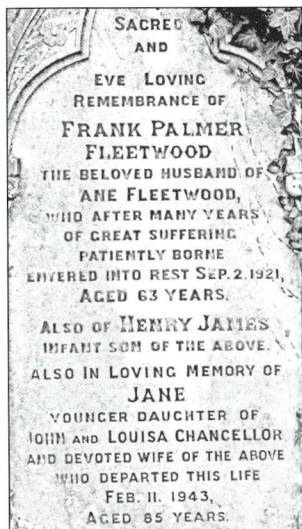

Frank Palmer Fleetwood was born in 1858, the son of Robert, a carpenter, and Ann Fleetwood. In one census his place of birth is given as Ashcott, only to be stated as Walton in the next. Following Robert's death in 1869 at the comparatively young age of 50, Ann kept a grocer's shop on Main Street. In the 1881 census Frank was described as a Grocer's Assistant living in Walton and, by that time, was married to Jane, the younger daughter of John and Louisa Chancellor who kept the shop on South Street. At that time they had two young children, Geraldine, aged two, and Gertrude, a baby, with another daughter, Nora Lucy, born later, in 1897. The inscription on the Chancellor family gravestone, which is to be found alongside the wall on the right just inside the church graveyard, shows that Jane's father died in 1877 *"in his 51st year"* in Australia; one does wonder as to what he was doing out there?

As we can see from the inscription on the Fleetwood family gravestone adjacent to that of Jane's family, Frank died in September 1921. As a widow, Jane continued with the shop and Post Office from 42 South Street. In the meantime, her youngest daughter Nora, in 1926, had married Cecil Arthur Reade and they were living with her right up until the outbreak of war in 1939. Indeed, Cecil was the named

The Post Box in Sharpham.
August 2004

sub-Postmaster in the *Kelly's Directories* after 1931, the same year when a telephone number was given for the Post Office, STREET 53. Unfortunately she died in 1943, then aged 85, and by 1945 Cecil and Nora had again taken over the business. Nora was in charge of the Post Office whilst George ran the shop as well as having another line supplying poultry to other shops as far away as Bristol. He also acted as a Special Constable in the area.

When she left school in 1944, Vera Rideout, came to help out in the shop. She was living next door to the Post Office in South Street in a house her father had bought from the Longleat Estate in the sale of July 1939. Although the price he paid seems very small by the level set in the early part of the 21st century Vera understood that, at that time, he even had to have an advance on his following week's wages to pay the required deposit. Unfortunately her Mother died young leaving Vera to look after her younger brother, who was still at school at the time, also her widowed father. Throughout the rest of her working life she continued to work here, the one constant in an ever changing world, only eventually retiring after giving the final owners of the shop, Roger and Abi Watts, the benefit of her knowledge for the first three weeks of their ownership in 2003. By this time she was 74 years of age.

Although the proposal to re-organise the local mail arrangements were first mooted in 1949 it was not until early 1957 that anything actually happened. In the initial plan all mail sorting was to be transferred from Street to Glastonbury; a number of changes to the delivery in Walton village were also planned. In 1949 the delivery round covering the village east of the Post Office as well as Asney road and the Sharpham area, and the round covering Walton and Bramble Hill area including the Windmill had started out from Walton Post Office each morning at 7.45am. and it was aimed to finish by 11.25. The planning of the re-organisation was meticulously carried out, it even said

who carried out these rounds, Elias Perry, a Permanent Auxiliary Postman and William Cottle. The latter was a retired policeman with a pension of £13 monthly from his police service, who was 59 at the time whereas Elias, who was then 62, had been working as a postman for the previous 14½ years although he was also self-employed as a carpenter and decorator in his own right as well as being responsible for the upkeep of the churchyard.

The Post Box on Whitley Road

Rather than the mail starting from Street, under the new scheme a mail van from Glastonbury would, in the morning, start out at 6.50am, bringing Postmen to the point of delivery in Street, to arrive at 7.00am. The van then to go to Clarks factory and hence to Walton Sub-office to drop off the early mail, before returning to Glastonbury by 7.25am.. The deliveries around Walton had formerly been carried out on foot or by bicycle including the mail for Ivythorn, Marshall's Elm, etc. Previously these had started out at Street at 6.30am. and ending at Walton by 9.10am, no doubt to pick up the incoming mail, before returning to Street Post Office by about 10.00am. Mail was also sent out again to Walton at 2.15p.m. in readiness for the afternoon delivery.

By 1969 Cecil & Nora Reade had retired to Chancellor Road, Walton. It is interesting that they called their new house "Fleetwood" after Nora's maiden name. Chancellor Road itself had been named after her grandparent's

A Post Card of Walton Post Office dated 28th September 1957.

family who had previously owned the land. Nora died in September 1978, aged 78 whilst Cecil, living to the grand old age of 92, died in early 1987.

George & Eileen Back, believed to have come from Devon, were then resident at No. 42 South Street, George found running the Post Office rather stressful particularly so when, on one occasion, just before a Bank Holiday when it was the practice to pay out double the money for pensioners in the prior week, they ran out of cash. George decided to make a special trip to Bridgwater Post Office to collect a further supply. Unfortunately he made the mistake of stopping at the Toby Inn on the way home and this was his downfall. He arrived home too late to make any payments that day.

It was not long before Denzil & Frances Moreton had taken over the business, they first appeared on the electoral roll in 1971 but this was period of frequent change in the ownership of village shops and it was not too long before another couple had moved in.

When researching the Parliamentary Electoral rolls in the Somerset Heritage Centre at Taunton a bit of confusion arose but, once it was realised that in 1972 the houses in Walton had been re-numbered, all became clear. No. 42 in South Street had become No. 14.

Walton Post Office.
14 South Street
in December 2002

GPO

NAME OF OFFICE
AND POSTAL ADDRESS

WALTON

WALTON, STREET, SOMERSET.

HOURS OF BUSINESS

| **WEEKDAYS** (EXCEPT WEDNESDAYS AND SATURDAYS) 9. 0 AM - 1. 0 PM 2. 0 PM - 5.30 PM **WEDNESDAYS** 9. 0 AM - 1. 0 PM **SATURDAYS** 9. 0 AM - 1. 0 PM 2. 0 PM - 4.30 PM | **SUNDAYS** **GOOD FRIDAY** **CHRISTMAS DAY** **BOXING DAY** **OTHER BANK HOLIDAYS** | CLOSED |

COLLECTIONS

| **WEEKDAYS** 9.15 AM 5. 0 PM (NOT SATURDAYS) | **SUNDAYS** **GOOD FRIDAY** **CHRISTMAS DAY** **BOXING DAY** **OTHER BANK HOLIDAYS** | 4.10 PM 9.15 AM NO COLLECTION 4.10 PM |

REGISTRATION LETTERS AND PARCELS MAY BE REGISTERED DURING BUSINESS HOURS. IF INTENDED TO CONNECT WITH A PARTICULAR COLLECTION THEY MUST BE HANDED IN AT LEAST **10** MINUTES BEFORE THE ADVERTISED TIME OF COLLECTION.

TELEGRAMS MAY BE DICTATED AT ALL TIMES FROM TELEPHONE KIOSKS.

PUBLIC TELEPHONES THE NEAREST TELEPHONE KIOSK IS AT JUNCTION OF MAIN STREET AND SOUTH STREET

P 756 E

This frame and contents were found in an outhouse of No.14 South Street.
It must have been issued to the Post Office prior to 1975 as there was
no Sunday collection after this date.

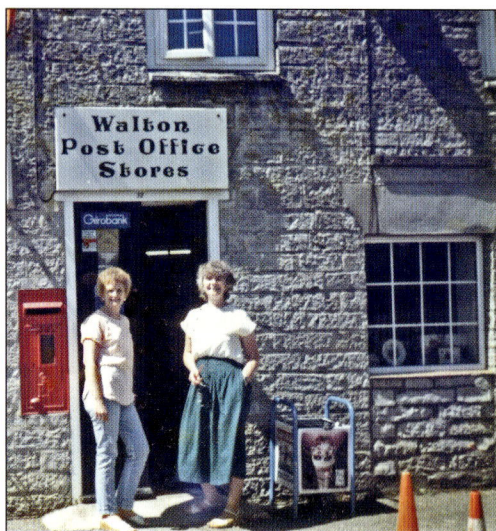

Kath Sully and Eileen Beese outside the Post Office in 1986.

For a short time around the years 1974/75 Roger and June Weaver, with their two sons, came to live in Walton but they did not stay long and in October 1975, Kath and Tony Sully, with Kath's sister Eileen Beese, purchased the business. Previously they had lived in Bristol. Kath had been working as a local government officer until the arrival of their children whilst Tony pursued a career in management accountancy. Kath and Eileen shared the running of the shop and Post Office. Each having two children, this arrangement suited them, being both free to devote time to their family when they needed it most.

Kath and Eileen found Vera Rideout a tremendous help as she knew everybody and everything about the business. Indeed, over time, she became a great personal friend to both of them.

At that time delivery of letters in the village was carried out by Hazel Wilkins, a job she had undertaken, by the time she retired, for some 37 years. The post was delivered from Glastonbury by van and, before setting out, Hazel first sorted the mail in a lean-to annex attached to the Post Office. To comply with postal regulations this was a self-contained unit having its own toilet and hand washing facilities supplied by the owners.

In a little booklet describing local properties produced by the Walton Women's Institute it was stated that the six paned bow windows on the shop front had been replaced by plate glass in 1946. An incident that Kath recalls

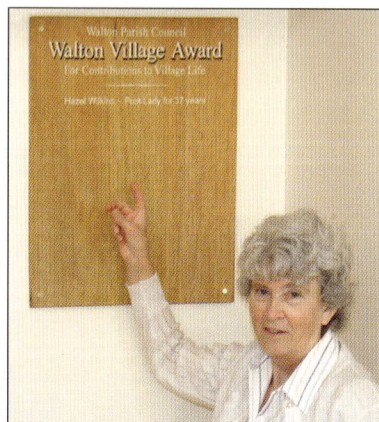

Hazel Wilkins and the plaque in the village Hall honouring her 37 years of service

well was when a motorcyclist broke one of these by allowing his bike to fall against it. To replace it was a major undertaking requiring a small crane, luckily the cost was covered by insurance.

In 1988 Kath and Eileen made the decision to retire and in October of that year they sold the business to Marian and Richard Gray. The Gray's had two children, Clare and Russell, the latter a young voter qualifying to vote on 2nd September 1992. Even after selling the Post Office, Kath did not break her connection with the service as she very soon took up a part-time post, working three days a week, in Glastonbury under the Postmaster, Ken Watkins. Whilst doing that it was not unknown for her to also act as a relief in other local offices, on more than one occasion helping out John & Janice Davies at Middle Leigh.

On 6th February 2003 Roger and Abi Watts came to Walton Post Office. Previous to this Roger had been working as a transport manager in Bristol, working very long hours; usually leaving home by 8.00am. and not getting back until around 8.00 - 8.30pm. whilst Abi was working as a nurse in a care home, undertaking the night shift. Roger had time to get the two children up and having their breakfast before leaving Abi, on her return, to get them to school. In turn he would be home to see them to bed after Abi had left to start her night shift. They decided that this life style was not really sustainable so that is when they started to look for a village shop to run jointly.

Abi and Roger Watts inside their shop

The Letter Box on Asney Road, on the left, December 2002 and, on the right, the new tinplate box, March 2015. BA16 253

Roger undertook two weeks of training at the special facility housed over the main Post Office in Weston-s-Mare after which he was the nominated Sub-postmaster. Abi was later trained so that she, too, could operate the Post Office side of the store. Just for their first two or three weeks Vera Rideout helped them to settle in before she finally took her well earned retirement.

By this time Walton had no other shops because, as seen in other villages, people had got into the habit of doing their main shopping in the local supermarkets and only used the village shop as a convenience store. With both Sainsbury's and Tesco having shops in Street together with Safeways in Glastonbury, competition was fairly strong. Roger and Abi realised this but they still did a good trade in alcohol in all its forms as well as turning over somewhere between £6 - £8000 a week in the Post Office. The hours the shop was open were 8.30am. - 5.30pm. with an hour for lunch from 1.00 - 2.00 on all weekdays except for early closing on Wednesdays and Saturdays. Wednesday afternoons have always been stock-taking time.

John Leech delivering the mail in Walton, March 2015.

Their newspaper business was good although it did entail getting up by 6.00am. to get the papers sorted for the three delivery rounds they operated. For these they employed one man and two boys, only operating six days a week; they

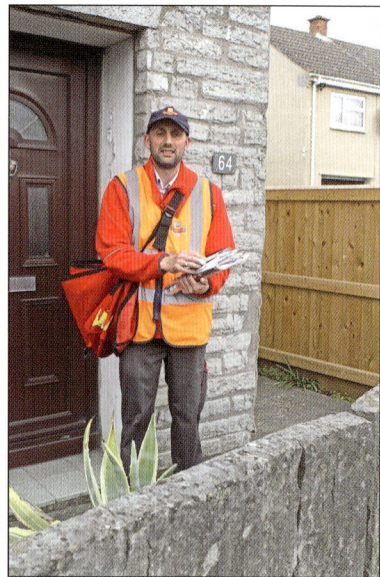

then opened on Sunday mornings for callers to buy their papers. This was well worthwhile as the people whose papers had been delivered during the week came in to settle their bills.

With the reducing turnover Roger and Abi decided, after five years of running the village shop, that it was time to move on to new challenges. Although the G.P.O. was offering a financial inducement to close many small Post Offices at the time this was not their main reason. The financial return for the hours worked had not been improving so Walton finally lost its last shop on the 14th August 2008 at 1.00pm. At one point in its history the village had supported at least three shops; there was even a barber's shop on the Post Office premises.

After retiring from the Post Office Roger took up garden maintenance together with part-time building in the winter, whilst Abi became an assistant teacher well on her way, in 2015, to becoming fully qualified.

The Letter Box (BA16 174) outside the church gate
replacing the one inset in the former Post Office wall.
Wendy Devenish illustrating the fact that initially it was too tall for disabled people's use.
After representation, it was then lowered.

ACKNOWLEDGEMENTS

With grateful acknowledgement to John Hanrahan, Adrian Howe,
Vera Rideout, Kath Sully, Roger and Abi Watts and Winston Williams.
Also all the people of Walton who have added to this story.

West Pennard

*W*EST PENNARD, *a village and a parish in Wells district, Somerset. The village stands 1 mile N. of the Somerset and Dorset railway, and 3½ W. by S. of Glastonbury; and has a station on the railway, a post-office under Shepton Mallet, and a fair on the first Monday of Aug. The parish contains also the hamlets of East-Street, South-Town, and Sticklinch. Acres, 3,063 . Real property, £7,289. Pop., 836. Houses, 177. There are a Wesleyan chapel, two national schools, and charities £29.*

From:- *"The Imperial Gazetteer of England & Wales"* by John Marius Wilson. Pub. A. Fullarton & Co. 1872

THE EARLIEST reference I can find to the post in West Pennard is from the village Vestry Meeting reports. In October 1830 there is an entry *"Paid for postage on two letters, 1/1."* (1 shilling and 1 penny) and again in November 1831 when the entry states *"Paid for a letter from Taunton, 5/-"* (5 shillings) which gives one an idea of the cost of postage although the letter must have been quite large. At that time the village support paid to maintain one child was 1/- per week. In 1845 the first postmarker was issued to the village by way of Wells Post Office indicating that the village postal service was administered from that head office.

The first reference to a possible Post Office in the village in the contemporary directories was in the 1859 *Harrison-Harrad Directory*. Here is listed Sidney Green as the *"Receiver of posts with letters through Glastonbury which is also the nearest Money Order office"*. In the 1861 census return his description is that of Grocer and Wesleyan preacher. By 1866 *Kelly's Directory* states -

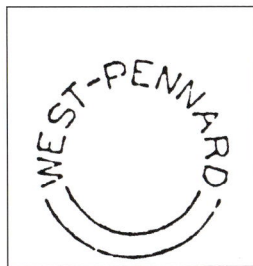

Issued to the Wells Post Office 13.11.1845

"Post Office - Sidney Green. - Letters now arrive from Shepton Mallet at 9.15am. and are dispatched at 4.50pm. and also 11am.Sundays and the nearest Money Order office is at Glastonbury"

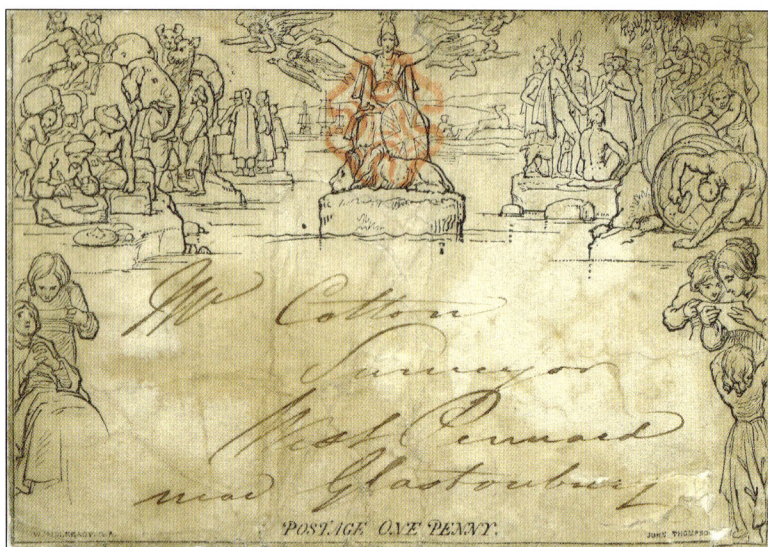

*The 1d. Pre-paid "Mulready" letter, issued in 1840, addressed to
Benjamin Cotton, Surveyor, West Pennard*

In the 1871 census return for West Pennard, William Shingleton and his wife
Harriet, both born in West Pennard, lived at the Post Office and he was also
described as a farmer with 11 acres and a dairyman, probably keeping a few cows
and selling their produce through the shop outlet. According to the introduction
to this census, carried out by Benjamin Cotton and Herbert Catford, the
Shingleton's house and the Post Office were on the Shepton – Turnpike Road
which fell into:-

> "that part of the village commencing from and including Green's late Post
> Office on the one side and Bible Christian Chapel on the other and taking in all
> cottages and houses on each side of the road to the boundary stone by Pilton, also
> Sticklinch and Mr Jno Creed's farm on the hill, Keate's farm by Redlake and any
> other cottage in the moor and after the railway."

Presumably, Sidney Green had run the Post Office from the house on the
corner of Laurel Street, opposite the turning to Newtown from the main road
and possibly, by 1871, William Shingleton had taken over the premises. Now,
in 2013, this house is lived in by the owner of the garage on the same side of the
main road.

Benjamin Cotton, the author's three times great uncle, was one of nine children,
born in Padstow, Cornwall, his mother's birthplace, but came to live in East
Street, West Pennard, where he carried out land surveying and map making. He

was responsible for producing a copy the West Pennard Tithe map as well as acting as the census enumerator for parts of the village in both 1851 and 1861

In the 1875 edition of *Kelly's Directory*, the very versatile William Shingleton had added Tailor to his list of occupations and continued as the sub- postmaster and he was still in post when he was aged 78 in 1880. His unmarried daughter, Emily, was his support as she was designated as the postmistress.

A report in the *Central Somerset Gazette* in July 1897 under the heading -

A RUNAWAY

> *"On Saturday last, Mr Hill, the well-known cheese dealer, of Evercreech, had his horse and trap tied up in Mr Sidney Creed's barton at Southtown, when the animal slipped the blind-halter, and started off in a mad career right through the village, its pace not being checked till it reached the Glastonbury Road, where, instead of taking the turning, it jumped over the wall into the flower garden adjoining the house of Mr Cory, the West Pennard postman. The horse was badly injured about the shoulder, and the trap much damaged."*

This is the only reference found for Mr Cory as he did not seem to appear on any of the census returns, held every 10 years, but obviously, by this time, the amount of mail must have justified a regular postman.

For the 1881 census the village was divided into two parts, the eastern part ran from the marker stone at Haviatt to "*the late Post Office occupied by William Davis (not inclusive) and then all the area taking in Coxbridge, New Town*" etc. on the south side of the village and there was a 32 year old shop-keeper, Samuel Rogers, included.

A bill-head on an account dated 2nd August 1887 (*illustrated*) is headed S Rogers, Grocer & Draper, General Stores, Post Office. Samuel, who was born in Semley, Wiltshire, and his wife, Sarah from Chard in Somerset, had taken over the Post Office. At this time letters were again being sent from the Glastonbury office, timed to arrive at 7.50am. and be dispatched at 5.40pm. The Sunday post went out at 9.55am. and Baltonsborough had become the nearest Money Order office.

Although the West Pennard P.O. was under the Wells head office this postmarker gives Glastonbury as the postal address

In the 1891 census returns we find two other references to postal affairs: William Lester aged 59, born in Glastonbury, a Rural Letter Carrier and in Church Lane: Richard Carter, aged 49, a Postman. A rather sad note also finds Harriet Shingleton, now over 80 and a widow, described as paralysed, living with her daughter, Emily, now a Nurse.

Postal orders were first issued nationally in 1881 and took the place of money orders for smaller sums and could later be cashed at most post offices. Obviously this was not universal as, at this time, West Pennard Post Office did not have the facility to cash them as the entry says that *"Postal Orders are issued here but not paid".*

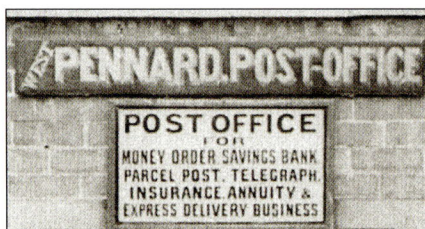

ROGERS' Supply Stores c. 1906 with Dorothy & Letitia Haimes, children from a neighbouring house, and an unknown boy in the picture

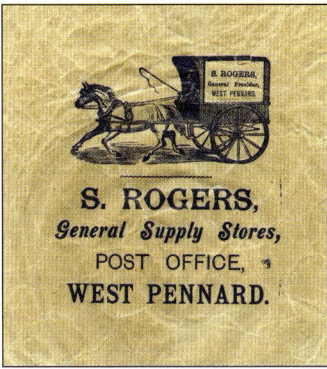

A Printed Paper Bag from the shop

It is interesting in that the Railway Station, on the Somerset & Dorset line, had an important part to play in that it is given as the nearest Telegraph Office for collection and also had a wall letter box which was cleared daily at 5.00pm. Baltonsborough, which was by now connected to the telephone, was responsible for the delivery of Telegrams although it was three miles distant.

It was early in 1900 that the Post Office at West Pennard was transferred from being a sub-office of Wells to being under Glastonbury. A new date stamp was despatched, as illustrated, to the Glastonbury Post Office on 25th January 1900.

It does seem that the Post Office was a little slow in taking up new technology. In August 1910 the quarterly meeting of the West Pennard Parish Council was held in the church school-room when a view was expressed that a telephone call office would be a great advantage to the parish. Obviously this was something not yet available in the village although it had been in Butleigh since well before this date; this probably prompted the request.

In 1902 we read that the letter box at Woodlands benefitted by being collected at both 7.30 am. and again at 6.50pm. together with one collection on Sundays. The one at the Station was only cleared once a day, at 5.00pm. and then only on weekdays which, at that time, included Saturdays as part of the working week.

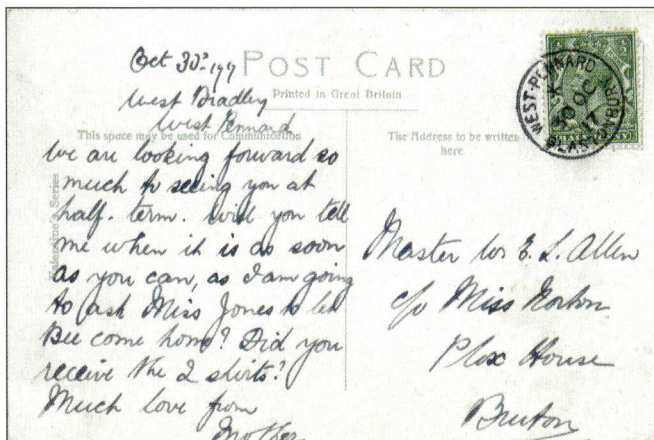

The Postmarker issued to West Pennard in 1900 was still in use in late 1917

An invoice from the Post Office Stores now under Joseph Henry Williams. Dated July 16th 1918.

Money Order certificate issued on August 30th 1918 and signed N. Williams

Samuel Rogers would have been 65 in 1914 and by 1918 he had retired and Joseph Williams and his wife were running the shop and Post Office, taking over at a difficult time due to rationing and the problem in getting supplies due to the war. The comment on the above bill "Sorry, we have no matches" gives an indication of this. The only reference to a Joseph Henry Williams in the census returns for 1901 is to one who was born in London in 1864, working as a *"leather grounder"* in a glove factory and living in Glastonbury with his wife, Mary Jane.

Ten years later he is doing the same job but now in a rug factory. In an extract of the deeds of the property, it can be seen that the freehold was passed directly from Samuel Rogers to Ernest Bray Senior in November 1918 so presumably Joseph Williams was only the tenant whilst running the business. The mystery of why the new Postmaster referred to himself as Ernest Bray Junior is also revealed in these deeds as the property was later conveyed, in 1939, from father to son, both being named Ernest Bray..

Ernest, with his wife Kathleen, remained at West Pennard for a considerable number of years, only retiring in 1946. They both took a very active interest in the community. Mrs Bray, a tall lady, was a stalwart of the village Women's Institute,

*Ernest Bray
in his Special Constable
uniform
and
Mrs kathleen Bray*

being treasurer in 1948, and took part in many of its activities whilst Ernest, as can be seen from his photograph, acted as a Special Constable as well as being the Sub-Postmaster.

In 1931 the Post Office telephone number was listed as West Pennard No.1 which very much indicated that the exchange was based here in the Post Office. By 1939, with the installation of the Automatic Exchange in the nearby village it was changed and became Baltonsborough No. 49.

By 1952 the Brays were living at Gable House, West Pennard, having sold the business to William and Kitty Alford from Christchurch, in June 1946. The Alfords stay was short-lived and Mr Frances Downing, a retired schoolmaster from Weston-super-Mare, purchased the business in January 1948.

Leila Chinn (nee Higdon) from Parbrook, who was later to take over the Parbrook Post Office from her uncle, worked here in the shop until Mr Downing retired. Mrs Downing providing a cooked lunch for the staff each day, the shop shutting from 1.00 –

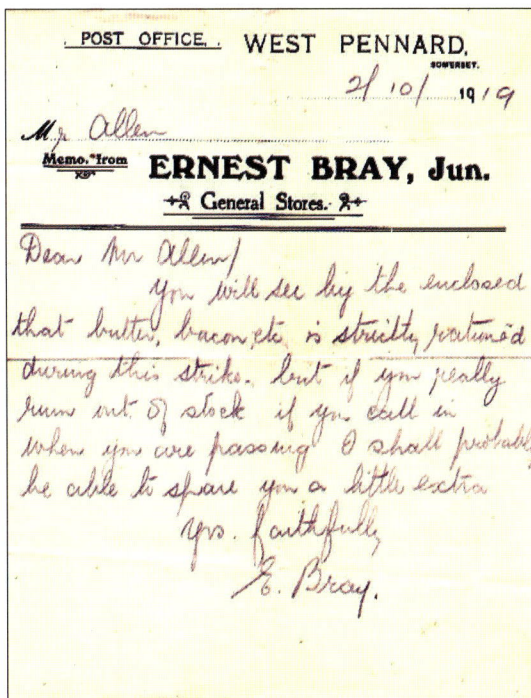

A Memo from Ernest Bray dated 2nd October 1919 showing loyalty to a regular customer.

*First Day of Issue of the first of the new Queen Elizabeth 11 stamps
on 31st August 1953*

2.00pm. and one of Leila's lasting memories was that, when they were having liver for lunch, Mr Downing always found an excuse to go to the George Hotel in Glastonbury as he could not abide it. At that time May Phelps was one of the post ladies who rode a bicycle delivering letters around West Pennard and some of the surrounding villages and is still well remembered in West Bradley. The author is very thankful to her for letting his father know that a certain gentleman in the village seemed to get some very nice stamps on his letters as she knew that I was a keen stamp collector. Maurice Sibson had come to live in West Bradley from Manchester where both he and his wife had been dentists. Maurice was a keen philatelist, as opposed to just being a collector, and subsequently he introduced me to the many of the finer points of the hobby.

The business changed hands again in May 1951 when Henry & Mary Piggott moved in and this is confirmed by the entry on the electoral rolls for the village in 1953 when the Piggotts were living in what was then named as the Newtown Post Office. A note in the sale documents leads one to believe that the property was worth £1000.00 and the fixtures and fittings were then valued at £35.00. One does wonder as to whether this also included the shop stock but probably this was valued separately.

By August 1957, when the Piggotts sold up and Bernard Riches bought the premises, the total value of the property had risen to £1900.00 and the ingoings amounted to £500.00. Did Mr Riches buy the building as an investment and lease it out?

By December in the same year Claude Douglas Hitchman and his wife were in charge. A *"Broadcasting Receiving Licence (including Television)"*, which cost a total of £4.00 for the year, dated August 1962 was signed by Ann Higgins and the one issued in August 1963 by Stanley Higgins. One could be misled by the grocery bill (illustrated), dated 19th June 1964, which, although it is under a C D Hitchman bill-head, the receipt is actually signed by Mr Higgins. This does seem to be a time when there was a lot of changes in the management of local Post Offices in the district and it was not too long before another couple had taken over.

Arthur & Sarah Smith were the signatories on TV licences issued to my Grandmother, Mrs Allen, in both June 1965 and 1966 although they, too, used old stationery as the illustrated bill, headed S. P. Higgins, is receipted by one of the next new owners, Ted Bowles.

With the arrival of Frederick (Ted) and Joy Bowles in May 1967 a long period of stability was about to occur and they were to stay for 30 years.

Mrs Sarah Smith's signature on a Television Licence of 1965

Security in rural Post Offices is always a major consideration, as with banks, they carry a lot of cash which is attractive to the criminal element in society. During the years following 1967 there were three attempts to break into the premises, only one of which was successful.

On one occasion the thieves removed a sky-light above the shop premises, only to be confronted by a very angry Alsation dog looking up at them from beneath. They quickly made their escape. The second attempt only got as far as throwing a gas bottle through the glass in the door. On the one successful attempt there was no dog present and not only did they get into

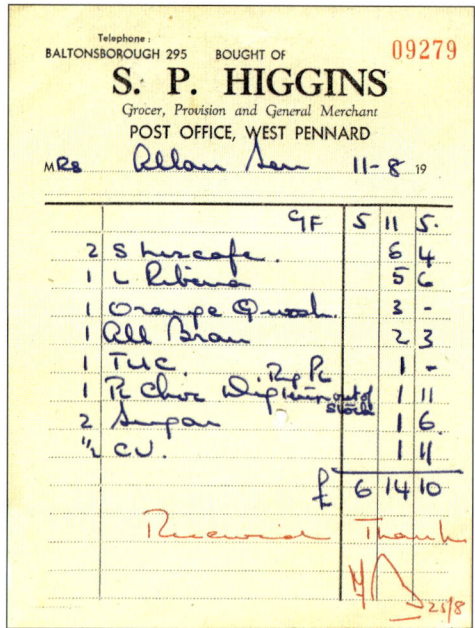

A bill headed S P Higgins, issued during the time that the Smiths ran the store, and receipted by Ted Bowles

the shop but they broke into the wall safe provided by the postal authorities. By all accounts this was not too difficult as it was not a very secure item. They stole not only a number of Postal Orders and the datestamps but also all the

tinned salmon from the shelves, salmon being expensive in the days before the advent of the farmed variety now so readily available. Luckily the bulk of the cash was in a much more secure safe in the living quarters attached to the shop. The

date stamps were later found in a ditch in a nearby village with all the date plugs scattered widely but, at least, they were re-instated. Some three years later the two robbers, whilst standing trial for other similar crimes, admitted carrying out this raid and were committed to prison for their offences.

Ted & Joy Bowles

"Ted", christened Frederick, was born in Calcutta, India, the son of a very long line of British people living in that country. As a schoolboy he excelled at table as well as lawn tennis, playing the former up to national standard and, indeed,

representing the country at that sport as a young man. He had a natural talent for all ball games and had played a lot of lawn tennis whilst in India. When he was called up for National Service in the army, having previously started training as an electrical engineer, he joined the Royal Signals Regiment. He then found himself, rather to his surprise, being posted to many different places where he could play and win for the regiment rather than take part in any actual soldiering. After two years of national service he joined the Colonial Police Force in East Africa, based in Tanganyika. It was there that he married Joy Parker, a qualified nurse and midwife whom he had met in Tripoli when he was stationed there. Still playing tennis at a high level, one year Ted won the East African Open Tournament

It was at the time of independence of the country, and its later joining with Zanzibar to form the new country of Tanzania, that he and Joy, together with their two children, Tim & Julienne, were on extended leave in Britain. As the country was changing so much they made the decision to not return. Ted found

*Ted and son, Tim, outside their new shop, shortly
after moving in, in May 1967*

a new job in Merthyr Tydfil, South Wales, as head of Security of the new Hoover factory. With government encouragement many new light industries were being established in South Wales to provide employment for those who had formerly worked in the, rapidly diminishing, coal mining industry. After a while Ted and Joy decided that a change was needed, Ted not taking kindly to being employed in the factory environment.

The idea of running a small business where they could both be self-employed appealed to them and so it was that they came to West Pennard. In spite of the fact that their house had dropped in value whilst in Wales, having found just what they desired, the village stores then being run by Bernard Riches, they sold up and moved in May 1967.

Ted and Joy were so very much involved with the children and the shop and Post Office, together with other village activities, that tennis playing was just a memory. That was until a near neighbour, Bill Carslaw, having heard that Ted was a bit of a tennis player, invited him round for a social game. Being always keenly competitive Ted's standard of play came as a bit of a shock to the locals and it was not long before both he and son Tim joined the tennis club at Wells. Ted soon got back to form and, having won a number of tournaments, became eligible to join the "45 Club of Great Britain", even playing in the veteran's section in the Wimbledon tournament in London. He not only played but also gave tennis tuition to an untold number of children locally. Also adding a new line to the goods sold in the village shop - tennis racquets and equipment as well as a racquet re-stringing service.

Even when later in life he had difficulty in concentrating he was still able to play a very keen game of table tennis, out-playing all his contemporaries.

The shop employed a number of local people, Brenda Kent, Anna Gifford and Marion Parsons. Marion was particularly helpful as she qualified to do Post Office counter work and could then give Ted & Joy time off as well as act as cover for the sub-Post Office run by Leila Chinn at Parbrook. Also working round about this time as a postman in the village named Louis Whitehead. Louis having previously been a self-employed painter and decorator, took on this job, cycling up to 12 miles a day, for over 17 years until his retirement in 1988.

It was during the 30 years of running the Post Office, in 1977, that one of Ted & Joy Bowles' regular customers achieved his 100th birthday. James Lomax not only received a special telegram from the Queen but, knowing that he was a keen philatelist, Ted organised the gift of a special presentation pack of the

James Lomax receiving his 100th birthday presentation pack.

Queen's Silver Jubilee stamps. These were then presented, as the picture shows, by the head of the Public Relations Division of the S.W. Postal region based in Bristol, at Mr Lomax's home on his birthday.

It was in 1997 Ted and Joy Bowles decided to retire and, having sold the shop, they continued to live in the village; Ted passing away quietly at home in February 2014 and Joy in early 2015.

Paul & Jenny Homer, the new owners, took over on September 1st but, as neither of them had passed the necessary examinations to qualify as sub-postmasters, Ted continued to run that side of the shop for a while after his retirement. In the meantime the new owners had reviewed the whole future of village stores in general and decided that, in its present form, they would be unable to make a living from it. Hence they soon lost heart in the project and it was not long before they were sending out a circular letter to the villagers announcing its imminent closure. *(See Appendix i.)*

In January 1998 Post Office Counters Ltd sent a letter (Appendix ii) to the Chief Executive of Somerset County Council informing him that, as they had been

Recorded Delivery receipts signed by Paul Homer in October 1997

unable to recruit a replacement, the West Pennard Post Office would be closing on 18th February. Helpfully they suggested that the nearest office to the village would be found at Baltonsborough, some three miles distant. After applying for planning permission to develop the site for houses, and having it turned down, it was not long before Mr & Mrs Homer decided to sell up and leave the village. And so ended a long association of the Post Office to the village of West Pennard.

ACKNOWLEDGEMENTS

With grateful acknowledgement for all their help to Julienne & Tim Bowles, Carol Clewlow, Betty Creed and the other people of West Pennard who helped with material for this story.

Appendix i.

Circular Letter re: West Pennard Post Office

<u>*The Closure of West Pennard Post Office Stores*</u>

Jenny & I are very sorry to announce that the Post Office Stores will shortly be closing down. Most of you will no doubt be sad,' though hardly surprised, at this news & we can assure you that it is with extreme reluctance & after exhaustive consideration of the options that we have reached the inescapable conclusion that the Stores are not viable in their current form.

We came to Pennard with real determination to see if somehow we could keep the village shop alive in full knowledge it would be an uphill struggle. We have sought advice from the Rural Development Commission & from other village shopkeepers. It seems the only possible future for shops such as ours in this age of the supermarket is as a convenience store open from "8 'til late." Apart from the additional hours, this would require a considerable investment in increased stock, refitting, & upgrading food preparation areas & electrical supply to comply with health & safety regulations, for what can at best be an uncertain future.

Post Office Counters are anxious to relocate the post office within the village & will be advertising the vacancy shortly. We or they would be glad to hear from anyone interested. Faced with the closure of their shop, some villages have organized community shops or weekly markets run by volunteers selling home produce/handicrafts on a commission basis to raise money for various projects. Jenny & I would be happy to support such a venture with fixtures & fittings out of the shop.

The shop and post office will remain open into the New Year and we shall continue to stock fresh produce until further notice. We would be appreciative if you could help us empty the shelves over the coming weeks & we also have several tennis, squash & badminton racquets which we would like to sell.

24/11/97

Appendix ii.

SWYDDFA'R POST   POST OFFICE

2 0 JAN 1998

The Chief Executive
Somerset County Council
County Hall
TAUNTON
Somerset
TA1 4DY

Cownteri Swyddfa'r Post Cyf
Post Office Counters Ltd

19 January 1998

Dear Sir/Madam

Re: West Pennard Post Office, Newtown, West Pennard, GLASTONBURY, Somerset, BA6 8NL.

I am writing to inform you that due to circumstances beyond our control Post Office Counter services will cease from the above named office on 18 February 1998. This action is very much regretted, but the subpostmaster has resigned and to date we have been unable to recruit a replacement.

The nearest office to West Pennard is *Baltonsborough Post Office, The Cross, Baltonsborough, GLASTONBURY, Somerset, BA6 8QW*, which is approximately 3 miles away. The hours of business transacted are:-

    Monday to Friday   09.00 - 13.00 and 14.00 - 17.30
    Saturday   09.00 - 12.30

I would like to apologise in advance for any difficulties that may result from the closure, but we are keen for service to resume and the vacancy has been advertised. In this respect anything you can do to stimulate interest would be helpful, and should you know of any interested party, they can contact Melanie Holland of our Agency Recruitment team on ☎ 01454 622444.

Yours faithfully

Martyn Lee
Post Office Counters
Helpline Administration

Cownteri Swyddfa'r Post Cyf
Post Office Counters Ltd
De Cymru a De Orllewin Lloegr
South Wales and South West
Network House, The Quadrant
Aztec West, Almondsbury
Bristol BS12 4QX
Teliffon/Telephone 01454 622
Ffacsimili/Facsimile 01454 62240819
Post Office Counters Ltd Registered in England
No: 2154540 Registered Office King Edward Building
King Edward Street London EC1A 1AA

Westhay

*W*esthay, a hamlet in the Meare parish, Somerset, 4¼ miles N.N.W. of Glastonbury.

From:- *"The Imperial Gazetteer of England & Wales"* by John Marius Wilson. Pub. A. Fullarton & Co. 1872

IT IS DIFFICULT to ascertain when the first Post Office in Westhay was opened. In the Post Office archives are kept what are known as the Postmaster General's Minutes and in 1884 in "Vol. 271. No. 6643." is a note to say *"Meare delivery extended to Westhay. Westhay Rural Postman's wages."* although I have not been able to discover what the payment was to be. And again in *Kelly's Directory* of 1902 it states that George Wilkins, was the Sub-Postmaster of Meare and the *"letters come through Glastonbury arriving at 8.20 am. dispatched at 5.40 pm. with the nearest Telegraph Office is at Glastonbury, 3 miles distant".* Details of the mail collection were mentioned with: *"Wall letter boxes- Westhay cleared at 5.10 pm. & Stileway 5.50 pm."* so at that time there still did not seem to be a Post Office in the village.

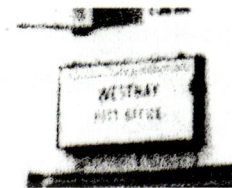

Pitts Farm with the
WESTHAY
POST OFFICE
sign over the window

In the book, *"Meare - Its place in history,"* published in 2001, on Page 122 in the article by Leonard & Margaret Gooding and compiled by Horace Toogood, it is written :-

> *"Westhay had its own little shops, the earliest being a room in Pitts Farm run by Esther Harper who later became Mrs Lewis Powell of the milk collection business"*

Esther Harper, born in 1855, was the daughter of John, classed as an agricultural labourer in the 1881 census, & Ann Harper. Esther is described as a grocer in the same census, and they all lived in Westhay, probably in what is now called Pitts Farm. Lewis Powell, born in Motcombe, Dorset the son of a Primitive Methodist Minister, had a sister, Mary, who was married to a Westhay farmer, James Toogood. Lewis, who was 18 at the time, was staying with this family when the 1881 census was taken; his stated occupation was *"Help on the farm"*. No doubt this was where they met as Esther and Lewis were married in 1886 and they moved to Homeway Farm on the Meare Road where they later ran a small milk collection business as well as the farm.

Pitts Farm. Photo - March 2014

The shop at Pitts Farm continued and a Post Office was later established and remained there until the Bassett family took over and ran the business from No. 62 Main Road, next to the "Bird in Hand" public house in about 1919.

Although the hamlet of Westhay has always been associated with Meare the post deliveries were undertaken from Shapwick from around 1900 when Westhay was transferred from the Glastonbury Head Office to Bridgwater, hence in 1902 the directory states that the postal address should be:- *Westhay, Shapwick, Nr. Bridgwater.*

Although, in the *Kelly's Directory* of 1906, under the Meare entry, we find that the letter box at Westhay was still cleared by the Postman from that village. But by 1910 we find an entry which names William Francis as the Sub-Postmaster. No doubt the postal authorities, wishing to open a new Post Office, would make use of an already established business.

As far back as 1883 we found that William Francis, a farmer's son who was born in Westhay in 1858, kept a grocer's shop in the village with his wife, Annie. She was formerly Ann(ie) Balch and was born in Crediton, Devon in 1860, and her father was a licensed hawker from Huntspill, Somerset. Her mother was also born locally, coming from the village of Mark, close to Westhay. In 1871 Annie, then aged 11, with her sister Louisa, was living in Westhay with their grandparents, Thomas & Betsy Balch. This couple were designated as shop-keepers in the Westhay census of 1871 and therefore it seems that soon after Annie & William were married, circa 1878, the young couple had taken over the shop. Initially William had probably worked in the Clark's shoe factory as his occupation in 1881 is given as "Slipper Maker".

With the passing of the compulsory Education Act of 1881, and the formation of schools in most villages, their children must have made good use of this opportunity as it is interesting to see that, in 1901, all three of their daughters were either teachers or school assistants.

The entry in the 1910 *Kelly's Directory* also shows how long the working day must have been for a village Post Office as it says letters, that at that time were coming through Bridgwater, were arriving at 7.20 am. & 6.45 pm. and were dispatched at 8 am. & 7.05 pm. although there was no Sunday delivery in Westhay. The hamlet has long been associated with the village of Meare, 1½ miles away, and this was where the nearest Telegraph and Money Order office was to be found. The only change by 1914 was that the Post Office was now being run by William's widow, Mrs Annie Francis, as the Sub-Postmistress. William was reported to have died early in 1913.

By 1919 we find another change as John Bassett is now being listed as the shop-keeper and Sub-Postmaster. John was born in Meare c. 1865 and at one point was living in Wedmore with the Watts family as an apprentice carpenter. In about 1900 he married Mary Ann Rogers, also from Meare, where their first daughter,

*John Bassett's signature in 1911. He was then a Carpenter and
Joiner in business in Meare*

Lena Maude, was born in 1901. They were later to have a son and another daughter, Leonard and Lillian. John died early in 1932 but his widow, Mary Ann, known to the family as "Annie" and described by some as a strong willed lady, took over the running of the Post Office and shop. She is still remembered by some of the older inhabitants, who knew her in her later years, as always wearing black, signifying widowhood. This was very much in keeping with many of the ladies of that generation.

*A Postcard sent by "Granny Bassett" showing the front of the house.
The Post Office was on the roadside on the left.*

In the Electoral Roll compiled in October 1939, Joseph H Simmons is recorded as a shopkeeper but, due to the outbreak of war, he was later called up for military service, joining the Royal Air Force. It seems that Mary Bassett then continued to run the business until at least 1945 and she then retired to live in Wincanton with her daughter. Ken Baker, who was living in the village in 2014, remembers that his mother used to help out in the shop and Post Office on a part-time basis when Mary Bassett needed to take time off.

Joe Simmons Shop and Post Office
with a Morris-Commercial J-Type van outside.
These vans were in production from 1949 - 57

In 1945 Joe Simmons' wife, Kathleen was living at the Post Office but Joe did not appear on the electoral roll until the following year, then giving their address as The Post Office. No.62, Main Road, Westhay. On Joe's return to the village, on his demobilisation after the war ended, there was a large party of children and adults from Westhay to meet him at the local railway station. Joe and Kathleen continued to run the shop and Post Office until 1962 when they retired to Bleadon. In a copy of the *"Extract of title deeds"* relating to the Post Office Stores, Westhay, found in the solicitors papers of Messrs Austin & Bath, in the Heritage Centre in Taunton, we have seen that on 26th February 1962 the shop was conveyed from the Simmons' to William James Dugan and Mrs Pauline Hunt. Mrs Hunt, who lived at the Post Office with her daughter, did not stay long as, in turn, on 18th July 1965, Mrs Hunt transferred it to David and Vera S. Adams. They, too, did not stay long as on 4th March 1967 we

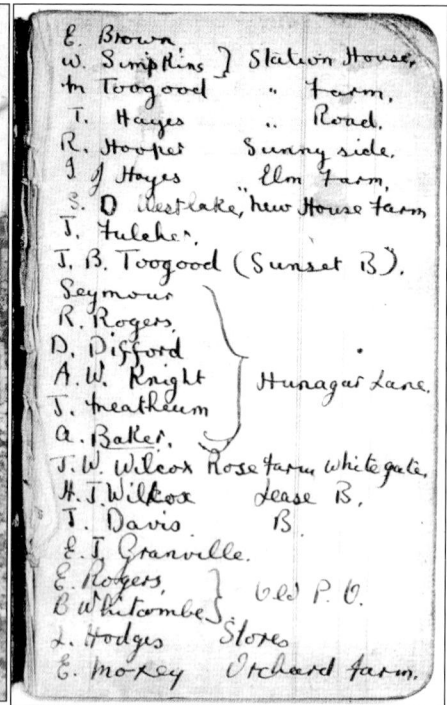

*Bert Howe of Shapwick signed on as a temporary Postman in 1940
and illustrated is a page from his notebook listing the houses and people
in Westhay to aid his deliveries*

find another entry: *Conveyance: Adams to James & Vera Carruthers.* James and Vera, who were still in position in 1973, are remembered as being the quite elderly parents of a young lad.

In the Register of Electors in 1974. Ernest & Mary Walters, known in the village as Ernie & May, gave their address as the Post Office, 25 Main Street, Westhay. It seems that the house numbers had been changed as, when the Simmons were there, its number was 62 Main Street. Ernie was a retired naval man and they were at Westhay for over seven years before moving to the nearby village of Mark.

Michael & Margaret Smith, who formerly lived in Rhodesia before the troubles in that country, had arrived by 1961 with their two children, Amanda & Jeremy - Jeremy was listed as a young voter on the list, being eligible to vote on reaching the age of 21 on 20th October 1983.

By 1987 we find that Patricia Wilkinson and Frank Macarthy were in residence but they were not long there as by 1988

John & Margaretta Sevenash had bought the business. John is remembered as being rather deaf and this probably explains why it was Margaretta was the one to notice the problem as reported in the *Central Somerset Gazette* of 23rd February 1989. This tells of an attempted robbery on the Westhay Post Office being thwarted by Mrs Margaretta Sevenash's pet dog, Fred. She is quoted as saying *"He is only small but he is very fierce and makes a lot of noise"* Mrs Sevenash was woken up by Fred's barking and, going downstairs to investigate, found him on guard outside the door of the Post Office. Fortunately the robbers failed to gain access to those premises although they did steal some jewellery and also Mrs Sevenash's handbag which they had found in the domestic part of the house.

As seemed to be happening in neighbouring villages the small shops, with a Post Office attached, seemed to change hands on a fairly regular basis; the Post Office salary was not particularly good and the hours were long. After less than three years Alan & Gillian Todd had come to Westhay. Alan had retired from the police service and this was their first experience of shop-keeping but, after a short spell they, too, had moved on and by 1993 the Brown family had moved in. Jeffrey & Patricia Brown (brother & sister) and their mother, Brenda, were, I was told, "proper" shop-keepers and, amongst other things, started a paper round in the village. They were later to move to a shop in Wells.

Westhay
Post Office & Shop
December 2002

Eddie Crocker in the shop

Jennie Bain in the Post Office

For the following five years, starting in 1997, Paul & Susan Janaway (Paul & Sue) kept the shop and Post Office. Then, on the 8th of August 2001, Eddie Crocker & Jennie Bain took it over.

Eddie and Jennie had formerly both lived in London. One thing that Eddie was known for was his habit of always keeping the shop door open in all weathers with the idea that it encouraged customers to come in. Eddie and Jennie were later married in Meare church at Easter 2003 and within a year they had made the decision to retire. After many years of serving the public they found that, after only 6 months of living in Poole, Dorset in retirement, they both missed the social side of their former life. It was not long before they again sought a similar small business. This they found at Cleeve in North Somerset, a village with a population of just under 1000, nine miles from Bristol. Eventually they did retire, coming back to Meare, only for Jennie to unfortunately pass away in the autumn of 2012 at the comparatively young age of 58.

Paul & Jan Watkins had first moved in on 15th December 2004 just in time for the Christmas rush in the Post Office. Before coming to Westhay, Jan had undertaken a two week training course in Clapham, London, not too far from their previous home in West Hoathly in West Sussex. On that course she was proud to say she obtained a mark of 88% in her final examination. Paul had spent the previous 20 years working for a bitumen company but, with a change of management, had become disillusioned with his job and desired a change. He had spent his early years in Wiltshire and, as they both felt comfortable

Jan and Paul Watkins outside
Westhay Post Office

in the West Country, they sought a business there. Once their two children had grown up, Jan had always worked in finance and management. After considering running a "Bed & Breakfast" establishment they opted for a village shop and Post Office and that is how they came to Westhay.

Paul concentrated on running the shop and Jan the Post Office. In spite of her initial training she still found it stressful but she was eternally grateful to Sandra Hillson, the Postmistress at Meare, for her help on many occasions. Her relationship with Post Office management did not get off to a very good start as, on her first day, attempting to use the "Help Line" number provided, found that there was no-one available to answer her questions. As the safe had broken and she was unable to open it this was a disaster; eventually they had to get a locksmith to come and solve the problem.

Westhay Post Office was classified as a community office and therefore only carried a basic salary, which was supplemented by the small commission available from selling tickets for the National Lottery. There were a lot of rules to be followed; in the contract it stated that within their first 6 weeks they were obliged to purchase, for £350.00, the new Post Office sign (illustrated) and they even had to fit it themselves. Another bone of contention was that, after purchasing one of the new self-inking date stamps for £80, there was no credit given for it when

they, after closing down, had to return it. They were even obliged to remove the Post Office safe themselves.

From around 2008 there had been much talk nationally about closing small local Post Offices and, with so much of the turnover being eroded by on-line sales of stamps and other products, they decided to quit. So, in May 2010, Paul & Jan made an agreement with the Hillson family in Meare that the latter should keep the Post Office, and the shop in Westhay would continue as a General Store. With the competition from the local supermarkets and the loss of the Post Office salary unfortunately the business proved to be unviable and so, in September 2012, it closed altogether. Luckily, with Paul's previous experience, he was able to obtain a good job in the County Highways department and they were therefore able to continue to live in the village.

Evan after closure of the Post Office, the letter box continued to be located in the garden wall. In January 2014 a notice concerning a revision in the mail collection times appeared on all the rural Post Boxes on the area. For most villages this meant that there would, in the future, be only one collection a day from henceforth.

With the increasing use of cell phones the telephone kiosk attached to the closed Post Office was declared redundant; in fact the Parish Council subsequently purchased it for £1 with the intention, in the future, of using it to house a defibrillator for use, in a medical emergency, by the general public.

The Post Box at the Old Post Office with a notice attached concerning collection frequency. January 2015

No. 25 Main Road, Westhay
January 2015

ACKNOWLEDGEMENTS

With grateful acknowledgement to Joan and the late Ken Baker,
Eddie Crocker, Paul and Jan Watkins and Horace Willcox. Also all the
people of Westhay who have added to this story.

Windmill Hill, Glastonbury

Windmill Hill Post Office & Shop, Glastonbury.
A Town Sub-Office. (T.S.O.)

The first pair of shops on the Windmill Hill estate were built for the Glastonbury Town Council on Chinnock Road in 1951.

Ronald Maddaford was born in Glastonbury and after leaving school he had joined Messrs Frisby's, a national footwear chain of shops, in their High Street store. Here he stayed until being called up to join the Royal Air Force at the start of World War II in 1939. After war service he came back to Glastonbury, later becoming the shop manager. This he continued to do until making the decision that he should go into business on his own account. This was how he came to run the shop next door to the Co-op, run by Bert Marsh, as a grocery and general store. The Co-op was to remain in its original premises until finally closing in the early 1990s.

Ronald & Rosalie Maddaford

The Windmill Hill Stores at the time they first opened.
*Photo - **Central Somerset Gazette**. 6th October 1961*

One of the window displays with a poster:
"WIN £450.00 and your SUNDAY JOINT
FREE for a YEAR"

The Post Box
outside the shop.
January 2009

The Spar Shop and Post Office in 1982
Note the Telephone Box

When the council commissioned a new pair of stores next door, in 1961, Ronald Maddaford forestalled them from letting them as separate units, by stating that he would take over both and run them as one general store. This would also incorporate a Post Office. His eldest son, Royston, had always helped his parents in this shop but, in 1965, when his father had purchased the Ivythorn Stores in Street, Royston moved over there to manage the new business.

In July 1966 Preston Maddaford, a younger son, left school and immediately came to work in the family business. It was he, joined by his wife Jenny, who later took over the running of the shop and Post Office on Windmill Hill, living in the flat above the premises all their married life until their eventual retirement.

Preston Maddaford

Jenny Maddaford

A Registered Cover posted in 1971 from Windmill Hill

After over 40 years of running the business they decided it was time to retire. So, in November 2006, the business was sold to McColl's, who ran a national chain of mini supermarkets. Unfortunately for the residents of Windmill Hill and Hillhead, Glastonbury, the Post Office side of the business was very soon closed and its last day of operation was the 7th July 2008. Later, Preston & Jenny moved to Baltonsborough to live.

The shop in January 2009 after the McColl take-over.
The Post Office now closed and the public telephone kiosk removed.

ACKNOWLEDGEMENT

With many thanks to Preston and Jenny Maddaford for all their help in preparation of this short history of a local Post Office.

Index

A

Abbey House, 26
Adams, David & Vera, 237
Aishcott, 70
Albion Inn, 154-155
Alford, Matt, 45-47
Alford, William & Kitty, 223
Allcock, Charles William, 78
Allen, W. T., 142, 145
Allman, Ida, 122, 128
Anderson, Jim & Pamela, 81
Aplin, Mr, 173
Archers Way, 45
Asney road, 208

B

Back, George & Eileen, 210
Badman, John, 89
Bagg, Reggie, 79, 161
Bailey, Emily, 23
Baily, Alexander, 23
Baily, John, 22-24, 26
Bain, Jennie, 240
Baker, Harold, 27-28, 122-124
Baker, John & Thirza, 120-122
Baker, Ken & Joan, 27, 120-121, 236, 243
Baker, Mrs, 74
Balch, Annie, 235
Balch, Thomas & Betsy, 235
Ball, Ellen, 14-15, 18, 86-87
Barker, Billy, 123-124
Barker, Hugh, 124
Barringer, Stuart, 30, 32, 34
Bartlett, William, 90
Bassett, John, 234-236
Beese,Eileen, 212

Bideford, 29
Biggs, Reginald & Florence, 110
Billings, Ellen, 24
Birch, Joan & Keith, 97-99
Bird, N A, 179
Bishop, Henry, 1
Bishop Mark, 12
Blandie, Major, 176
Bond, Louisa Mary, 91-92
Bonham, Neil, 47
Booker Group, 83
Boon, Ernest, 29
Bowles, Julienne & Tim, 229
Bowles, Ted & Joy, 225
Boyce, William, 170-173, 175
Boyce, Caroline, 31,
Bragg's Directory, 15, 69-70, 168
Bray, Ernest & Kathleen, 222-223
Brewham, 169
Bridgeman, Thomas & Elizabeth, 12
Bridgwater, 3, 6, 24, 27-28, 32, 69-70, 74-77, 81, 119, 121, 142-143, 145, 149, 151-152, 159, 161, 169, 171, 173, 179, 198, 205-206, 210, 235
Bridgwater, Nick, i
Bristol Aeroplane Company, 159
Bristol Evening Post, 161
British Postal Museum and Archive, ii
Britton, William, 103, 116
Brooks and Sons, 31
Brooks, Arthur & Ellen, 93-96
Broome, Mary, 96
Browning, Clive, 41
Brown, Jeffrey, Patricia & Brenda, 239
Bruton, 22, 150
Burnham on Sea, 22, 152

Index

Butleigh Court, 101-102, 104-105, 108
Butleigh Wootton, 106

C

Calcutta, 36, 226
Cannon, William 104-105
Carroll, Graham & Mrs, 33, 124
Carroll, William, 19
Carruthers, James & Vera, 238
Carslaw, Bill, 228
Carter, Richard, 220
Catford, Herbert, 218
Cavill, Henry, 79, 161, 207
Cavill, Keith, 161
Central Somerset Gazette, i-ii, 6, 23-25, 41-42, 44, 90-91, 113, 125, 137, 172-173, 178-181, 219, 239, 246, 250
Champion, John & Joan, 130
Chancellor, John & Louisa, 207, 209
Chapman, George, 70, 73
Chapple, James Sandy, 75
Chapple, Walter John, 74
Chard, 2, 11, 219
Chesterman, Mr, 127
Chinn, Judith, 147
Chinn, Leila, 143-147, 223-224, 228
Chinnock Road, 245
Clapp, Louise, 199
Clark, Alan, 42
Clark, Ralph, 183
Clarks Shoes, 46, 146, 167, 195, 197,
Cleeve, 240
Clewlow, Carol, 229
Cook, Benjamin, 88

Cory, Mr, 219
Cottle, William, 209
Cotton, Benjamin, 218
Cotton, Max & Maxine, 98
Coxbridge, 94, 219
Cox, Eric, 79-80
Cox, Victor & Annie, 80
Cox, V W & Sons, 79
Cranhill Road, 79, 173, 185
Creech St Michael, 131
Creed, Betty, 229
Creed, Sidney, 219
Cresswell, W, 17, 20, 150
Crewkerne, 2, 11
Cridland, Thomas, 24, 173, 206
Crocker, Eddie, 240, 243
Cross, Gerald, 43-44, 47
Crossman, Jack, 34
Crown Inn, 120
Cruse, William, 19

D

Davey, Henry & Betty, 110
Davies, John & Janice, 131, 133, 138, 213
Davis, Joan, 112-113
Davis, William, 219
Davys, Cecil, 154
Devenish, Wendy, 215
Difford, Alan, 120, 123, 128
Doncaster, Earl of, 201
Downing, Frances, 41, 146, 223-224
Dugan, William, 237
Dunkerton, Bill, 94, 99
Dunster, 130, 156
Dunthorn, D. R., 31
Dunthorn, Ken and Diana, 138

Index

Dyer, Annie, 105-108
Dyer, Charles, 107-110
Dyer, Edith, 106-107
Dyer's Orchard, 110
Dyer, Sylvia Georgina, 108
Dyer, Wilfred, 107-108

E

East Pennard, 139
East Street, 218
Edgarley, 17, 48-49
Eglington, Dr, 32, 176
Elkin, Robert & Julie, 127
Evercreech, 43, 152, 219
Everett, Jim, 97
Exeter, 2-3, 5, 1-12, 14, 22, 70, 95
Eyers, Clara, 24

F

Filton, 46
Flagg, Reuben & Mrs, 139-140
Fleetwood, Frank, 207, 209
Forde Abbey, 1
Forden, Miss, 79
Fordington Green, 19
Francis, William & Annie, 235
Freeling, 5, 14, 69, 102-103, 119, 149,
      165-166, 202
Frisby's, 245
Fry, George, 169-170
Fullbrook, Arthur and Ethel, 130

G

Gainey, Sharon, 44
Gane, Ken, 47, 182
Garrett, Les, 36-40, 47
George Inn & Hotel, 12-13, 224

Gifford, Anna, 228
Gifford, Dawn, 98
Gilbert, George, 139
Glastonbury Canal, 22
Glastonbury Penny Post, 14, 69, 71,
      149-150, 166
Godney, 118-119, 121
Godwin, Johnnie, 154-155
Godwin, Noah, 79
Golledge, Susan, 24
Gooch, Charles, 35
Gooding, Leonard & Margaret, 234
Goodland, Arthur and Emma, 129
Gould, Edwin & Arthur, 97
Grange Avenue, 176-177, 187
Gray, Marian & Richard, 213
Greedy, Charlotte, 93
Green, Mike & Anne, 111-112, 116
Green, Sidney, 217-218
Greinton, 202, 204
Grenville, Neville, 87, 101-105
Griffin, Arthur, 170
Griffin, Emily, 28-29
Griffin, Minnie & Joe, 140-146
Griffin, Robert and Marjery, 97
Griffiths, Fred, 83
Groves, Catherine, 164

H

Hampherson, Albert, 91
Ham Street, Baltonsborough, 90, 92,
      95-96
Hanrahan, John, 215
Harper, Esther, 234
Harrison-Harrad, 22, 70, 104, 150,
      170, 204, 217
Harvey, Thomas & Ellen, 151-155

Index

Harvey, Violetta, 153, 155
Harwood, Paul & Glynis, 113, 116
Haworth, Peter & Margaret, 125-126, 128
Hecks, John & Mary, 130, 138, 182
Heeley, Ann & David, 108, 110, 116
Hewlitt, Elizabeth, 104
Higdon, Leonard & Margaret, 144
Higgins, Ann & Stanley, 225-226
Higgins, Rosie, 96
Highbridge, 22, 117, 119, 152, 178
Hilburn, Ray, 164
Hillson, Paul & Sandra, 127, 241-243
Hiscox, William, 169
Hitchman, Claude Douglas, 225
Hoddinott, Jessie Ellen, 157
Hodges, Frank & Bill, 94
Homer, Paul & Jenny, 229-230
Homeway Farm, 234
Honiton, 2, 11
Hoover, 228
Howden, Angela & Simon, 163
Howe, Adrian, i, 84, 156, 215
Howe, Bert, 238
Howe, Bertha May, 156
Hucker, Wm, 31, 32
Hunt, Pauline, 237
Huntspill, 235

I

Ings, Geoffrey, 164
Ings, Leonard & Ivy, 158-159
Ings, Percy & Jessie, 157-159, 164
Ivythorn, 130, 176-177, 185, 188-189, 209, 247

J

James Barry, 180-181
Janaway, Paul & Susan, 240
Jennings, Trish & Fred, 154, 164
Jesson, Graham & Olga, 82
Johansson, Simon & Denise, 132, 138
Jones, Frederick & Beryl, 130
Jones, Michael, 84

K

Keen, Les, 83
Kelly's Directory, 26, 48, 73, 75, 78, 90, 92, 105-106, 117-120, 122, 129, 140-141, 143, 151, 171, 174, 204, 206-208, 217, 219, 233, 235
Kent, Brenda, 228
King Edward VII, 76
Kingsteignton, 150
Knight, John & Marie, 80

L

Lambert, Tracey, 44
Lamport, Mary, 91
Langport, 14, 102-103, 166, 202, 205
Lanham, Pat, 164
Leech, John, 214
Lester, William, 204, 220
Lewis, John, 31
Lewis, Rev. Lionel S, 34
Lewis, Trevor & Beryl, 124-125
Little, Maureen, James andTerrance, 176
Lock, Mr, 74
Lockwood, Albert, 76
Lomax, James, 228

Index

LONDIS, 82-83
London House, 31-32
Longleat Estate, 208
Lord Glastonbury, 101-102
Lottisham, 90, 95, 139-141, 143-144
Lott, Samuel, 165
Louis, Mr, 18, 69-70, 167, 202, 208
Luckwell Cross, 156
Ludlow Letter Boxes, 152, 160
Luscombe, Rev.d Mr, 202, 204

M

Macarthy, Frank, 238
MacGowan, Bede, i
Maddaford, Preston & Jenny, 247-248
Maddaford, Ronald & Rosalie, 247
Maddaford, Royston, 133, 247
Mail Bag Seal, 202
Maisey's Bakery, 161, 253
Manning, Pat, 44
Marazion, 30
Mark, 122, 235, 238
Marshalls Elm, 177, 188
Marsh, Bert, 245
Marsh, Joan & William, 155-157
Martineau, John, ii
Martin, Robert, 150-151
Martins Stores, 137, 181
Maryborough, 202
Maydon, Lynch, 181
McClurg, Gloria, 125, 128
McColl's, 134, 137, 248
McLaughlin, Ina, 45
Meare Heath, 122
Meare & Westhay Drama Group, 127

Mechanised Letter Offices, 8, 39
Mere, 2, 11, 122, 126
Merthyr Tydfil, 228
Miles of Minehead, 83
Millener, John, i
Minehead, 13, 74, 83, 117
Modbury, 29
Montevideo, 36
Moorlinch, 78, 157, 202, 204
Moreton, Denzil & Frances, 210
Morris and Co, 23, 140, 151, 205
Morris-Commercial, 237
Mortimer, William, 174-175
Motum, John & Margaret, 158-160, 164
Mullins, John, 86
Munt, Tessa, 47

N

Nanking, 36
Nelder, Reginald Charles and Mary, 125
Neville Grenville, 101, 103
Newe, Steven & Janice, 163
Newton Abbot, 35
Nicholls, Ken, 175, 182
Nicholson, Sir Bryan, 41
Northwood, 90
Nutt, Mary Ann & Elizabeth, 117

O

Oberholzer, Jon & Sue, 42, 44, 47
Old Down, 76, 203
Orchard, David, 47
Oxley, Geoff, 14

Index

P

Packer, Ralph, Maureen & Simon, 161-162, 164
Padstow, 218
Palfrey, Jaqui & Karen, 161
Parcel Force, 39
Parcel Post, 6, 24, 38, 75, 94, 171, 193
Parsons, Marion, 228
Passmore, Henry, 29
Patten, M. A., 89-92
Paulton, 36, 39
Pearce, James, 142
Pedersen, Svend Bek, i
Pedwell, 69, 79, 81
Pembroke House, 144-146
Penny Post, i, 13-14, 69, 71, 85, 103, 149-150, 166-168, 201
Perrett, Mr & Mrs Brian, 160
Perry, Adeline, 207
Perry, Elias, 209
Phelps, Ernest & Georgina, 111
Phelps, May, 145, 224
Phillips, Charles, 205
Phillips, Gilbert, 91
Piggott, Henry & Mary, 224
Pigot's Directory, 14, 17, 166, 168, 254
Piper's Inn, 76
Pitts Farm, 234
Plumley, Gladys & Gloria, 96, 99
Plumley, Hazel, 96
Plymouth, 2, 11, 30, 36
Polkinghorne, George & Dorothy, 176
Pontypridd, 174
Porter, Charlie, 139

Porter, Mary, 96
Post Office Counters Ltd, 8, 39, 41, 127, 229
Pople, Dorothy Mary, 178
Powell, Lewis, 234
Prichard, F R, 179
Prideaux, Edmond, 1
Puriton, 178
Pursey, W, 168

R

Rangoon, 36
Reade, Cecil, 207, 209
Reakes, Ernest, 139
Redlake, 218
Reeves, John Fry, 15, 17, 20
Rhodesia, 42, 238
Riches, Bernard, 224, 228
Rideout, Vera, 208, 212, 214-215
Roberts, Nick, 137
Robinson, Harold & Joan, 125
Rogers, Mary Ann, 235
Rogers, Samuel & Sarah, 219, 222, 235
Rood, James, 13-14
Royal Mail, 1, 9
Royal Mail Group, ii
Royal Signals Regiment, 227
Rural Life Museum, 104, 116

S

Sawtell, Ellen Elizabeth, 152
Seccombe, H.E., 32
Semley, 219
Senior, Robert, 102, 104, 116
Sevenash, John & Margaret, 239

Index

Shaftesbury, 2, 11

Shapwick, iii, 14, 24, 69, 73-75, 81, 121, 149-164, 167, 169, 201-203, 234-235, 238

Sharley, Arthur & Catherine, 111

Shave, Ann, 12

Sheppard, Albert & Thelma, 176

Shepton Mallet, 2, 11, 31, 43, 89-90, 139-140, 169, 217

Sherborne, 2, 11, 129

Shilton, Bruce & Pam, 82, 84

Shingleton, William & Harriet, 218-219

Sibson, Maurice, 224

Simmons, Joseph & Kathleen, 236-238

Simons, Walter, 35

Skudder, Ivor & Doreen, 81

Smith, Arthur & Sarah, 225

Smith, Michael & Margaret, 238

Society of Friends, 169

Somerset and Dorset Postal History Group, ii, 117

Somerset County Council, ii

Somerset Heritage Centre, i, 210

Somers, Nellie, 92

Somerton, 14, 166

Southgate, Basil, 35-36, 199

Southtown, 219

SPAR, 82

Stevens, Ron & Linda, 83

Sticklinch, 217-218

Stileway, 120-121, 233

Stone, Bernard, 84

Stonehill, 186

Stone, Hugh & Martha, 73, 84

Stone, Richard, 84

Stow, Mr., 102-103, 204

Strange, Brian, 41

Strangways, Miss, 156

Street Inn, 166, 168-169, 184

Stride, Henry, 141

Sully, Kath & Tony, 212, 215

Swanton, Stephen, 22

Sweet, Angela, 182

Swinton, Thomas, 22

T

Talbot, Caroline, 170

Talbot, Ron, 30, 39-40, 47

Tanganyika, 227

Tanzania, 227

Taunton, 3, 30, 45, 70, 81, 83, 102, 131, 145, 210, 217, 237

Taylor (of Shapwick) 69

Taylor, Mr & Mrs, 125

Templeman, Alfred & Elizabeth, 170, 174-177, 181

Templeman, Alice, 174-175

Templeman, Joseph, 174

Templeman, Margaret, 179

Thornfalcon, 131

Thynne, Rev. Lord John, 167, 201-202, 204

Todd, Alan & Gillian, 239

Todman, Jenny, 81, 83-84

Toogood, Horace, 234

Toogood, James, 234

Tripp, Roger & Jean, 111

Trollope, Anthony, 21, 91

Turnbull, Mr, 32

Index

U

Uniform Penny Postage, 16, 87
Universal Directory, 11

V

Vernon, William, 19
Vincent, Anna Maria, 21-23, 89

W

Wake, John, 89, 104
Walters, Ernest & May, 238
Wanstrow, 2, 11
Warman, John, 79, 84
Watkins, Dora, 155, 164
Watkins, Ken & Margaret, 41-42, 47, 213
Watkins, Paul & Jan, 240, 243
Watts, Geoffrey & Christine, 97
Watts, Mary, 156, 164
Watts family, 237
Watts, Roger & Abi, 208, 213, 215
Weaver, Roger & June, 212
Welch, Mike, ii, 191
Wells, i, 2, 3, 11-12, 2, 27, 41-42, 44, 53, 64, 69, 85, 101, 111, 117-118, 133, 139, 149, 165, 168, 172, 179, 201, 217, 220-221, 228, 239
Wells Philatelic Society, i
West Hoathly, 240
Westlake, George & Sarah, Henry & Elizabeth, 205-207
Weston-s-Mare, 28, 35, 122, 177
Westonzoyland, 145, 162
West Quantoxhead, 104

Whetstone, 82
White, Charles, 169-172
White, George & Mary, 168-169
White Hart inn, 14, 74
White Lion, 12
Whitehead, 15-16, 86
Whitehead, Louis, 228
Whitehead, Miss, 144
Whiting, Samuel & Mary, 120
W H Smith, 182
Wilkins, George & Jane, 118-120, 233
Wilkins, Hazel, 212
Wilkins, Mrs, 123
Wilkins, Sarah, 117
Wilkinson, Patricia, 238
Willcox, Horace, 243
Williams, Cathy, 137
Williams, George, 155
Williams, Joseph & Mary Jane, 222
Williams, Winston, 215
Wimbledon, 228
Windmill Hill, i, 54, 133, 137, 245-246, 248
Winter, Alfred & Dorothy, 178, 199
Wiveliscombe, 70, 131
Wooden Books Ltd, ii
Woodlands, 221
Woodward, 69
Woolley, Nora, 110, 112, 116
Worrall, John, 144
Wren, Frederick & Emily, 153-154, 157
Wride, Thirza, 122

Y

Yeovil, 2, 11, 18, 45, 151

The Author

Allen Cotton was born in West Bradley, five miles from Glastonbury, into a long established local farming family.

After first attending Glaston Tor School he moved to Wycliffe College in Gloucestershire. He spent a year on a farm in Wiltshire prior to a course at the Somerset Farm Institute at Cannington. He was awarded one of three distinction certificates for that year. This completed his formal education.

Coming home to the farm he took an active part in the local Young Farmers Club, not only culminating in a travel scholarship to Australia and New Zealand in 1958 but also meeting his future wife, Mary; she, the daughter of a local farmer, was one of the joint secretaries of the club.

His interest in stamp collecting started at very young age but really took off when he met Maurice Sibson, a retired dentist from Manchester, who came to live in the village around 1940; a true philatelist, as opposed to just being a collector of stamps, who introduced him to the finer points of the hobby.

He initially specialised in Australian stamps, having family connections going back to Tasmania in 1802, then formed a collection of Postal Stationery which, in turn, led to an interest in Postal History.

The finding of a large hessian sack full of his grandfather's business correspondence, dated 1917-19, furthered this line of collecting and led into the study of the postal history of the Glastonbury area. A subject on which he has been quietly researching, storing up envelopes, post cards, press cuttings and photographs, for nearly 30 years. So, encouraged by his wife, he has, at last, committed his research to print.

He was proud to be presented, at Buckingham Palace in 2013, with an O.B.E. for his "Services to Agriculture and the Community in Somerset".